THE MIDLIFE MIND

November 2020

To Susan,

for the (mid)life beyond the commissies.

With respect and admiration,

Ben.

THE
MIDLIFE MIND
Literature and the Art of Ageing

BEN HUTCHINSON

REAKTION BOOKS

Published by
REAKTION BOOKS LTD
Unit 32, Waterside
44–48 Wharf Road
London N1 7UX, UK
www.reaktionbooks.co.uk

First published 2020
Copyright © Ben Hutchinson 2020

All rights reserved

No part of this publication may be reproduced, stored in a retrieval system, or transmitted, in any form or by any means, electronic, mechanical, photocopying, recording or otherwise, without the prior permission of the publishers

Printed and bound in Great Britain by
TJ Books Limited, Padstow, Cornwall

A catalogue record for this book is available from the British Library

ISBN 978 1 78914 350 8

CONTENTS

Prologue: The Incremental Inch 9

1 CRISIS AND GRIEF
   The Invention of Midlife 16

2 THE PIGGY IN THE MIDDLE
   The Philosophy of Midlife 38

3 HALFWAY UP THE HILL
   How to Begin in the Middle 52

4 A ROOM AT THE BACK OF THE SHOP
   Midlife Modesty 76

5 GETTING ON
   The Tragicomedy of Middle Age 99

6 PERPETUAL INCIPIENCE
   The Midlife Gap Year 117

7 REALISM AND REALITY
   The 'Middle Years' 143

8 'THE YEARS THAT WALK BETWEEN'
   Midlife Conversion 165

9 LESSONS IN LESSNESS
   Midlife Minimalism *188*

10 FROM THE PRIME OF LIFE TO OLD AGE
    How to Survive the Menopause *206*

11 STREAMS OF CONSCIOUSNESS
    Middle Age in a New Millennium *229*

Epilogue: The End of the Middle *250*

REFERENCES *259*

FURTHER READING *270*

ACKNOWLEDGEMENTS *272*

PHOTO ACKNOWLEDGEMENTS *273*

INDEX *274*

'I dare not tarry. I am already at an advanced age, and perhaps fate will break me in the middle of life and the Tower of Babel will remain an incomplete stump. At least they should be able to say it was a daring attempt.'
JOHANN WOLFGANG VON GOETHE, 1780

'Poetry has always been understood to start in the middle.'
GEORGE ELIOT, 1876

'We do not free ourselves from something by avoiding it, but by living through it.'
CESARE PAVESE, 1945

Prologue:
The Incremental Inch

One morning, I awoke from uneasy dreams to find myself transformed into a monstrous middle-aged man. Lying on my stiff, ageing back, when I lifted my head a little I could see my soft belly divided into spreading segments, on top of which the blanket could hardly keep in position and was about to slide off completely. My aching legs, which were pitifully thin compared to the rest of my body, waved helplessly before my eyes.

Kafka's metamorphosis happens to us all. The question is not how to resist it, but how to respond to it. Time is the one universal element of the human condition; although all organic beings are subject to it, we are – we think – the only species that is fully conscious of it. We may not turn into bugs, but we do turn into cruel caricatures of our younger selves. No wonder that neurosis is the default setting of humanity.

Unlike Gregor Samsa's dramatic transformation, however, ageing does not occur overnight. It begins slowly, almost imperceptibly, as we edge tentatively into our forties, youthful zest receding ever further into the distance. Initially, the change is in fact anything but dramatic; only gradually do we coarsen and spread. Yet this very gradualness is both consoling and terrifying. While we have time to get used to our new selves as we inch incrementally forward, we also have a dawning sense of the sheer ineluctability of age. We see the train coming, but can do nothing to get out of its way.

This book is about such incremental inching. With the help of some of the greatest figures in the history of literature, it examines how we have understood middle age in the past, how we understand it in the present and how we might make it as productive as possible in the future. What does it mean to start slipping from the 'prime of life' towards a long, slow decline? How does it feel to become conscious of starting the second half of one's existence? And how do we even define a period that has no clear beginning and no obvious end? As lifespans have evolved over the centuries, so the understanding of middle age – when it begins, what it entails and what it signifies – has evolved accordingly. We know about the seven-year itch of marriage, but what about the incremental inch of middle age?

If we rarely stop to think about what it *means* to be in the thick of life, it is because we are too busy *being* in the thick of life. What does it mean to be a man; what does it mean to be a woman? Poised between youth and dotage, between innocence and experience, middle age is what we make of it. And yet by making so little of it, we make so much of it. By refusing so stubbornly to acknowledge its arrival, contemporary culture renders it conspicuous by its absence. We think of ageing as the most natural of processes, but it is also the most culturally constructed of phenomena; how we 'age' – how we see ourselves *as* ageing – has always been determined by the norms and models surrounding us. We are only as old as others make us feel.

As I finish writing this book, I am 43, married with two children. I am no longer young, but far from old. The biology is irrefutable: I am in the middle of my life. But what of the anthropology? What of the culture? The question is not so much about how I feel middle-aged as how I feel *about* being middle-aged. The answer, for me as for everyone else, derives from a constantly shifting process of triangulation between my own self-image and that of the society around me. In the twenty-first century we are told to feel 'young' in our forties and fifties in a way that would have been unimaginable in the nineteenth century, let alone earlier. Life expectancy has changed, in the sense that we expect more from life – not (just) because we are living longer, but because we have access to so much more in the way of opportunity and experience. Our expectations are accordingly that much harder to satisfy. Capitalism depends on keeping us permanently dissatisfied, permanently vulnerable to the elixir of advertising. Middle age is as much a demographic as a development.

Why have we allowed midlife to be hijacked in this manner? While the psychology of middle age is far from merely negative – it is, after all, the period in which by and large we enjoy the greatest power and prestige – it is striking that it is so often depicted as such. Men have the midlife crisis, women have the menopause; in the popular imagination, nothing good seems to happen in the middle years. Colloquially, such terms function as all-purpose insults; even the economy, in the infamous words of the deputy governor of the Bank of England, can be 'menopausal.'[1] And yet the dawning of middle age can also be the spur to unprecedented levels of creativity. Some of the greatest works of art and literature have been driven by the sense of finding oneself, all of a sudden, in the middle of life's way – an idiom that suggests nothing so much as being in *harm's* way, overrun by the unstoppable force of ageing. Aesthetic virtue emerges, as so often, out of existential necessity.

Identifying these virtues is the aim of the present book. Its premise is that the middle of life is as worthy of attention as its ending or beginning. What, indeed, does it mean to speak of *middleness*? Is it simply the default setting for our understanding of the human lifespan? One of the most iconic of all images of humanity suggests as much: drawn when he was in his late thirties, around the midpoint of his own life, Leonardo da Vinci's so-called Vitruvian Man amounts, among other things, to a portrait – some claim a self-portrait – of the artist as a middle-aged man. Inspired by the architectural reflections of the Roman writer Vitruvius, its perfect symmetry places Man at the very centre of the known universe, his navel the *umbilicus mundi* of Renaissance humanism. Leonardo's drawing suggests, in other words, that midlife man is the measure of all things.

Why, then, does he receive such a bad press? Why do we cringe when thinking of ourselves as 'middle-aged'? If the term has been so negatively constructed by modern culture, it is high time to think about how we might reconceive it positively, or at least about how we might strip away the accretions of contemporary cliché. Middle age is a metaphor, but what are the terms of the comparison? Following the work of Michel Foucault, we are increasingly familiar with the notion of the 'history of the present', a history that seeks to reconstruct not the past but the values and presuppositions underlying the contemporary era. What I propose in this book, analogously, is a *memoir* of the present, as seen through the eyes of major figures of Western culture. Rather than excavating the past, I want to examine, as honestly as possible, the perspective of my present – which is to say, of incipient middle age. That is not to say that I will not also consider the past, both my own and that of cultural history more generally; but I will explore it in terms of how it affects the present. People normally write memoirs looking back over the whole of a life, or at least something close to it, but I want to think about what it means to have lived *half* a life – to register feelings as I have them now, rather than as I used to have them. 'What I want', to borrow the words of a 45-year-old Susan Sontag, 'is to be fully present in my life, to be really where I am, contemporary with myself *in* my life, giving full attention to the world.'[2] What I propose, in short, is a memoir of the middle.

Such a memoir must of necessity be both personal and impersonal. For ageing is the most universal, but also the most individual of experiences; not just how we age, but how we *perceive ourselves* as ageing, changes from person to person, from culture to culture, and – not least – from gender to gender. We

Prologue

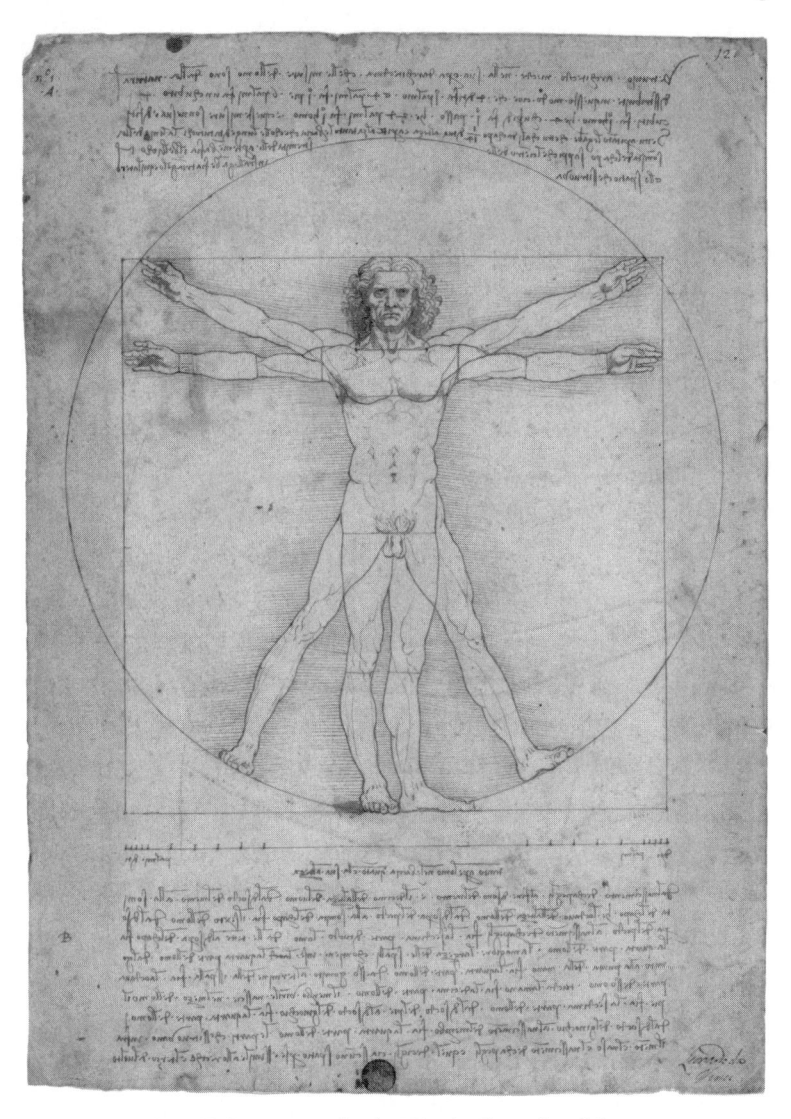

The circle of midlife: Leonardo da Vinci, *Vitruvian Man*, c. 1490, wash over metalpoint on paper.

do not all cross what Joseph Conrad calls 'the shadow-line' of maturity at the same age, nor indeed do we cross it definitively; on any given day we are liable to take off the tie of adulthood and put back on the T-shirt of adolescence.[3] The tick of one life is the tock of another. Even professions have their distinct biological clocks, with footballers and mathematicians middle-aged well before judges and politicians. Writers and critics, it seems to me, enjoy the 'privilege of being "in the middle"', not just because they require a mixture of energy and experience, but because they mediate between finished texts and unfinished contexts, between intellectual emissions and psychological emotions.[4] Literature, the most interiorized and self-critical of all art forms, constitutes a privileged site of reflection on what it means to be in the middle of life since it tells us not only *about* middle age, but how it *feels* – which can help us, in turn, to marshal our own emotions. Words and ideas can master moods and feelings; the trick is to edge into them sideways, to undo the deadening, monolithic status of 'great works' by resituating them within the lived experience not only of their authors, but of their readers. Bibliotherapy, in short, can help us come to terms with ageing.

The closest literary analogy for ageing in this regard is the essay, which ever since Montaigne has sought to combine reflection with citation, anecdote with authority. An essay is nothing if not a meditation on time, and on our attempts to capture and convey it. The very etymology of the term – behind the French *essai* or 'attempt' stands the Latin *exagium*, indicating the way that we 'weigh up' or evaluate a question – evokes the degree of maturity necessary to the genre, implying as it does the careful calibration of several sources. 'What is it that requires such weighing?' asks the great twentieth-century Swiss essayist Jean Starobinski. 'It is the life that we feel in us, the life that both asserts itself and atrophies.'[5] Middle age, equally, is nothing if not a period that both asserts itself and atrophies, a self-unfulfilling prophecy of the second half of our lives. As we move into our forties, what we essay, however inadequately, is to weigh things up; what we essay, however inadequately, is maturity.

Memoir, history, criticism, essay: the midlife mind draws on all these genres and more, producing a composite construct that blends both intellect and affect, thinking and feeling. Taken as a whole, the authorities adduced suggest that middle age, despite all the negative clichés and preconceptions, may in fact be the most productive period of life. There is no need, in other words, to panic. Hold your chin up and your stomach in; there is life on the other side of forty. The major writers can show us where, and how, to find it. The best response to the consciousness of getting older is to cultivate this consciousness, to run towards rather than away from it. The unexamined midlife is not worth living.

1
Crisis and Grief:
The Invention of Midlife

Crisis: Do *or* Die

Like sex, the midlife crisis was invented in the 1960s. If intercourse began, according to Philip Larkin, in 1963, the midlife crisis arrived shortly afterwards, in 1965. First published as an academic article in the *International Journal of Psychoanalysis*, Elliott Jaques's essay 'Death and the Midlife Crisis' launched the term in scientific – and rapidly also popular – discourse.[1] Although the term 'midlife' had first appeared in 1895 (defined in the dictionary as 'the part of life between youth and old age'), it was only in the 1960s that it became automatically associated with the idea of having a crisis. That the two terms have become so indissoluble testifies to the concept's resonance; equal parts self-justifying myth and self-fulfilling prophecy – you fear you are going to have a breakdown, so you do – the midlife crisis has become a staple of films and novels. No narrative of achievement, no biography of becoming is complete without the moment of self-doubt in the middle act, the crisis of confidence that must ultimately – such is our cultural obsession with success – be triumphantly overcome. In part this corresponds to our lived experience as we settle into the long, slow process of getting older, but it also reflects the nagging sense of hollowness behind the modern Western story of security and prosperity. The idea of the 'midlife crisis' crystallizes not just our dawning sense of personal mortality, but the way we come to question the very meaning of our lives as we reach middle age. Is that all there is?

How we answer this question depends, according to Jaques, on whether we conceive ourselves as creative. The biological facts of the crisis, as he sees them, are rapidly established: it occurs around the age of 35, it can endure for several years, and it varies in intensity according to individual circumstances and temperament. It is also, in Jaques's telling, decidedly male; 'Death and the Midlife Crisis' is most definitely not 'Death and the Maiden', neither in the examples adduced nor in the understanding of the crisis as essentially 'creative' in nature. Although the post-industrial era sees the midlife mind becoming increasingly female, its conceptualization as 'crisis' remains resolutely male well into the post-war world. The male menopause (the 'manopause') seems to invite psychoanalysis, no doubt because it is metaphorical rather than physiological, but perhaps also because it is (supposedly) only temporary, a passing lull presaging renewed productivity. Men merely pause where women menopause.

Reading Jaques's essay more than half a century after it was first published, it is striking not only in how old-fashioned his attitudes now seem – his exclusive focus on men, his assumption that family life 'ought to' have become established by the time one reaches one's mid-thirties – but in how problematic any attempt to universalize the midlife crisis must surely be. Whether or not it actually exists as anything more than a popular myth (a point much disputed by specialists), it takes different forms in different people: one man's meltdown is another woman's maturity. Yet Jaques reduces these many narrative threads to a single story: the midlife crisis as discernible in the work of 'great men'. While his impressionistic approach to the crisis seems problematic from a scientific point of view – he 'gets the impression' that the death rate between the ages of 35 and 39 jumps markedly in creative artists, and his invocation of predetermined 'genius' is little more than rehashed romanticism, underpinning as it does his reading of artistic biographies ('the closer one gets to genius . . . the more striking and clear-cut is this spiking of the death rate in midlife') – the popular success of his diagnosis suggests that he has a point. Creativity changes – pauses, pivots and metamorphoses – as we reach middle age.

What new forms does it take? Jaques terms the post-crisis period that of 'sculpted creativity'. By this he means to indicate a newfound attentiveness to 'externalized material' as well as to internal, immaterial thoughts, an interest in execution as well as inspiration. While there is an element of circularity about this argument – Jaques derives his models of Romantic, intuitive youth and Classical, reflective middle age from the canon of male artists (Beethoven, Shakespeare, Goethe and so on), and then applies this model back on to them – it is clear what he means. Desire and impatience give way to serenity and acceptance.

Attaining this enlightened state, however, requires passing through what Jaques terms the 'purgatory' of the midlife crisis. What has to be purged are any remaining illusions about one's own immortality – fantasies of which, according to Sigmund Freud, we all secretly maintain. As we stop growing up and begin growing old, we are forced to face up to the brute reality of our eventual death; we can no longer continue pretending that only other people die. The future tense becomes the future past.

Jaques may have been the first to popularize the term, but his conceptualization of the midlife crisis was hardly new. Popular culture has long held that men, in particular, tend to experience, around the age of forty, what the French call *le démon de midi*. That psychologists have repeatedly sought to quarantine this demon is hardly surprising. In 1881 the neurologist George Miller Beard, the man who coined the term 'neurasthenia', published *American Nervousness*, written as a sequel to his previous study of nervous exhaustion. In it, he included a chapter on the 'longevity of brain workers and the relation of age to work', surveying 750 of the most eminent names in history as well as a series of less prominent figures. With quasi-mathematical certainty, he concludes that 'the year of maximum productiveness is *thirty-nine*'. Creativity, for Beard, is a young man's game: 'the essence of poetry is creative thought, and old age is unable to think.'[2] On this basis, he even awards medals to the passing decades: the thirties are the golden years, the forties the silver decade, and so on all the way to the wooden spoon of the seventies and eighties. Beard's neurasthenic vision of ageing thus reverses the hierarchy of value traditionally ascribed to wedding anniversaries; the older we get – the further we drift from the golden mean of the middle – the less valuable we become. We walk up our 39 steps, and then we start walking down them again.

Unsurprisingly, subsequent psychologists sought ways of reversing Beard's law of diminishing returns. Even before Walter Pitkin published his best-selling self-help book *Life Begins at Forty* (1932), his colleague G. Stanley Hall had made the point more seriously.[3] In a study of 1922 entitled *Senescence: The Last Half of Life* (intended as a sequel to his study *Adolescence* of 1904), Hall coined the term 'middle age crisis', which he defined

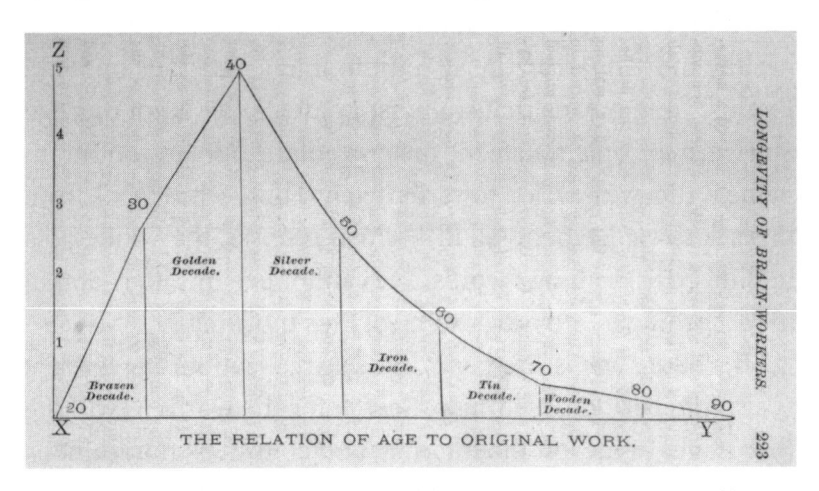

'The relation of age to original work', a diagram from George Miller Beard's book *American Nervousness* (1881).

19

as a 'meridional mental fever' that afflicts men in their thirties and forties.[4] Hall views this crisis, however, as marking the beginning of true maturity. 'Modern man was not meant to do his best work before 40,' he claims, before adding, in strikingly Nietzschean language, that 'the coming superman will begin, not end, his real activity with the advent of the fourth decade.'[5] Hall can retain such a positive view of middle age because he views it – to cite the title of his first chapter – as 'the youth of old age'. Writing from the vantage point of his late seventies (born in 1846, he would die two years later, in 1924), Hall looks back wistfully to the supposed vitality of midlife: between adolescence and senescence, he implies, comes essence. It is all a question of perspective.

For another, far more celebrated psychoanalyst, middle age is the period in which 'self-realization' begins to take place. After falling out with Freud in 1912, Carl Jung underwent his own midlife crisis, rebelling against the tyranny of the unconscious and arguing that we in fact continue developing beyond childhood and into adulthood. Jung identified four stages of development, from childhood and youth to middle life and old age. The middle stage – which he famously calls 'the second half of life' – begins at around 35, and is characterized, in the healthy individual, by the attempt to find a 'religious outlook'. By this, Jung means that we must gradually let go of our ego and learn to contemplate the meaning of the human condition: namely, that we develop towards death. Those who shrink from this acknowledgement fall ill – which is to say, they undergo a midlife crisis. In Jung's words, 'we cannot live the afternoon of life according to the programme of life's morning.'[6]

If middle age is the period of self-realization, however, it is also the period of self-help. Search for the words 'Carl Jung four stages of life' on the Internet, and countless mindfulness, consciousness and personal development websites scroll invitingly down the screen. Jung even gives alternative names to his four stages – the 'athlete', the 'warrior', the 'statement' and the 'spirit' – implying a developmental relationship between them: we (should seek to) evolve from one stage to the next. The 'statement' stage – becoming a parent, losing a parent, reaching maturity – corresponds to middle age and its 'psychology of the afternoon'; its implied sense of stock-taking reflects the increasingly 'religious' attitude that Jung would have us assume as we grow older.[7] Although it is supposed to turn us away from our own concerns towards those of others, in encouraging selflessness this attitude still foregrounds the self as the measure of all things. Know thyself, in the words of the Delphic dictum – but especially in middle age.

As Jaques notes, though, there is a paradox not just in the conceptualization, but in the timing of this selfless self-realization. For, viewed from a more positive perspective, middle age is also the very zenith of our life, the period in which we come into our full powers of experience and maturity. Why should we be unhappy in the prime of our lives? The answer, of course, is that this prime is now end-stopped, or more precisely that we now *realize* that it is end-stopped. Jaques quotes the spatial allegory outlined by a patient in his mid-thirties: 'Up till now ... life has seemed an endless upward slope, with nothing but the distant horizon in view. Now suddenly I seem to have reached the crest of the hill, and there stretching ahead is the downward slope with the end of the road in sight.' The summit, in other words, is also the start of the descent.

Jaques's patient exemplifies the problems we all face as we reach middle age. Even for those of us who are not geniuses, the question of how not to 'plateau' takes on renewed significance. Success and a busy life are no defence against this; indeed, the more successful and active we are, the more we risk simply deferring the inevitable – and psychologically necessary – reckoning. In the words of the Italian poet Cesare Pavese, we do not free ourselves from something by avoiding it, but by living through it.[8] Jaques quotes his patient as stating one day that his favourite slogan was 'do or die' – but that under analysis he now remembered he had always shortened it simply to 'do'. In the prime of his life – the 'time for doing', in Jaques's words – the patient functioned by convincing himself, even into his very motivational slogans, that death was to be denied.

Defined in these terms, having a midlife crisis might seem to be a very 'first world' problem, a modern luxury made possible by the spread of the bourgeois Western lifestyle. The peasants and subsistence farmers of the Dark Ages had more pressing things to worry about, one imagines, than whether they were going grey. Did they even live long enough to enjoy a 'middle' age? We tend to think of the average lifespan as having expanded considerably with the advent of modern medicine, and this is indeed the case if one surveys all the population, including those who (used to) die young. If one considers only the intellectual classes, however, then once one factors out infant mortality rates the life of the educated man remains relatively consistent over the centuries. Consider, for instance, the following statistics:

Life expectancy of men throughout history[9]

	Date	Mean age
Kings of Judah	1000–6000 BC	52
Greek philosophers, poets and politicians	450–150 BC	68
	After 100 BC	71.5
Roman philosophers, poets and politicians	30 BC–AD 120	56.2
Christian Church Fathers	AD 150–400	63.4
Italian painters	1300–1570	62.7
Italian philosophers	1300–1600	68.9
Monks Roll of Fellows of the Royal College of Physicians	1500–1640	67
	1720–1800	62.8
	1800–1840	71.2

	Date	Mean age
Lifespan at fifteen years	1931	66.2
	1951	68.9
	1981	72.0

While life-expectancy figures are notoriously volatile – it all depends on the sample size and sources – there is no doubt that those who survived into maturity have historically had a better chance of a long life than we might now think. By the late twentieth century, we had gained around ten years on the aggregate of previous millennia; by the early twenty-first century, we have gained the best part of another decade, with most estimates for life expectancy in the developed world hovering somewhere around eighty. From antiquity onwards, nonetheless, if you made it past childhood and into education you had a fair chance of reaching somewhere near the biblical three score years and ten (with the notable exception of the bloodthirsty Romans). By the Victorian period, moreover, life expectancy for males once they reached the age of five was well past seventy.[10] Such figures belie the standard Hobbesian view of pre-twentieth-century life as nasty, brutish and short.

What these figures also suggest, by extension, is that the middle of life has remained relatively unchanging throughout history, hovering somewhere around our mid-thirties. To be sure, this does not mean that it has always been *understood* as unchanging, whether in the West – Shakespeare and Montaigne had a different sense of what it means to be in your thirties from the one we have now – or in the East, where the Japanese idea of the *ossan* has historically hovered between meaning 'old man' and 'middle-aged man', recently even morphing into a commercially viable category of 'middle-aged man for rent'.[11] But the biology is, surprisingly, relatively consistent.

Such is the story, at least, for educated *men*. For women, the picture looks startlingly different:

THE MIDLIFE MIND

Life expectancy of women throughout history (at fifteen years)[12]

Date	Mean age
1480–1679	48.2
1680–1779	56.6
1780–1879	64.6
1891	61.6
1901	62.6
1911	66.4
1921	68.1
1951	73.4
1961	75.7
1971	76.8
1981	78.0
1989	79.2

Two obvious conclusions suggest themselves from these rising numbers: for most of history, women have lived significantly less long; from the twentieth century onwards, they have been living significantly longer. If the single most important factor in this shift has no doubt been the improved quality of medical care during childbirth, the implication of this is that modern women enjoy an extended period of middle age beyond their childbearing years. Patricia Cohen seems to be on to something, then, when she suggests, in her cultural history *In Our Prime* (2012), that 'middle age' itself emerged as a demographic category only in late nineteenth-century American women's magazines. Only then, in the era of mass production and 'Taylorized' working practices, were newly liberated middle-class women free to pursue their own self-interest; only then, in the post-industrial era, could midlife become the good life. The machine age had created middle age.[13]

This modern bias, however, is as much commercial as conceptual. The mass media of the nineteenth century hardly invented the anxiety of ageing; they merely exploited it for financial gain. The sixties hardly invented the midlife crisis; they merely codified it for popular consumption. With their finely tuned antennae, writers and thinkers have always intuited the crisis and anxiety of ageing, well before there were magazines to sell them beauty products or psychiatrists to tell them what they were feeling. Writing in the early twelfth century, for instance, the Andalusian poet Yehuda Halevi is almost Metaphysical in his wit and concision:

> When a lone silver hair appeared on my head
> I plucked it out with my hand, and it said:
>
> 'You've beaten me one on one –
> but what will you do with the army to come?'[14]

Which of us doesn't feel this way? Ancient or modern, male or female, we are all racing against time, and we are all losing. Denial is a very powerful tool – as Friedrich Nietzsche noted, forgetting is the gateway to good mental health – and for a time it can work very well. But sooner or later we must come to terms with the fact that we are no longer young, and that we now have less time ahead of us than behind. Sooner or later we must reckon with the army to come. There is no easy way to say this, so I'm just going to have to put it bluntly: we do *and* die. Better to start the grieving process sooner rather than later.

Grief: The five stages of middle age

If the 1960s invented sex and the midlife crisis, they also invented grieving. In 1969, in a book enticingly entitled *On Death and Dying*, the Swiss psychiatrist Elisabeth Kübler-Ross established what have been known ever since as the five stages of grief.[15] Abbreviated collectively to the acronym DABDA, the five stages described what Kübler-Ross took to be the standard phases through which the dying patient necessarily passes: denial (and isolation), anger, bargaining, depression and acceptance. While neither clear-cut nor rigorously successive – at any given time, the patient may move backwards and forwards between the various stages – they nevertheless offered a powerful model for one of the most overwhelming of all emotions, and rapidly gained traction in popular, if not always in professional, discourse. Perhaps the most important reason for the popular success of this model was that it implicitly views death as a *process*, since in doing so it implies that one may yet come to terms with it, that life, in due course, may yet continue. Time may not heal everything, but – crucially – it does offer serenity.

Can the same be said of middle age? If grief, in Kübler-Ross's model, mourns the mortality of the body, middle age mourns the mortality of the self. It represents an incipient form of death, bringing with it the first unmistakeable intimations of mortality as the brute finitude of life – long observed in others, but only now integrated into the self – slowly dawns. If their shared success in the public imagination is striking – the 'midlife crisis' and the 'five stages of grief' have both gained significantly more traction in popular than in scholarly circles, suggesting a general need for such models – the big difference between the two is that in the case of middle age, time precisely does *not* offer serenity; physically speaking, things can only get worse, not better. Psychologically, however, the standard experience seems to be that as we get older we learn to live with ageing more readily, as the memory of youth recedes ever more fuzzily into the distance. As with grief, then, acceptance – the final letter of the acronym – is the endgame of middle age.

Denial

One of my most vivid memories as a child is of my father's fortieth birthday party. I must have been ten years old (I have strikingly few memories of my childhood before then, so this one really stands out), and I had never consciously observed someone reaching this milestone before, my mother being three years younger. I remember how happy my father was, with his long, leonine hair swept back over his ears and his freckles catching the light as he beamed at the assembled well-wishers. The thing that bothered me, though – and the reason, no doubt, that it has stuck in my memory – was that everyone kept telling him that 'life begins at forty'. I can still recall the feeling of bafflement that this produced in me: how could life 'begin' halfway through? Why then and not earlier? What had my father been doing for the last forty years?

Now that I have reached that age myself, I can only smile at the literal-minded child I once was. If children don't really do irony, nor do they understand the ways we gently attempt to console each other for the inevitability of the human condition. The clichés of consolation are the disclaimers of denial: we tell each other that life is only just beginning precisely because it is *not* only just beginning, precisely because it has now, undeniably, reached its middle phase. Forty-one and a half as I type these lines, I am exactly halfway through the life expectancy of the average English male. But to say that life merely *continues* at forty is hardly the stuff of inspiring birthday-card sentiment.

Denial, then, is the inevitable first phase of middle age. As the first hairs turn grey and fall out, as the first wrinkles creep across our faces likes cracks in a mirror, we do everything we can to avoid noticing. Vanity in the banal sense becomes *vanitas* in the baroque sense; like slaves at an imperial procession, our grey hairs whisper to us *memento mori*. We have all had the experience, as we look into the mirror, of seeing the skull beneath the skin – and we have all had the experience of trying to deny it to ourselves. Perhaps the experience of this – or rather of its social and cultural codification – is different for men and women: where before the age of forty men can for the most part avoid interaction with the biological realities of their bodies, from early on in their lives women are subject to an almost incessant pressure – from the cosmetics industry, from the culture industry, from the very idea of the 'body clock' – to remain 'young' and gamine. Middle age, in this regard, is implicitly constructed as a psychology of loss before women even reach it; little wonder, then, that they risk feeling diminished when they do.

Yet denial is essential to us all, whatever our gender. If consciousness of mortality constitutes the human condition, so does the attempt – as in Halevi's poem – to suppress it. In her dystopian novel of late romanticism, *The Last Man* (1826), Mary Shelley captures this psychology memorably:

> Ye are all going to die, I thought; already your tomb is built up around you. Awhile, because you are gifted with agility and strength, you fancy that you live: but frail is the 'bower of flesh' that encaskets life; dissoluble the silver cord that binds you to it.[16]

The fancy that we live is the denial that we die; no human life can be enjoyed without it. Middle age, in this sense, functions as the very essence of the mortal human condition. In order to experience it fully, we must deny it.

Anger

When I myself turned forty, I did not, surprisingly, receive any cards telling me that my life was now beginning. Perhaps this kind of gentle irony about middle age, as with so many other approaches to the topic, has gone out of fashion. Having married into a French family, however, I did receive a range of knowing comments about *la crise de la quarantaine*. Forty, then, is not only the age at which life begins; it is also the age of the midlife crisis.

Why should this be? If 35 marks the middle of the biblical three score years and ten, there is an equally well-established tendency to locate the true turning point five years later. The staging post seems to be almost universal – beyond modernity, beyond even the Judaeo-Christian culture of the West. Writing in fourteenth-century Andalusia, for instance, the Arabic scholar Ibn Khaldūn stakes the claim in his classic history of the Islamic world, the *Muqaddimah* (1377): 'Reason and tradition make it clear that forty years mean the end of the increase of an individual's powers and growth. When a man has reached the age of forty, nature stops growing for a while, then starts to decline.'[17] If the subtext to Khaldūn's claim is no doubt the Islamic convention that Muhammad received his revelation from the Angel Gabriel at the age of forty, what is striking in his analysis is not only his invocation of both logic and history (or his implication that one's forties form a plateau where things seem to stand still for a time), but his subsequent anthropological argument. For forty is equally the limit, he suggests, for the 'sedentary culture' that emerges out of nomadic life in the desert, after which elegance and economy are followed by 'subservience to desires' and the 'human soul receives a multiple stamp that undermines its religion and worldly well-being'. Translated into the terms of our all too sedentary modernity, the completion of our fourth decade forms the natural – and, it would seem, quasi-universal – moment for a crisis.

'Forty' is as much a psychological as a physiological staging post, however, and it is in this regard that middle age emerges as a contingent, culturally conditioned phenomenon. When that bland little letter from the National Health Service drops, unsolicited, through the letterbox one morning – announcing that now you have reached your fifth decade you should have a check-up once a year to ensure that your heart is in good condition – it is as though middle age itself has arrived, unsolicited, through the front door. In the terms of Roland Barthes, one could say that such an event constitutes the 'caesura' marking the beginning of the middle of life. Without such a moment, Barthes argues – he cites the much more dramatic example of the founder of the Trappist order of monks, Abbot Rancé, who according to legend at the age of 37 discovered the decapitated body of his mistress and immediately withdrew from society – we will of course physically still slide into middle age, but psychologically we will not be conscious of the transition. For Barthes, middle age is as much a state of mind as of body.[18]

That such a state leads to anger as well as denial is hardly a surprise. To be middle-aged is to be at the bottom bend of life's U-shaped cultural cachet, neither nimbly young nor nobly old. If the U-bend has emerged as the standard image for the development of our 'happiness quotient' over the span of a Western life, it is because we are at our least happy, according to the statistics, between the ages of 40 and 55 – which is to say, during the onset of middle age. This unhappiness may be, indeed often is, more internally than externally manifested; the embittered middle-aged colleague is a cliché because, alas, it is all too real. Resentment and self-righteousness have long been the mood music of midlife. Threatened by younger, shinier versions of ourselves, none of us is immune to insecurity or 'feeling our age'. Popular psychology, interestingly, lacks terms for this midlife impasse; we all have a sense of what Freud means by the Oedipus complex – but who identifies with the mother or father? Instinctively, we all think of ourselves as the young man (or as his female counterpart, Electra). Perhaps we need to complement the Oedipus complex with an Odysseus complex, understood as the middle-age counterpart to the neuroses of youth.[19]

As with all the psychological mechanisms of middle age, the anger at being usurped by the next generation reflects the shifting terms of the lifelong dialogue with the self. How can we not resent the sense of the rug being pulled from under our feet (or indeed, off our heads)? To get angry about encroaching middle age is to get angry about the human condition – and who does not do this from time to time? Anger in the face of mortality just means that we are alive.

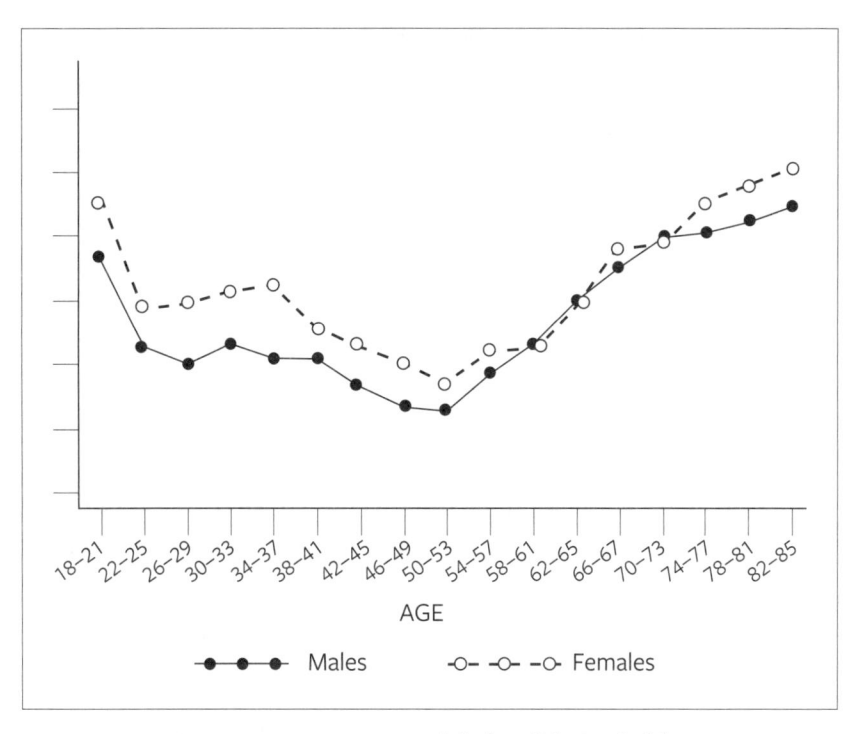

Happiness is a warm U: global well-being ladder
(plotted by four-year age groups), from a 2010 U.S. study.

Such anger is also, however, constitutive of the productive, positive side of middle age. Provoked by anger, we undertake new projects; prodded by pride, we find new energy, new ways of attempting to stay young. The clichés of the midlife crisis – the flashy new car, the trashy new partner – represent vulgar versions of this, overcompensations of the ageing libido. Channelled creatively, however, such energies result in some of the finest works of art that we have. The anger of the midlife crisis can also, in short, be the precursor to midlife maturity.

Bargaining

Whether we can take this step depends on our attitude to ageing – an attitude that is itself, of course, always ageing. When young, we don't feel the same way about the abstract notion of getting old as we do when it actually starts happening. Accepting the ageing process is itself a process, and one that involves constant recalibration, constant reassessment of how we see ourselves. If middle age is defined, in contrast to youth and old age, by its incremental nature, bargaining is an inevitable part of its psychology.

Mathematically speaking, the very notion of being in the 'middle' of life can only ever be hypothetical, since of course we don't know at what age we will die. As Barthes notes, the 'middle of our life is obviously not an arithmetical point: how, at the moment of writing, could I know my life's total duration so precisely that I could divide it into two equal parts?'[20] The shifting nature of this midpoint means that, for a time at least, renegotiation is always possible: am I still in the first half or have I now begun the second half of my life? Am I still 'young' or have I become 'old'? If we are defined by the stories we tell ourselves, self-identification on the spectrum of age is one of the most fundamental of our fictions.

We can all recall wishing to be older when we were younger, but at what point do we start wishing we were younger? The constant bargaining with the self that middle age occasions – I may be getting wrinkles, but at least I now have children; I may have children but at least I now have greater status – amounts to a Relativity Theory of ageing, according to which time passes faster or slower depending on our (always shifting) perspective. Our place within the generations has a particularly strong influence in this regard; losing a parent makes us feel as though we have shuffled up the mortal queue, but so, in a different way, does becoming one, if only because time now takes very visible form in the shape of our rapidly changing children. Ageing, in short, is anything but absolute.

From the creative point of view, an increasing awareness of time passing can bring the sense of urgency necessary to undertake previously deferred projects, or indeed to begin new ones.

I once asked a friend in her late thirties why she was starting a course in psychoanalysis and writing a novel while also teaching, researching and raising a baby; because we're running out of time, came the striking answer. 'Running out' is a concept we normally associate with the end of something, not the middle, yet here it was being co-opted as an expression of midlife urgency. Such urgency, if we are lucky, affords us the agency we crave.

Whether explicitly written *about* middle age or implicitly inspired *by* middle age, examples of this newfound urgency – what one might term the 'middle as muse' – punctuate the history of Western literature. For creativity is one of the central ways that humans combat mortality. We may be finite, but at least we can write a novel, or have children, or build a house; we may be mortal, but at least we can leave something behind. Yet this awareness of time passing can equally be perceived as paralysing, as throwing a ruthless searchlight on everything that we have left undone, or done badly. Middle age can also be a time of stasis.

Depression

That such stasis can lead, if untreated, to an extended period of depression is one of the recurring experiences of middle age. The much-mythologized 'crisis' constitutes an attempt to shake oneself out of this stasis, but many of us don't have the courage (or foolhardiness) to pursue it. As the initial energy of youth burns away, as relationships, career and children settle in for the long haul, the danger of drifting into apathy and repetition – into existential ennui – is all too real. Arthur Schopenhauer, the great miserabilist of modern philosophy, famously argued that life consists of either boredom or pain; on bad days, it is a close call which of the two sensations is worse. Lacking the *jouissance* of youth, middle age can tend towards the tedious. No wonder we feel blocked at the bottom of life's U-bend.

Alongside this default position of *taedium vitae*, the principal mode of middle-aged depression is disillusion. It is the privilege of youth to harbour that great cliché, 'hopes and dreams', and indeed the future-orientated impetus of youth – the Austrian author Jean Améry, who as an Auschwitz survivor knew a thing or two about midlife disillusionment, wrote of the 'credit' accorded to the young and withdrawn from the old – is unthinkable without them.[21] With the passing of time, however, comes the dawning realization that even in the best-case scenario, only a fraction of these aspirations will be fulfilled, and even if they are, new ones will simply take their place. Experience, to paraphrase Oscar Wilde, is the name men give to their middle age.

Illusions are of course indispensable to psychic health, so it is no wonder that the middle years of life are so awkward to negotiate. It would be emotionally intolerable to confront the truth about mortality and finitude daily, and that is why we busy ourselves with projects of one sort or another. 'Looking forward' to life is more than a mere idiom; it is an existential necessity. The burnt-out middle-aged man – the typical hero of a Graham Greene novel, for instance – is defined by his inability to do so. But even the most inextinguishable among us will only write so many books or travel to so many places; even the busiest of lives leaves a great deal undone. As we get older the future slowly shrivels, leaving fewer and fewer corners to hide in. Either we do things now or we will, in all probability, never do them.

As we 'grieve' for our youth, then, depression of some sort is an obvious danger. The sheer irreversibility of time can be overwhelming, particularly if we feel that life has not (yet) kept its promises with respect to all the things we are constantly told we should want: love, success, self-esteem. Even achieving these things is no guarantee against dissatisfaction; the very fact of feeling fulfilled can produce a burning desire to throw it all up in the air, to start again. Satiety, in this regard, is as dangerous as hunger. If desire is the human condition, its fulfilment is among the most insidious of punishments. When the gods wish to punish us, they answer our prayers.

For the sake of our sanity, then, we have to keep wanting. As anthropologists have long noted, we are defined – linguistically, psychologically, culturally – by the future tense, since we are the only species that can conceptualize the future in any abstract sense. The past is a foreign country, and we have only visiting rights; the present is ever ephemeral. Future-orientated projects of some kind are thus indispensable. But so is the final stage of Kübler-Ross's acronym, since it is only by acknowledging our exile from the past – and our ever-dwindling call on the future – that we will feel in step with our biology. As with grief, so with middle age: acceptance is the consummation devoutly to be wished for.

Acceptance

What form might this acceptance of middle age take? That is, in effect, the key question posed – and to differing degrees answered – by the works and writers explored in this book. My own answer emerges from the trajectory of the book as a memoir: by outsourcing our anxiety to minds greater than our own, we can use literature and culture to help us channel our thoughts and feelings. Through bibliotherapy, we can learn to accept growing older. That is not to say that there is any 'correct' way to do so; the very breadth of voices evoked in this book suggests the range of possible responses to middle age. For, while the writers gathered here all find ways to transform angst into art, they do so in markedly different forms. From the religious to the aesthetic, from the political to the personal, literary responses to finding oneself in the middle of life's way vary with the centuries and cultures. One thing they all share, however, is the desire to make creative virtue out of chronological necessity. To do so requires accepting middle age, wrinkles and all, for what it is.

In one sense, it is in fact startlingly easy to depict the middle of life in positive terms. Substitute 'maturity' for middle age and suddenly the U-bend becomes a bell curve, with the middle years representing the top, not the bottom, of life's way. Certainly this is the implication of Shakespeare's celebrated comparison of life to a play: the fourth and fifth of Jaques's 'seven ages of man' are the clear high point of our development, the courageous soldier and wise judge representing his culmination as a social and ethical being.[22] Maturity, it is implied, is tantamount to morality.

Yet the problem remains, of course, that behind the soldier and judge lurk the 'slipper'd pantaloon' and 'second childishness'. Accepting maturity with all its advantages – the power and judgement represented by those fourth and fifth stages – also means accepting middle age with all its disadvantages. Above all, it means abrogating the fantasy that we can control everything, starting, most obviously, with our own mortality. It hardly needs saying that this is an almost impossibly difficult thing to do. So what we do instead – the most supremely creative among us the most compellingly – is try to control what we can: the project of our lives.

It is in this sense that the great works of literature adduced in this book can be understood as both accepting and defying the passing of time. By making their self-consciousness about being in the middle of life the very premise of their project, they paradoxically transcend it; the five stages of midlife come full circle. Reflecting on middle age in the light of literature, I have come to realize that my own obsession with words has always been an obsession with time, and that I am now, in the middle of life's way, in the best possible position to explore it. Past and future, adolescence and maturity: all perspectives converge on the vanishing point of youth. If time is the true measure of the human condition, then what we can learn from such writers as Dante, Montaigne and Goethe – or from their latter-day descendants such as T. S. Eliot, Beckett and Beauvoir – is that middle age is both motif and motivation for some of the most searching reflections on this condition that we have. For this much is certain: there are few conditions more uniquely human than that of middle age.

2

The Piggy in the Middle:
The Philosophy of Midlife

In the beginning was the word. In the end was revelation. In the middle, however, was silence.

Such, in essence, is not only the biblical, but the contemporary view of the three main stages of life. Births and beginnings have their narratives, their 'grammars of creation': to the genesis the glory, to the *incipit* the divine spark of glamour. Endings, too, have their pathos, the sudden urgency of mortality: late style, lateness and late-life creativity have become recurring concerns of an ageing population. What, though, of the pivotal period in the middle, the great stretch of time that constitutes the defining period of life in terms of professional achievement, personal satisfaction and social prestige? What of middle age?

In a society for which youth is the measure of all things, the topic has remained largely taboo. If God is dead, in the words of Nietzsche's lucid lunatic, Youth has taken his place, universally worshipped and unflaggingly flattered, beseeched for favours that can only ever be temporarily bestowed. Old age, at the other end of the spectrum, is increasingly asserted as a counter-model, a dignified mode of resistance to the tyranny of youth. With the ageing of the baby-boomer generation, memoirs and studies on 'the pleasures and the perils of ageing' have proliferated since the turn of the millennium.[1] The hole at the heart of this spectrum, however, points to the trauma that binds the two poles of life; the real terror of the contemporary West is not so much age as *ageing*, the scandalously irreversible sense of time passing, with all its attendant coarsening of ambition and energy into stasis and apathy. The real terror is middle age.

That the topic suffers from such a bad reputation is testament to the taboo. A quick word-association game with the phrase 'middle age' summons up, for most people, some version of physical decay: sagging bodies, menopause, middle-aged 'spread'. Add to this the concomitant psychological anxiety – the frustration of unfulfilled ambition, the fear of being left behind by one's peers, the burden of care for both young and old – and it is clear that the term is anything but positive. In the youth-obsessed West, no one wants to acknowledge that they are ageing, until, as middle age digs its crow's feet in, it becomes unavoidable. Accordingly, a colossal cultural apparatus is mobilized in a desperate rearguard action against the passing of time, resulting in the virtual repression of an entire life stage. As we shall see over the course of this book, that has not always been the case; nowhere are the changing cultural attitudes to ageing more apparent than in the middle years of life. In modern Western societies, however, we go from being 'young' to being old, seemingly with little or no transitional phase.

Well I, for one, would like to accept the age that I am. Why are we ashamed of ageing? Why are we embarrassed when we see ourselves in old photographs? Perhaps the process shames us more than the result: to be 'aged' is to have made it to the end of life; to be middle-aged is merely to be struggling like everyone else. Critics often equate late style with great style – figures as disparate as Rembrandt, Beethoven and Shakespeare are all said to have had sublime, culminating periods at the end of their careers – but middle age offers no such nobility. Midlife style is simply *style*; the middle has been so little theorized as an epistemological position because it is defined by what it is *not*. Boasting neither the thrill of initiation nor the pathos of completion, it falls, quite simply, in the middle, forming the great grey mass of which most of life actually consists. To get a handle on this intractable matter, we can begin by situating the middle within some of the foundational models of modern philosophy.

Underlying any articulation of 'middleness' is an implicitly dialectical structure: it is only the tension between two poles that creates the space in between. In his *Phenomenology of Spirit* (1807), the German philosopher Georg Wilhelm Friedrich Hegel claimed that the development of 'world-spirit' is driven by a recurring pattern of thesis-antithesis-synthesis. An initial idea or 'thesis' calls forth a countermanding reaction or 'antithesis'; out of this interaction there then emerges a 'synthesis' of the two positions. This synthesis in turn forms the basis of a new thesis, and the whole cycle starts again, like an Archimedes screw carrying water ever higher. The median element in the three-part model thus has purposive force, an antithetical energy that transforms early ambition into later achievement by setting itself against the initial thesis. Within the constellation of Hegel's triad, the middle period functions as what Samuel Taylor Coleridge would term a 'salutary antagonism', goading the naive creation of the past into the noble consummation of the future. Out of tension emerges resolution.

Mapped on to the stages of life – Hegel also maps it on to the stages of history – the 'antithesis' would thus apply to the middle. It suggests an optimistic vision of the process of ageing, whereby the struggles and doubts of middle age function as a necessary precursor to the fulfilment of old age. Of course, Hegel's dialectic can also be recast as what the twentieth-century thinker Theodor Adorno would call a 'negative dialectic', such that it remains *stuck* in the middle and *un*fulfilled, incapable of leading to the synthesis of a serene old age. Either way, the dialectical model foregrounds the middle stage as the pivotal, indispensable moment. *The Empire Strikes Back*, to put it in terms of perhaps the most famous of all trilogies, is almost universally acknowledged as the best of the three Star Wars films precisely because it reacts against the self-sufficiency of the first instalment while setting up the possibility of closure in the final one. The middle requires the margins, then – but the margins also require the middle.

The problem with this three-part model, however, is that the margins demonstrably dislike the middle. One has only to think of the many ways in which the term is used pejoratively – the dreaded judgement 'middle-of-the-road', the dead hand of 'middle management' – to see that culture abhors a medium. 'Mediocrity' is the worst fate of all; far better to be a splendid failure. To be sure, such judgements are culturally specific; the English, for instance, like nothing more than eccentrics, defined by their distance from a supposed centre. Yet in every culture, in every language, there lurks a recurring sense that to be in the middle is to be mundane, unoriginal and uncreative. The piggy in the middle is the one without the ball.

Yet sporting metaphors also suggest a more positive model. Cricketers and baseball players speak of 'middling' a delivery, of timing a stroke so sweetly that the ball rockets away seemingly without effort. The idiom is suggestive, since it implies that to 'time' something properly means to find the middle; one might, in this regard, reconceive the middle in terms of the more positively inflected 'centre', understood as the source of all power and glory. Middling a stroke is the opposite of a middling stroke.

The most influential of all theorists of the good life would agree. In Book Two of his *Nicomachean Ethics*, Aristotle (382–322 BC) famously develops what he terms 'the doctrine of the Mean'. Extrapolating from mathematical formulae, he understands this mean as 'that which is neither excessive nor deficient' (although he also views it as a relative concept, varying with our capacities and stage of life).[2] Sometimes referred to as the 'Golden Mean', the doctrine as Aristotle formulates it regulates – or should regulate – every aspect of our character and behaviour; the 'habit' (*hexis*) of moral virtue 'is in each case a middle state', as he writes elsewhere in the *Eudemian Ethics*.[3] We should be neither too joyful nor too doleful, neither too upbeat nor too downcast. Just as craftsmen and artisans aim for balance in their work, so should we as moral beings. Virtue, for Aristotle, lies in the middle ground: in all things, moderation.

Writing in his *Rhetoric*, Aristotle extends this logic to the stages of life. The young are bold, the old timid; 'men in their prime will evidently be of a character intermediate between these, abating the excess of each.'[4] The questionable nature of the claim aside – his adverb 'evidently' is doing a lot of work here – Aristotle's assumption about the nature of maturity tells us much about the implicit cultural expectations of the day: men (and only men) are supposed to be 'courageously temperate and temperately courageous'. But the model is also explicitly mathematical; the prime of life – the *akmē* – is 'the fitting mean. The body is in its full vigour from thirty to five-and-thirty; the mind at about forty-nine.' The perfect man, in short, would be a chimera, with a body in its early thirties and a mind in its late forties.

Between the Hegelian antithesis and the Aristotelian mean, the middle can thus represent both tension and balance, failure and success. The cultural history of the middle points both ways because the category itself points both ways, torn between an irretrievable past and an unknowable future. Humans may be defined, anthropologically speaking, by their ability to conceive competing forms of the future, but they are equally defined by their ability to conceive the present. This present, suggests Aristotle in Book Four of his *Physics*, can be understood only 'when we think of the extremes as different from the middle'; it is only through perceiving 'before' and 'after' that we can identify 'now'.[5] The middle is not just a moral or mathematical category, but a metaphysical one. As I type these words I can delete, edit or reformulate, not only because of the obvious fact that I live in the present tense, but because of my capacity to *conceptualize* the present tense as a series of more or less articulable possibilities. It is because we are self-conscious that we are human.

Such self-consciousness is, of course, the very symbol of maturity. For Immanuel Kant, famously, enlightenment constitutes a process of growing out of self-imposed immaturity. In order to be able to do this, however, one must be *aware* that one is immature in the first place. Without such self-awareness, there can be no maturity. To be in the middle of life, similarly, one must be aware that one has stopped developing and is now 'developed'; one must step back and wonder how the present can avoid merely repeating the past. Where the Hegelian dialectic instrumentalizes the middle as the means to an end – as the means, in terms of the parabola of life, to *the* end – Kant would resist such instrumentalization, on the basis, as he argues in his *Groundwork of the Metaphysics of Morals* (1785), that one must act in such a way that one treats everyone never merely as a *means* to an end, but always at the same time as an end.[6] The middle, in this Kantian reading, must have force and validity on its own terms, not as the precursor to some further stage.

That middle age is in this sense as much cognitive construct as biological fact surely chimes with our everyday experience of ageing. We are constantly being told that we are only as old as we feel; but we are also – and perhaps especially – only as middle-aged as we feel. This shifting relationship between psychology and biology echoes René Descartes' doctrine of mind-body dualism, a doctrine that is generally taken to mark the start of modern philosophy. In his *Meditations on First Philosophy* (1641), Descartes claims to prove the 'real distinction between mind and body', grounding the distinction on his celebrated claim *cogito ergo sum*: I think therefore I am. From this basic premise, he proceeds to show that such self-consciousness implies – indeed, requires – the division of the 'thinking thing' (*res cogitans*) from the 'extended thing' (*res extensa*), which is to say the division of the mind from the body. Since the mind can apprehend the brain separately from the body, it follows, in this Cartesian argument, that they are separate entities; the self-consciousness of the cognitive faculty grounds itself in itself. With his *Meditations*, Descartes thus establishes mind-body dualism – and the self-consciousness that it implies – as the starting point of modern philosophy.[7]

The stories we tell ourselves about middle age depend on how we tip the scales of this dualism. For one of the essential markers of reaching middle age is that we start becoming *aware* of our bodies again, as changes start to occur for the first time since puberty: hair begins to go grey and fall out, eyesight worsens, bellies bulge. Even if we can keep such unwelcome phenomena at bay through exercise or lucky genes, we have to work ever harder for the privilege, and with ever-diminishing returns. The body, in short, once again asserts its dominion over the brain. Our minds, on the other hand, are arguably just reaching their peak, as mature experience comes to temper youthful enthusiasm. A scissors effect begins to obtain, as mind and body start cutting into each other.

If Cartesian dualism provides the foundation of modern philosophy, then, it is because it goes to the heart of the defining modern obsession: the self. Modernity is nothing if not the era of narcissism; on both the personal-psychological and collective-cultural levels, we define ourselves through our 'identity'. Majority or minority, straight or gay, in the twenty-first century we are how we see ourselves: I self-identify, therefore I am. But does this identity remain stable as we age? One of the most celebrated arguments regarding the malleability of identity is the so-called prince and cobbler passage in John Locke's *An Essay Concerning Human Understanding* (1690). Locke suggests that 'should the soul of a prince, carrying with it the consciousness of the prince's past life, enter and inform the body of a cobbler', we could say that it would be the same *person* as the prince, but not the same *man*. This is because the prince – even transported into another man's body – would see himself from the inside (the 'person'), whereas everyone else would continue seeing only the cobbler from the outside (the 'man'). 'The body too goes to the making of the man,' as Locke laconically notes.[8]

The resonance of this line of reasoning for how we age is obvious. On the inside, you're only as old as you feel ('Inside I still feel twenty'); to the outside world, however, you are as old as you look. Seen subjectively, a princely consciousness of youth may continue to determine self-identity; seen objectively, it is the cobbler's ageing body that determines the identity of the self. The scissors effect of middle age cuts these subjective and objective senses of the self ever further apart, to the point that some moral philosophers – most famously the latter-day Lockean Derek Parfit in *Reasons and Persons* (1984) – have gone so far as to argue that the supposed unity of a human life is to all intents and purposes an illusion.[9] Even consciousness, on this reading, cannot ensure uninterrupted continuity of the self, since we change so dramatically from birth to death that we are effectively (at least) two different people. The prince is not the same prince, irrespective of whether he borrows the cobbler's body. The inner prince is *not* the inner child.

Middle age thus makes us aware, once more, of the uneasy marriage between mind and body. It renews the wedding vows only to discover that the terms have changed. Middle age might be said, in this regard, to equate to Descartes' pineal gland, which he famously declared to be the meeting point of mind and body, since it controls the flow of 'animal spirits' around the nervous system (a system that he held, erroneously, to be uniquely human). While middle age, as a biological fact, is clearly not uniquely human – all living things will find themselves at some stage in the midpoint of their lives – 'middle age' as a cultural and psychological construct surely is.

The Cartesian doctrine of dualism came under attack from the moment it was formulated, and it has been under attack ever since. One particularly influential assailant was Henri Bergson, whose thought did so much to set the terms for modernist art and literature in the early twentieth century. In his *Matter and Memory* (first published in French in 1896), Bergson argued that the Cartesian distinction between mind and body should be located not in space, but in time: the mind is the realm of the past – the memory – while the body acts always in the present. His famous notion of *la durée* – of the inner duration of time as perceived by the mind – functions as 'the continuous life of a memory which prolongs the past into the present, the present either containing within it in a distinct form the ceaselessly growing image of the past, or, more profoundly, showing by its continual change of quality the heavier and still heavier load we drag behind us as we grow older'.[10] Middle age, in Bergson's hands, becomes metaphysical.

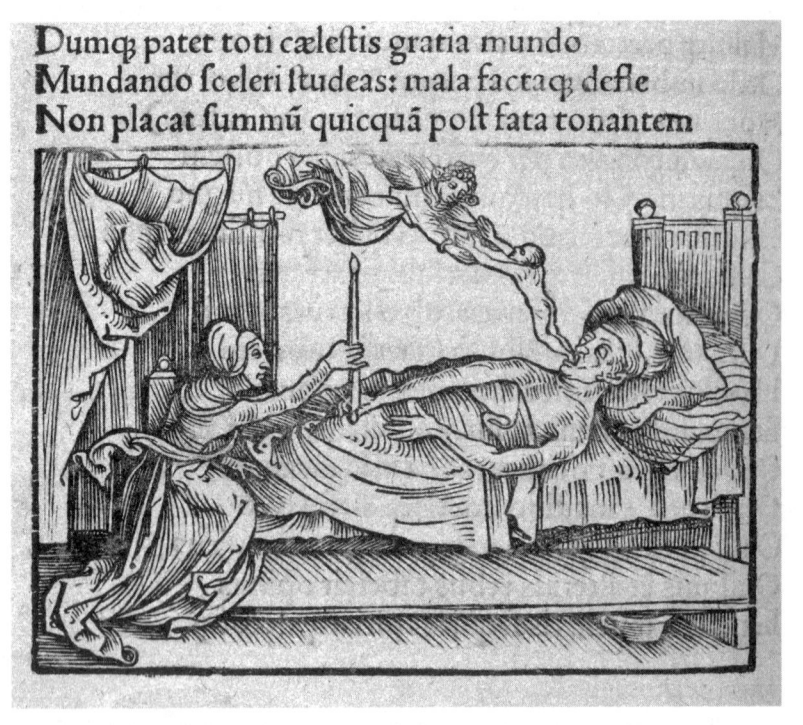

The inner child?: the illusion of identity, from Conrad Reitter's book *Mortilogus* (1508).

It is also, however, demonstrably physical. In his study *The Phenomenon of Life* (1966) – dedicated to the 'existential interpretation of biological facts' – the German-born philosopher Hans Jonas claimed that Descartes' dualistic antithesis leads 'not to a heightening of the features of life through their concentration on one side, but to a deadening of both sides through their separation from a living middle'.[11] As a way of foregrounding this living middle, Jonas emphasizes, as an alternative to dualism, the centrality of metabolism to organic life. Our metabolism, as is well known, changes as we age: from 25 onwards our metabolic rate slows by at least 2 per cent every decade. As we enter middle age, then, we are burning up the food we consume less and less efficiently, which is what leads to the notorious phenomenon of 'middle-age spread'. Midlife is about metabolism if it is about anything.

For Jonas, as for organic biologists more generally, metabolism is the basic engine of life. But Jonas goes further in making metabolism metaphysical: we remain ourselves only inasmuch as we perpetually renew ourselves. In this argument, our changing rate of metabolism, and the changing shape of our bodies that it occasions, functions like the old paradox of the philosopher's axe: if first we change the handle, and then we change the blade, is it still the same axe? To be in the middle of life – whether symbolized through Descartes' pineal gland or Jonas's decelerating rate of metabolism – is to know the force of this paradox, as we gradually feel both our minds and our bodies changing us into people almost unrecognizable from our youth.

Contemporary science, meanwhile, has begun to show that this is as true on the inside as on the outside. Under the aegis of the pioneering project 'Midlife in the United States', researchers at the University of Wisconsin-Madison's Institute on Aging have undertaken a series of longitudinal studies on the ways that not just our bodies, but our *brains*, age.[12] 'Neuroplasticity' has emerged as a key idea in the field, and just as photographs taken at annual intervals show our appearance gradually changing, so MRI scans show that our brains, too, alter as we get older. At around the age of forty, the brain begins to shrink by about 2 per cent every decade – that is to say, at exactly the same rate as our metabolism. The prefrontal cortex – the part of the brain just behind the forehead, which is thought to control judgement, self-awareness and restraint (what Freud would have called the Superego) – seems to be particularly vulnerable to such programmed obsolescence. What is striking, however, is that this same prefrontal cortex reaches full maturity only once we are in our thirties, which is to say at the point when we are fully developed adults. From the point of view of neuroscience, then, the middle of life seems to offer something of a bittersweet spot: just as our brute brainpower is starting to decline, increased confidence and maturity begin to compensate for the attenuation in processing speed. Experience, in short, comes to temper intelligence.[13]

If such a conclusion feels intuitively plausible, it is because we all want to feel that we are learning from our errors as we get older. Yet the response to our changing brains differs from person to person. Our circumstances, our character, our genetic make-up and (not least) our gender: these and other variables all play an important role in conditioning midlife mentality. Women inevitably experience middle age differently from men, since the female experience of ageing is linked at a very visceral level to the onset of menopause. Culturally speaking, women often report an external shift, too, as (they feel that) men stop looking at them so much; they have the sensation of becoming, as the saying goes, increasingly 'invisible'. This may or may not be welcome – invisibility is a superpower, after all – but for all the progress of feminism there is no doubt that the male gaze still dominates Western society, meaning that its absence, fairly or unfairly, is often perceived as a lack. Perhaps the nearest equivalent for men – equivalent in that it is a specifically *male* experience – is the loss of hair, the ostentatious cultivation of which, from Samson to Donald Trump, has always figured as a crown of potency. Physiological factors aside, the experience of the two genders is in any case hardly comparable, since as they become older men still attain to positions of power far more often than women – power that men use to compensate, however egregiously, for the humiliation of ageing (clearly this can also be true of women, although, as the Harvey Weinstein and MeToo scandals suggest, it is far less common). The piggy in the middle can also be the pig in the middle.

I don't know about you, but I for one struggle to find any appeal in the accumulative – and no doubt very male – model of ageing. It casts life as an unceasing Olympiad, driven ever onwards by the competitive, comparative motto *citius, altius, fortius*: 'faster, higher, stronger'. The history of thought and literature suggests a far worthier counter-model, it seems to me: not to compensate for the perceived indignity of ageing, but to cultivate it. One of the great lessons of the cultural history of middle age is that humility is the best antidote to humiliation. From the ancient Stoics to the modern Existentialists, from Seneca and Dante to T. S. Eliot and Beauvoir, those who reflect most rigorously on middle age understand it not as a culmination of the will to power that characterizes youth, but rather as an attempt to *divest* oneself of that power. Any honest appraisal of the intellectual achievements of middle age must include the realization that while we now know more than we did in youth, we are also much more aware of everything we *do not* know. The known unknowns, to use Donald Rumsfeld's infamous but insightful terms, are so much greater in middle age than in early adulthood. I have certainly read much more than I had twenty years ago, but I have also come to realize how much remains – and no doubt always will remain – unread. While I can keep adding to my stock of knowledge, by now its holdings are essentially established, my mind mapped out, for better or for worse, by the compass that will steer it for the rest of its existence. This is not necessarily a bad thing – as Ludwig Wittgenstein notes in his *Philosophical Investigations* (1953), 'problems are solved not by reporting new experience, but by arranging what we have always known' – but it does foreclose the freshness vouchsafed to youth.[14] Middle age oscillates, in this regard, between the known unknowns and the always already known.

Understood in these terms as a function not just of biology but of epistemology, one of the most poignant statements of middle age emerges from the life and work of Samuel Beckett, or more specifically from the relationship *between* his life and his work. Returning to Dublin after having spent the war hiding in the South of France, he was shocked to discover that his mother had Parkinson's disease. His reaction tells us much about the way what we might call 'middle ageing' – a feeling elicited here in response to maternal mortality – can lead to a tipping point, to a sense of wanting to throw out everything that has been so carefully accumulated over half a lifetime:

> Her face was a mask, completely unrecognizable. Looking at her, I had a sudden realization that all the work I'd done before was on the wrong track. I guess you'd have to call it a revelation. Strong word, I know, but so it was. I simply understood that there was no sense adding to the store of information, gathering knowledge. The whole attempt at knowledge, it seemed to me, had come to nothing. It was all haywire. What I had to do was investigate not-knowing, not-perceiving, the whole world of incompleteness.[15]

Beckett's subsequent response to this 'revelation' – his attempt to pursue a *via negativa*, to develop a 'literature of the unword' – comes to define his work, as we will see in Chapter Nine. At this point, however, it is the revelation itself that matters, almost literally; as his mother puts on one mask, Beckett takes off another. The mother's physical transformation prompts the son's metaphysical transformation, when at the age of 39, Beckett suddenly realizes that all his efforts at accumulation – of knowledge, of insight, of experience – have been in vain. In the second half of his life, he decides, he will pursue precisely the opposite agenda. The unmaking of him will be the making of him.

The broader lesson of this revelation as it relates to the creative life is that biological, physical processes have aesthetic, metaphysical consequences. Middle age, in this Beckettian model, should be not simply more of the same, but *less* of the same. Ageing is a lesson in lessness. In the words of the great Polish diarist Witold Gombrowicz (1904–1969), 'it would seem that there should be two separate languages: one for those who have more and more of life and another for those who have less and less.'[16] By the time we reach the middle of life, doing less arguably has greater value than doing more, since reaching middle age means not only achieving maturity, but accepting mortality. There comes a tipping point in life when, rather than collecting *more* books – or money, or cars, or stamps – you start getting *rid* of them. We will never have read every last book, and that's just fine; life is finite. We must learn to divest ourselves of the banality of ego. Perhaps, indeed, this is the defining aspect of middle age: the acceptance that we don't stay young and self-centred forever. If to philosophize, in the phrase made famous by Montaigne, is to learn how to die, it is also to learn how to age.

3

Halfway Up the Hill
How to Begin in the Middle

I

How does it feel to be in the middle of life? One of the greatest works of world literature ponders precisely this question. The opening lines of Dante Alighieri's *Divine Comedy* describe perhaps the most famous midlife crisis in history:

> *Nel mezzo del cammin di nostra vita*
> *Mi ritrovai per una selva oscura,*
> *ché la diritta via era smarrita.*[1]

> When I had journeyed half of our life's way,
> I found myself within a shadowed forest,
> for I had lost the path that does not stray.[2]

Begun in 1308, Dante's great poem constitutes the culminating statement of the medieval world view, with its rigid, scholastic theology and arcane allusions to long-forgotten debates. But it is also the most pressingly personal of epics, driven by Dante's allegorical journey through the three spheres of Hell, Purgatory and Paradise and peppered with reckonings with his own real-life enemies, whom he condemns – who wouldn't like to do that? – to various levels of imaginatively conceived punishment. The technique of *contrapasso* – 'counter-suffering' – allows him to assign an appropriate fate to anyone who has sinned: false prophets walk backwards with their heads turned to the past, the wrathful tear each other limb from limb. Equal parts physical and metaphysical, visceral and visionary, the *Divine Comedy* constitutes a symbolic representation of how it feels to be in the middle of life's way, to step back and reflect on the road taken and the road to come.

For Dante, such stepping back had a very particular context. Longstanding hostilities in northern Italy between supporters of the Pope and the Holy Roman Emperor – Guelphs to the left, Ghibellines to the right – saw Dante, a so-called White Guelph, exiled from his native Florence in 1302. The opening lines of his great poem indicate that he set it in 1300; given that he was born in 1265, the middle of the way in the biblical terms of the Psalms ('three score years and ten') places the action of the poem at the precise turn of the century. Symbolism and a sense of numerical neatness aside – the *Divine Comedy* is nothing if not obsessed with numerology, its 34 cantos in the first book and 33 in the last two adding up to a perfect century – this matters because it enables Dante to look back to the time before he was exiled. The poem represents a middle-aged man's enquiry, in short, into where it all started to go wrong.

Yet it is equally a meditation on where it all starts to go right. To be sure, the *Divine Comedy* can be read as a revenge fantasy, particularly in those cantos of the *Inferno* that describe in such visceral detail the poet's enemies roasting in the flames. But it can also be read as a reckoning with time. As an ageing, exiled poet – in his forties when he began the poem, Dante would die in 1321 at the age of 56 – the author frames the entire metaphysical edifice within his own process of coming to maturity. He will undergo many obstacles and encounters along the way, first in the company of the pre-Christian Virgil, who will guide him through the circles of Hell and the cornices of Purgatory, then in the company of the blessed Beatrice, who will lead him up through the celestial spheres of Paradise. But the direction of travel is ultimately upwards, and it is because he starts *nel mezzo* that he can look both backwards to pre-Christian beastliness and forwards to post-Christian beatitude. The end begins in the middle.

Dante's poem brings out the essential ambivalence of his starting point. Like all metaphysics of the middle, it looks back to the past in order to look forwards to the future. In Dante's case, the path to maturity that his epic outlines is not only personal, but religious, national and even linguistic. His decisive influence on the history of European culture derives, in fact, from this multifaceted resonance. In religious terms, the *Divine Comedy* functions as a *summum* of the theology of the Middle Ages – the periodic term is itself suggestive, as we shall see – on account of its implicit teleology. Pre-Christian antiquity, however impressive its cultural achievements may have been, was fated to come before Christ; the Christian era was blessed as the *Anno Domini*. Seen from the point of view of the Christian West, the true historical turning point was the birth of Jesus.

Dante's work describes not just one pilgrim's progress, that is to say, but that of an entire culture. Although Italy was not officially unified until the *Risorgimento* of 1861, the process had been made possible by the creation of a common vernacular initiated some 550 years previously. In his treatise *De vulgari eloquentia* – written, ironically, in Latin – Dante had advocated the use of vernacular Italian in literature; in the *Divine Comedy* he made good on his promise, establishing his own Tuscan dialect as the basis for what would become the national language of Italy. Between its mythical origins in Aeneas' arrival in Rome and its ultimate establishment as a modern, Christian state in the nineteenth century, Italy found in Dante's Tuscany its own halfway house.

The *Divine Comedy* broke new ground not just in its language, but in its prosody. Dante introduced into European literature a new meter, known ever after as *terza rima*. The pattern of this 'third rhyme' constitutes a three-line stanza, with interlocking rhymes following the model A-B-A, B-C-B, C-D-C and so on. It is difficult to reproduce in English owing to that language's scarcity of rhyming words, but in a Romance language such as Italian *terza rima* is relatively easy to construct, since there are so many words that end in rhyming syllables (see, for instance, the feminine endings of the opening tercet *vita/smarrita*). The interlocking rhyme scheme creates a constant sense of momentum, appropriate to the movements of Dante's pilgrim as he travels through the various circles, cornices and spheres. It also places emphasis on the rhyme words, creating conceptual pairs out of coincidental sounds. Dante's *vita*, to return to the example of the opening tercet, is now *smarrita* (lost, frustrated), rather than *nuova* as it had been in the title of his hybrid work of prose/poetry *The New Life* (1295). Out of such opposites emerges a middle ground.

As the poem moves into its second and third stanzas, these opposites become increasingly apparent:

> *Nel mezzo del cammin di nostra vita*
> *mi ritrovai per una selva oscura,*
> *ché la diritta via era smarrita.*
>
> *Ah quanto a dir qual era è cosa dura*
> *questa selva selvaggia ed aspra e forte*
> *che nel pensier rinnuova la paura!*
>
> *Tanto è amara, che poco è più morte:*
> *ma per trattar del ben ch'i' vi trovai,*
> *dirò dell'altre cose ch'io v'ho scorte.*

When I had journeyed half of our life's way,
I found myself within a shadowed forest,
for I had lost the path that does not stray.

THE MIDLIFE MIND

> Ah, it is hard to speak of what it was,
> that savage forest, dense and difficult,
> which even in recall renews my fear:
>
> so bitter – death is hardly more severe!
> But to retell the good discovered there,
> I'll also tell the other things I saw.

That the poem begins in the middle is, of course, striking enough. Dante begins *in medias res*, not in the narrative sense of taking the reader straight into the thick of a story, but in the biographical sense of taking the reader straight into the middle of his life. The central image of these opening verses, the forest ('shadowed' in the first instance, 'savage' in the second), expands allegorically on what it means to be in the middle. Through this forest – understood not only as an allegory of life itself, but as a purgatorial version of the paradisiacal Garden of Eden – Dante must find the 'path' that he has temporarily lost. Echoing the obvious imagery of light and dark, good and evil, there emerges a subtler distinction between moving in a straight line (the path) and going around in circles (the forest). The heavily stressed transition at the start of the second line from the first person plural to the first person singular – from '*our* life's way' to finding '*myself* within a shadowed forest' – parallels this negotiation between the universal and the particular. In order to find himself, Dante first needs to lose himself; to 'tell the good', he must also tell the bad.

Purge, purgation, purgatory: counterpoint and dialectic are built into Dante's enterprise from the very start. The poor souls trapped in hell 'suffer the opposite' of what they did on Earth, but Dante too is trapped in his own *contrapasso*, exiled into an inauthentic existence away from his native Florence. Within the poem, his constantly shifting narrative presence contrasts pointedly with the static, unchanging nature of Hell; where the poet keeps moving, like a trauma tourist ushered from one catastrophe to another, the condemned are frozen for all time in their baroque, symbolic contortions. For the reader, too, this is surely one reason why the *Divine Comedy* continues to fascinate; we are both hypnotized and horrified by the idea of eternity. As Woody Allen once remarked, eternity is a long time, especially at the end, and this open-ended metaphysics runs counter to every instinct of human consciousness. If life is defined by time, the afterlife, terrifyingly, is defined by the absence of time. Dante keeps on walking (along that opening image of the path); the condemned can only stand still. Life can only have a middle, in short, because it has an end.

Dante was nothing if not Aristotelian in his conception of this middle. Aristotle, as we have seen, defined time as a midpoint between past and future. In Book Four of *The Banquet* (known in Italian as the *Convivio*, and written between 1304 and 1307 as a sort of compendium of medieval mores), Dante follows the philosopher not only in adopting this metaphysical sense of the middle, but in sketching out a related moral sense of the term as it applies to middle age. Defining 'maturity' (*gioventute*), with mathematical precision, as the twenty years either side of the midpoint of 35, he holds that the middle period thus starts at 25 and ends at 45, this latter year marking – somewhat dispiritingly from a modern perspective – the beginning of 'old age'. Even if our actual lifespan may vary according to circumstances, the proportion of the four life stages ('youth' and 'extreme old age' completing the cycle at either end) does not.[3]

Beyond the maths, however, it is the morality that holds our attention. Dante identifies five necessary qualities that define the mature man: he should be temperate, strong, loving, courteous and loyal. His great exemplar of maturity – and one that would remain extremely influential throughout the medieval period – is Aeneas, whom Virgil is forever praising as 'pious' for having lovingly carried his father, Anchises, out of the burning ruins of Troy. But he is also temperate (he tears himself away from the

Detail from Carle Vanloo, *Aeneas Carrying Anchises*, 1729, oil on canvas.

temptations of Dido), strong (he has the courage to go down to the underworld), courteous (he honours the dead) and loyal (he rewards his supporters handsomely). Aeneas, in short, is not only the ideal *middle-aged* man; he is the ideal *man*.[4]

Arriving at the middle of his own life, then, Dante implicitly aspires to be Aeneas; the choice of Virgil as guide suggests as much. But, like the rest of us – Dante is nowhere more human than when he doubts – he also fears that he is not up to the job.

The *Divine Comedy* is premised on the assumption of *gioventute*, the maturity of middle age embodied by the classical hero struggling manfully with both father and child. Just like Aeneas, Dante will go down to the underworld; just like Aeneas, he will emerge at the other side. Yet the path through the middle is anything but straightforward. Triumph and culmination require crisis and confusion; the path points both ways. Maturity may be the most perfect state of the 'noble person', but it is also cruelly, heartbreakingly brief. Like Franz Kafka's Gregor Samsa, Dante's pilgrim starts in the middle, in that fleeting moment of existential equilibrium between the past of youth and the future of old age. But as he begins to write, Dante has in fact already moved well beyond this median point, and is now looking back at his younger self with retrospective pathos. Metamorphosis, whether swift or slow, instant or incremental, is the meaning of midlife: we are changing under our own eyes. The middle announces itself as the most promising, but also the most problematic, of beginnings.

II

I first read Dante on a tropical island in the Indian Ocean. At the age of twenty – exactly halfway to my age as I began writing this book – I had decided to spend six months on La Réunion, a tiny speck of land lost in the immense stretches of water between Madagascar and Mauritius. Arriving in September, with the southern spring getting hotter by the week, I was there to speak as much French as possible (no easy task, given the local preference for Créole). I was also there, it turned out, to take a decisive turning in my own life's way.

My introduction to the island began before we had even landed. As the plane sat refuelling on the tarmac in Antananarivo, the capital of Madagascar, I began talking to my neighbour, a student of my own age returning from a year in Sheffield. Frédéric, it emerged, was the son of a prominent local journalist; his father could often be seen on television commenting on the complicated politics of La Réunion, an island administered from Paris but anchored in the Indian Ocean. His mother, I would later discover, ran a nursery from home, complete with miniature furniture and age-appropriate reading material; we would sit around their swimming pool in the evening perched on comically small chairs, pallid Gullivers in a world of swarthy Lilliputians. Fresh from his experiences in the north of England, Fred clearly wanted to continue speaking English; nervous about flying thousands of miles away to the other side of Africa, so did I. I still remember the phrase he used as we got off the plane and exchanged contact details: 'Don't be a stranger.' I had found my guide to this island paradise.

La Réunion in the summer is a hot, sweaty delight. To anyone raised in the northern hemisphere, there is a guilty, transgressive pleasure in spending the winter months under the southern sun. The indices of exoticism – to transpose Edward Said's notion of 'orientalism' on to the ways in which we construct our distant idylls – are vividly present on the island: gently wafting palm trees, glistening beaches, translucent water. The inland mountains and jungle paths are extraordinary, a lost world of unique birds and luxuriant flowers lifted directly from an adventure story by Conan Doyle or Rider Haggard. And at the far end of the island is one of the world's most active volcanoes, a glowering, vaporous crater sitting squat in a mud-red Martian landscape. This could be, one feels while clambering timorously up to it, Avernus itself, the very entrance to Hell.

Under the punishing sun, I began to appreciate the full force of Fred's advice. Camus' *The Stranger* had been a set text at school, and I was starting to sympathize with the hero Meursault's sense of addled alienation on his Algerian beach. *Un étranger* was exactly what I was on this tropical island, and it was exactly what I was becoming. The heat, the isolation, the long, empty days, the intoxicatingly strong local marijuana – all created an impression of distance from one's own life, a percussive numbness at once vivid and vertiginous. Our addled brains were primed to believe anything, all the outlandish stories of how slaughterhouses next to the sea attracted sharks, of how foreigners had never returned from the inland *cirques* and were still wandering around up there in a daze. The sheer sensual overload of the tropical climate was almost too much. Simple tasks such as walking around a food market were overwhelming, a synaesthetic smorgasbord of colour, smell and texture. Often I would end up buying nothing, too stunned by the sultry charisma of the spices and pulses, the fish and the sugar beet, to settle on any single choice. Daily hitchhiking, too, encouraged an equal sense of immersion and alienation; dropping in and out of people's lives, we were also dropping out of our own lives. Like Odysseus' lotus-eaters, we were at the edges of our selves.

Into this languid air, maturity dawned. Discipline, self-control, a long-term perspective: precisely at a time when I had none of these things, I started to desire all these things. Like millions before and since, I was beginning to realize that maturity is not just a biological fact; it is also an idea, and a consciously cultivated one at that. I had to *decide* to begin the adult phase of my life, I had to *decide* to escape the dither and drift of post-adolescent aimlessness. In my case this meant discovering, and taking a very deliberate decision to pursue, the life of the mind. At the height of my self-indulgence, I found myself surprising, like Larkin's churchgoer, a hunger in myself to be more serious. The island was functioning like a purge, a purgation, a purgatory. In order to possess what you do not possess, as T. S. Eliot observes in the first of his *Four Quartets* (1936), you must go by the way of dispossession. In order to attain maturity, I went by the way of immaturity.

Eliot was well into middle age by the time he wrote his quartets, and they feel like the work of someone older still, an 'aged eagle' looking to Beethoven's late quartets as his inspiration. Maturity is a relative concept; 'coming into it' is not the same thing as fully possessing it. When I look back now to how I was then, I see, for the first time, an incipient adult, drawn out of himself by a distance both geographical and intellectual. The island helped me to gain purchase on my life up to this point; literature, as I was just beginning to discover, helped me to gain purchase on my life to come, and provided a sense of purpose hitherto absent from my comfortable, complacent upbringing. My own identity, I was starting to realize, could go by the way of others.

There is in fact an intimate, if rarely considered, connection between late adolescence and middle age. Reaching full maturity inevitably requires reconsidering its formation; *middle* age looks back, with its accumulated critical distance, on *coming* of age. The common element to both milestones, the thing that actually makes them milestones, is their shared self-consciousness (whether as cause or effect is an open question). During the majority of adult life we drift from activity to activity, too focused on the task at hand to reflect on its greater meaning or significance. To be middle-aged, however – and perhaps in particular at the beginning of the period – is to be (painfully) aware of being 'middle-aged', just as one is vividly aware of being merely at the start of adult life during late adolescence. Joseph Conrad's notion of the 'shadow-line' of maturity is predicated on precisely this self-consciousness: 'Youth is a fine thing, a mighty power – as long as one does not think of it. I felt I was becoming selfconscious.'[5]

My own emergence from adolescence was defined by an almost crippling degree of self-consciousness regarding my place in the world. No doubt this is a common experience, particularly for anyone intellectually inclined, but for several years around the age of twenty I was repelled by what I saw as the futility and superficiality of ordinary adult life, its dull banality and dutiful compromise. This was the arrogance of youth, to be sure – I wanted nothing to do with the standard concerns of my peers, preoccupied as they seemed to be with sporting and alcoholic prowess – but it was also the dawning sense of something more compelling beneath the surface of everyday existence. As the nineteenth-century Italian poet Giacomo Leopardi noted (at the age of thirty), for an imaginative man

> the world and its objects are, in a way, double. He sees with his eyes a tower, a landscape; he hears with his ears the sound of a bell; and at the same time his imagination sees another tower, another bell, and hears another sound. The whole beauty and pleasure of things lies in this second kind of objects.[6]

If adolescence produces this split sensibility, with maturity – and with a bit of luck – we find our way out of the dead end as we settle into an established, autonomous sense of self. But as we enter middle age the vanity recurs, this time in the baroque form of *vanitas*. Mortality now replaces 'identity' as the defining concern; we are no longer discovering what we don't (yet) have so much as protecting what we do. Self-consciousness returns, but this time it is concerned more with what we stand to lose than with what we stand to gain.

When I had set out for La Réunion, I had found room in my luggage – at the last minute, as I recall – for three big books and one slim one. Alongside C. H. Sisson's translation of the *Divine Comedy*, I had squeezed in the Penguin edition of James Joyce's *Ulysses*, an anthology of French lyric poetry and the Faber edition of Eliot's *Collected Poems*. When I returned from the island, from the southern summer of the tropics to the northern winter of Vienna, I spent six months reading Goethe's *Faust*, Montaigne's *Essais* and Miguel de Cervantes's *Don Quixote*, as well, only slightly later, as Shakespeare's *Collected Plays* and Marcel Proust's *In Search of Lost Time*. Reading these major texts – defining works of the Italian, English, German, Spanish and French traditions – marked, I realize now, my passage to intellectual maturity. If they furnish my mind to this day, it is because the middle part, the major part of my life, began with them. To write of the past, in this sense, is also to write of the present.

Looking back at these works that I encountered during the formative period of late adolescence, I see now that I set myself something like a 'Great Books' course of reading. At this pivotal point in my life I looked to literature for guidance; I posited the person I wanted to be – subtle, capacious, cultivated – and tried to live up to it. That I have no doubt fallen short – that we all fall short – is beside the point; it is the discrepancy between the two, the inevitable failure to become exactly what we had imagined, that constitutes maturity. Or perhaps it is rather that what we had imagined was not precise enough in the first place. Middle age reproaches, but it also revises, the dreams of early adulthood. Gaining lucidity about this is itself an invaluable lesson. Clarity begins at home.

The great books give us structures of feeling and modes of expression, but they also change with us over time. The way I read Dante now, the way I read Eliot or Joyce, differs markedly from the way I did when I was twenty. The field that has changed the least in my perception – probably because I still associate it so strongly with my time on La Réunion – is French lyric poetry, particularly that of the nineteenth century, which with its luminaries such as Charles Baudelaire (who visited the island at the age of twenty, exactly my age when I was there) and Leconte de Lisle (who came, as his name suggests, from the island) retains for me a strongly tropical flavour. The famous closing exhortation of Baudelaire's poem 'Voyage' – 'plunge to the void's depths, Heaven or Hell, who cares? / Into the Unknown's depths, to find the *new*' – always evokes, to my mind, the Indian Ocean through which he travelled in 1841.[7] This suggests, in fact, that too vivid an initial contact with a writer may actually prevent a later, more mature reassessment of their work.

More broadly, however, the middle of life offers an intellectual perspective foreclosed to early adulthood. Partly this is, quite obviously, a function of greater experience: we find more in a text because we have more to find. It is also, however, a function of the fact that the passing of time is built into the major works – one is tempted to say into *all* major works – of literature. Goethe's *Faust* and Proust's *In Search of Lost Time*, to take just two of the canonical texts I read in these years, are both explicitly about the metaphysics of time, the attempt to recuperate youth and purpose. That Joyce set himself the deadline of his fortieth birthday to finish *Ulysses* is as suggestive as any of the book's many references to Homeric myth, for it tells us that he was haunted by his own maturity (*im*maturity being of such enduring importance to his aesthetics). And Eliot, it would seem, was always already middle-aged, trading the nonchalance of youth for the neurosis of footnotes.

But it is Dante who marks most vividly my altered perspective. Ironically, he is perhaps the least obsessed with time of all the major authors, since the *Comedy* takes place in a world outside time, outside youth and ageing. Yet this very timelessness is itself a comment on time, a metaphysical promontory that allows Dante to peer into the purgatory of human life from the outside. *Purgatory* is in fact the one book of the *Comedy* in which movement is possible, since it is there that repentant sinners can hope, with sufficient expiation, to work their way up to Paradise. Lost in the middle, it is the book that everyone forgets – lacking as it does the horror of Hell or the bliss of Heaven – but it is also the most human of the trilogy, since it is not theologically predetermined. Purge, purgation, purgatory: the passage from one form of expiation to the next, the passage from one temporal regime to another. From moral damnation to metaphysical redemption, the middle of the afterlife contains the greatest potential for self-improvement, the greatest possibility of change. As such, it forms the template for the middle of life: how to keep developing beyond the halfway point?

III

Dante's epic poem opens up a whole hinterland of echoes and allusions. It is one of the most storied works of literature in the European tradition, both in the sense that it contains other stories and in the sense that other stories refer to it. Representing as it does the very summit of medieval thought, it could be said to constitute a middle point in the history of Western culture; saturated with classical culture, it in turn saturates modern culture. Seen from our post-millennial perspective, the *Divine Comedy* is in the middle not only of life's way, but of history.

It is worth pausing to reflect on what this means. Why have we come to understand the 'middle' period of Western history the way we do? The very term 'Middle Ages' – which designates, broadly speaking, the millennium between the end of Classical antiquity in the fifth century and the beginning of early modernity in the fifteenth century – implies the *post hoc* perspective of modernity; without this third phase of history, there can be no middle phase. It is perhaps not surprising, then, that the Middle Ages have long suffered such a bad press, struggling, like the proverbial middle child, to establish their own identity. The Early Moderns – from Renaissance humanists to Enlightenment *philosophes* – paid the period little attention, patronizing it, in their rush to look back to the perceived glories of antiquity, as little better than an extension of the Dark Ages. Witchcraft and feudalism were the watchwords of their anti-medievalism, its strict religious dogma a laughing stock for increasingly secular modernity. To be 'medieval' was to be lost in the middle, sandwiched between two superior eras. The fact that this was a grotesquely selective reading of history – completely ignoring, to take just one example, the manifold glories of Spain's 'three cultures' during the period of the *Reconquista* (711–1492) – mattered little. For the cultural self-esteem of modernity, the Middle Ages had to be mediocre.

All this started to change with the advent of Romanticism. Emerging in reaction to the hypertrophied rationalism of the French Revolution, Romanticism developed in late eighteenth-century Germany as a way of emphasizing imagination and passion over argument and reason. One of the key avenues for doing so, historically speaking, was the rediscovery of the Gothic mystery of the Middle Ages. Writers such as Ludwig Tieck began looking to the fairy tale as a model for the modern short story; poets such as Novalis began praising the Christian faith of the medieval period as a model for modernity. The 'Gothic' was at times even conceived as superior to modernity; when crossing the Danube, the French diplomat and memoirist Chateaubriand memorably decried the 'vulgarity and *modernité* of the customs officer and passport [which] contrasted with the storm, the Gothic gateway, the sound of the horn and the noise of the torrent'.[8] Bucolic medievalism had become a viable alternative to bureaucratic modernism.

In the spirit of this new zeitgeist, it didn't take long for historians and critics to get in on the act. The Romantic theorist Friedrich von Schlegel's *Lectures on the History of Literature Ancient and Modern* (1815) give a fair sense of the nineteenth-century revaluation of the Middle Ages. He begins his lecture on the topic by assessing the standard view of the period:

> We often think and represent to ourselves the middle age, as a blank in the history of the human mind, an empty space between the refinement of antiquity and the illumination of modern times. We are willing to believe that art and science had entirely perished, that their resurrection after a thousand years' sleep may appear something more wonderful and sublime.[9]

Schlegel here brings to the fore the obvious fact that the Renaissance, understood as the founding period of early modernity, required a foil against which to define itself. The very idea of 'rebirth', after all, is predicated on the 'death' that precedes it. In order to triumph, modernity *needed* a dormant middle phase out of which it could re-emerge, like a butterfly from its chrysalis.

Yet Schlegel rejects this view by shifting the terms of the metaphor. Far from being a dead, pre-natal period awaiting rebirth, 'the middle age' now becomes the 'youth of modern Europe'. Schlegel's conversion to Catholicism plays a major role in this revaluation (the poet Heinrich Heine later mocked his 'view from the belfry'), since it allows him to identify, alongside a 'chivalric' strain of knights and crusades, an 'allegorical' strain of medieval literature – of which the *Divine Comedy*, unsurprisingly, is the supreme exemplar. Given that it comprehends 'the whole science and knowledge of the time, the whole life of the later middle age', Dante's epic comes to function, following Schlegel's anthropocentric argument, not only as a bridge to Classical antiquity, but as the nursery to modernity. 'Middle age' is repurposed both historically and conceptually.

Our understanding of Dante's great poem depends, then, on these several senses of middle age. If the *Divine Comedy* encapsulates medieval thought and theology, it also captures its anxieties, chief among which is how to reconcile the worldly and the spiritual. To say that Dante's iconic *incipit* is rooted in medieval scholasticism is to say that it emphasizes Man's place within the cosmic order, caught in the middle between the sublime consciousness of angels and the non-consciousness of animals. Being in the middle of life's way, from a medieval point of view, is not only a physical condition, it is a metaphysical one; halfway through our earthly existence, we are also halfway to heaven. Time and again this double perspective emerges as the underlying concern of medieval literature, whether in its chivalric or allegorical strains: not just how to justify the ways of God to man, in the celebrated phrase of Dante's heir John Milton, but how to justify the ways of man to God? The midlife crisis as we understand it in the twenty-first century poses precisely the same question, albeit in suitably secularized form. For what is this crisis about if not the meaning of life?

It is no surprise, then, that ever since Dante's death, poets and novelists have found themselves turning back to his work whenever they require a vocabulary of the middle. The difference, of course, lies in the ontological underpinnings of this middle; where the medieval writer might have suffered a crisis of faith, the modern writer suffers a crisis of faith in *herself*, in her own ability to fill life with purpose and meaning. The shift can already be felt in Early Modernity, even in an avowedly Christian thinker such as Descartes. In his *Discourse on the Method of Rightly Conducting One's Reason and of Seeking Truth in the Sciences* – published in 1637, shortly after he had turned forty – Descartes adumbrates a series of maxims for how to proceed not only intellectually, but morally. His so-called 'provisional moral code' consists of three principal axioms, the second of which is 'to be as firm and resolute as possible in my actions'. Descartes' image for this resolution is strikingly Dantean:

> [In this I would be] imitating travellers who, when they find themselves lost in a forest, should not make the mistake of turning in one direction or another or, even less, of staying in the same place, but should always walk in one direction in as straight a line as possible and not change it for trivial reasons, even if initially it was only chance that determined them to choose it. For, in this way, if they do not arrive exactly where they wish, they will eventually arrive somewhere, and they will probably be better off there than in the middle of a forest.[10]

As a guide to midlife morality, Descartes' travellers echo Dante's pilgrim in his *selva oscura*. As long as we keep moving in one direction, Descartes argues, we will eventually find our way out of the forest; the trick is simply to continue advancing. This presupposes, however, that there is indeed a way out of the forest, that there ultimately *is* meaning on the other side of the trees, if only we are determined enough to find it. The image mediates between our sense of making life up as we go along on the one hand – what Descartes terms his *morale par provision* – and a teleology that ultimately underpins this provisionality on the other. There can be a middle, in short, only if there is also an end. Descartes' shifting of the image away from an exclusively Christian framework and towards the question of personal morality marks the beginning of a recognizably modern sense of individual agency; in his faith that the path will actually lead somewhere, however, he remains demonstrably Dantean.

As early modernity moved into modernity, such faith began to waver. The shift from a world in which Christianity was essentially unquestioned as a source of meaning (the medieval period), via its first unmoorings in the Deism of the Enlightenment (the eighteenth century) to its increasing articulation as a pre-modern anachronism (the nineteenth century), has far-reaching implications for how we conceive of middle age. As long as the path of life is understood as inexorably orientated towards heavenly succour, reaching the notional halfway mark need ultimately hold no fears; so much is implicit in the Dantean-Cartesian image of finding one's way through the woods, and explicit in the upward progression towards Paradise. As soon as this goal disappears, however, one is no longer halfway to heaven but halfway to oblivion.

Historicizing the issue in this way helps us to understand, then, that being in the middle of life depends not just on how we conceive of the middle, but on how we conceive of life. That is perhaps obvious, but it is easily overlooked; it is not much good being in the middle if you don't know of *what*. Post-Romantic articulations of the position betray this anxiety time and again

– indeed, they are constituted by it. Perhaps the most representative example is Friedrich Hölderlin's brief, gloriously limpid poem of 1804, 'Half of Life':

> With yellow pears hangs down
> And full of wild roses
> The land into the lake,
> You loving swans,
> And drunk with kisses
> You dip your heads
> Into water, the holy-and-sober.
>
> But oh, where shall I find
> When winter comes, the flowers, and where
> The sunshine
> And shade of the earth?
> The walls loom
> Speechless and cold, in the wind,
> Weathercocks clatter.[11]

The title of Hölderlin's poem suggests that it stands consciously within the Dantean tradition of being *nel mezzo del cammin*. Yet its content, as it begins, bears strikingly little relation to the promised topic, revealing rather an unmistakeably Romantic landscape of earthly delights. It is only as the poem unfolds that it makes good on the title's promise, developing, through its three deceptively simple sentences (four in German), into a haunting meditation not merely on being in the middle of life, but on what this even means within a natural, rather than a supernatural framework. One can almost feel the poet grappling with his search for higher meaning.

The poem unfolds as a series of oppositions, most obviously between the summer of the first stanza and the winter of the second. The lake functions as a mirror for the earth, both literally for the pears and roses and metaphorically for the poet as he reflects on the passing of time. The fruit and flowers of the first half of the first stanza contrast with their absence in the first half of the second stanza; in the corresponding second halves, the lovely swans become speechless walls. The whole force of the lyric thus crystallizes, in a sense, into the little sigh 'but oh' (*weh mir*), pivotally positioned in the very middle of the poem; swans and roses may swoon invitingly into the lake, but not for long. Summer's lease hath all too short a date.

Perhaps the most potent image of the poem is that of the swans, and it is in them that the poet's anxiety regarding his midlife status – and, by extension, that of all creative figures – is most clearly articulated. Traditional emblems of elegance, the 'loving swans' are associated with an idiom of intoxication: 'drunk with kisses', they dip their heads into the 'water, the holy-and-sober'. These enigmatic lines have attracted much attention from scholars, particularly given the intriguing tension between the intoxicated animals and the sobering lake. Is the action of dipping their heads into the water an artistic or a religious image? Is it sexual? The invented adjective 'holy-and-sober' – in German the single, almost mystical compound *heilignüchtern* – perhaps suggests that they are being baptized, but it also implies that their spell is being broken. What begins as a Romantic image *par excellence* ends as a solemn, sad moment.

The middle of life's way for Hölderlin, then, emerges as a metaphysical hangover. After the sensuous thrill of late summer and early autumn, the prospect of winter can be figured only as a rhetorical question to which there is no answer: after such knowledge, what forgiveness? The move from animate swans and roses to inanimate walls and weathercocks tells its own story. Language – the very stuff of poetry – has deserted Hölderlin in the middle of his life, as he looks ahead to the mute indolence of old age. Meaning itself has fled, like the fleeting shadows of summer.

That Hölderlin would lose his mind the year after he wrote this poem only reinforces its pathos. His life in fact displays a striking symmetry. Born in 1770, he reached – and wrote – the 'half of life' in his mid-thirties, before spending almost exactly the same amount of time living, in a state of attested madness, in a tower in Tübingen (he would die in 1843). It is well-nigh impossible, in other words, not to read the poem as an uncanny anticipation of his fate, whereby the pivotal expostulation 'but oh' at the heart of the poem assumes an almost tragic force. The poet is bemoaning the passing of not only time, but his powers.

In the year before Hölderlin's death, another, very different poet reached the middle of life's way. Henry Wadsworth Longfellow marked the occasion with a sonnet entitled simply 'Mezzo Cammin':

> Half my life is gone, and I have let
> The years slip from me and have not fulfilled
> The aspiration of my youth, to build
> Some tower of song with lofty parapet.
> Not indolence, nor pleasure, nor the fret
> Of restless passions that would not be stilled,
> But sorrow, and a care that almost killed,
> Kept me from what I may accomplish yet;
> Though, half-way up the hill, I see the Past
> Lying beneath me with its sounds and sights, –
> A city in the twilight dim and vast,
> With smoking roofs, soft bells, and gleaming lights, –
> And hear above me on the autumnal blast
> The cataract of Death far thundering from the heights.[12]

Written in 1842 (although not published until 1886), Longfellow's poem is more overtly biographical than that of Hölderlin, less concerned to find what T. S. Eliot would call 'objective correlatives'. The poem's principal aim is simply to express the poet's midlife angst. And angst there was in the life of Longfellow: his first wife died following a miscarriage in 1835 (this, presumably, is the 'sorrow' and 'care that almost killed'); his second wife would die in a horrific accident in 1861, having set fire to her dress with candle wax. The muted, minor key of this and other poems by Longfellow is eminently understandable.

Yet the poem is also explicitly indebted to Dante in ways that make it as much a literary as a biographical reckoning with middle age. As the first American translator of the *Divine Comedy*, Longfellow was intimately familiar with the Italian poet's work: 'Midway upon the journey of our life, / I found myself within a forest dark', runs his translation of the opening lines of the *Inferno*.[13] The title and first line of his own sonnet suggest that he is not simply borrowing Dante's iconic moment of crisis, but also measuring himself – and finding himself wanting – in the light of his great predecessor's achievements. For the architecture of ageing, in 'Mezzo Cammin', is based on the *Commedia*: Longfellow's life, like Dante's afterlife, winds higher and higher up the mountain of time. The echo of Elliott Jaques's patient, who describes his midlife crisis as the sudden realization that he is at the crest of the hill with nothing but a downward slope in front of him, is inevitable, although the difference is equally significant; for Longfellow, the direction of travel is not down but up, like Dante's pilgrim climbing the cornices. 'Half-way up the hill' at the point of writing, the poet finds himself in the purgatory of middle age.

Seen from this sobering perspective, Longfellow's 'cataract of Death' equates to Hölderlin's rattling weathercocks. Both poets fear a grim, icy future on the far side of summer. Yet what is equally notable is that they both frame these fears in the self-referential language of the lyric poet; where Hölderlin anticipates seeing speechless walls in his future, Longfellow regrets not having constructed a 'tower of song' in his past. It is not so much old age that scares them as decelerating creativity. The attempt to understand middle age through reference to one of the greatest poets of world literature – as well as the striking conflation, in both poems, of language with architecture, as though this could somehow confer enduring solidity on their words – suggests that writing functions as a way of coming to terms with ageing. Literature as catharsis: one of the oldest tricks in the book.

As we begin to trace our path through the shadowed forest of middle age, then, a first function of literature starts to emerge. From Penelope unspooling her thread to Scheherazade keeping her head, from Boccaccio's *Decameron* to Chaucer's *Canterbury Tales*, literature has always been about 'buying' and passing time. We write, we read and we narrate so that we may forget, however fleetingly, our mortal condition; we tell stories to mark time, in the several senses of this resonant phrase. Now that I am halfway up the hill myself, I see this with ice-cold clarity: to write – and to read – is to wrestle with the anxiety of ageing. Middle age is the point at which our finite allotment of time becomes inescapably apparent, but the crisis that this realization can occasion also provides the creative spark necessary for a *Divine Comedy*. If the art of middle ageing is to keep developing and to keep creating, then literature – its production and its reception – can both conceptualize and constitute this process. Elsewhere in his poetry, Hölderlin asks 'what poets are for in destitute times', and to the version of this question as it applies to middle age we might reply that they are for helping us think through our own mortality – while showing us that we can, in fact, transcend it.[14] Time is a disease that literature hopes, however quixotically, to cure. Such, we will see, is the wager that it stakes.

4

A Room at the Back of the Shop
Midlife Modesty

I

How do those of us who are not Dante come to terms with getting older? It is all very well finding solace in writing one of the great masterpieces of world literature, but such gifts are hardly given to all. An achievement as exceptional as the *Divine Comedy* is by definition no sustainable solution to middle age. For those of us who don't have Dante's talents – which is to say, all of us – more modest aims may be appropriate. Self-acceptance, career reassessment, new challenges: turning inwards can be as productive as turning outwards. It all depends on working out what we want from (mid)life – more, or less, of the same?

The first thinker in modern Europe to ask himself this question with any degree of rigour was the French essayist Michel de Montaigne (1533–1592). A lawyer, humanist and public servant, Montaigne withdrew from court when still at the height of his very successful career, not so much beginning *in medias res* as ending in it. In a statement that he had engraved, in his native Latin, above the door to his reading room, Montaigne explained – above all, to himself – why he was retiring from the public sphere while still relatively young:

> In the year of our Lord 1571, aged thirty-eight, on the day before the calends of March, the anniversary of his birth, Michel de Montaigne, long weary of the court [and of] the servitude

of the Parlement and public offices, still in the prime of life, retired to the bosom of the learned Virgins, where, in peace and security, he shall spend the days that remain to him to live. May destiny allow him to complete this habitation, this sweet retreat of his ancestors, which he has devoted to his liberty, his tranquillity, and his leisure.[1]

With the inscription of this epochal statement above his library lintel, Montaigne inaugurated the modern sense of identity that is still with us today. The audacity of his ambition, so common in our age of narcissism that nowadays it barely merits remark, is hard to overstate. In an era of rigorously policed religious dogma, Montaigne's subject matter, scandalously, was to be himself. On a range of subjects both weighty and trivial – from cowardice to thumbs, from solitude to smells – he set out to record his warts thoughts and all. His chatty, conversational style was designed to appeal to the general reader of the Renaissance, an emerging market by the end of the sixteenth century. The fifteenth century had been marked by a series of era-defining discoveries, including Johannes Gutenberg's invention of the printing press, Filippo Brunelleschi's calculation of the laws of perspective and Christopher Columbus's claiming of the Americas; by the sixteenth, the Renaissance reader was ready to discover himself. Reminiscent of Leonardo's 'Vitruvian Man', the wager of Montaigne's *Essais* – one of the most spectacularly successful in the history of Western culture – was that the experiences of one human were those of humanity more generally. One small step for Montaigne, one giant leap for mankind.

Anyone who has ever kept a diary owes the Frenchman a debt of gratitude. If all philosophy, in the famous phrase of the twentieth-century mathematician and philosopher Alfred North Whitehead, is a footnote to Plato, all autobiography is a footnote to Montaigne. This very book that you hold in your hands sits in his shadow; to write about one's own development, and the ways that it relates to literature and culture, is to reinforce Montaigne's position at the beginning of the modern self. Memoir, newspaper column, blog: writing more than four hundred years ago, Montaigne had already invented the tools of our confessional age. But he also invented, on closer inspection, the tools of our middle age. Like Dante at the start of the *Divine Comedy*, Montaigne consciously resolved to undertake his project of self-examination only once he had reached the middle of his life.

The tone of his inscription, to be sure, is markedly different to that of the beginning of the *Inferno*. Where Dante *loses* his way in a dark wood, Montaigne *finds* his way back to his childhood home, meaning that the image of the doorway takes on a particular significance, symbolizing as it does the portal both to intellectual enlightenment and to the second half of life. Hanging above the entrance to his library, Montaigne's statement functions almost as the exact opposite to the inscription that Dante and Virgil notoriously encounter above the gate to Hell: 'Abandon all hope ye who enter.' As he enters the second half of life, Montaigne inscribes hope into the very structure of his existence.

There are doorways behind doorways, however. Hiding behind both Dante's and Montaigne's thresholds is the biblical precedent of Hezekiah, king of Judah. In Isaiah 38, the titular prophet comes to the king, who has been struck sick in the prime of life, to announce that he will shortly die; Hezekiah, unable to accept his fate, prays to God and pleads for clemency on account of his lifelong piety. Moved by his devotion, God grants Hezekiah a further fifteen years of life, setting the sun back by ten steps of the stairway as a sign of their agreement. Divine intervention seemingly forestalls the midlife crisis.

Yet closer inspection suggests that it also creates it. For Hezekiah is far from unambiguously grateful, since he realizes that this now means his days are, quite literally, counted: 'In the middle of my days / I must depart; / I am consigned to the gates of Hell / for the rest of my years.' By granting him the extra fifteen years, the Lord has also marked out the day of his death, since the sun will still climb inexorably higher up the stairway. The concept of the midlife crisis, if not the term, thus exists already in the Old Testament; *nel mezzo del cammin*, Hezekiah suddenly becomes horribly aware of the brevity of human life. His story teaches us that while middle age may be about mortality, it is above all about confronting our *consciousness* of mortality.

Hezekiah's gates of Hell hover, then, behind both Dante's opening and Montaigne's entrance. But the two writers' responses differ. Where Dante maps out a suitably pessimistic mood, Montaigne pursues a more optimistic path, paying due deference to the ineluctability of death ('may destiny allow') and striking a fatalistic tone about 'the days that remain to him to live'. Modesty, in Montaigne's view, is the best defence against mortality; neither in his library inscription nor anywhere in the *Essais* does he plead for extra time beyond his allotted span. Eschewing the *deus ex machina* for which King Hezekiah pleads, Montaigne accepts his ageing and foreswears worldly pursuits. Where before he had been a busy politician and public servant (he would end up as a reluctant mayor of Bordeaux, as well as a key adviser to Henri de Navarre before the latter became Henri IV), now he pledges to devote himself to calm self-examination. From the *negotium* or business of court and marketplace, Montaigne turns to the *otium* or leisure of home and culture.

The *Essais* can be read, then, as a series of attempts at what one might term 'midlife modesty'. Over the course of three collections of essays and three succeeding editions (published in 1580, 1588 and 1595), Montaigne interrogates his feelings about the human condition as unsparingly as possible. The thousand-plus pages of the *Essais* rank as one of the greatest achievements of the Early Modern mind, a compendium of Renaissance culture. Yet what is perhaps most impressive about them is their enduringly – and endearingly – provisional status. Unlike so many of us, Montaigne manages to keep an open mind even into middle age, as the continuing revisions to his manuscript suggest. The very term *essai* (a term that he effectively coined) implies this experimental approach – the twentieth-century Austrian author Robert Musil would describe 'essayism' as the continuation of science by other means – since it defines Montaigne's whole intellectual project as so many 'attempts' on meaning. Intermittent failure is an inevitable consequence; midlife modesty consists in accepting this. As we get older, the only realistic ambition is to fail better.

For Montaigne, the prerequisite for such an ambition – although the word is too forceful, since he is precisely *renouncing* ambition – is solitude. Solitude, he argues, helps to secure the self; by setting aside a 'room at the back of the shop', we can refocus our thoughts on our own well-being.[2] Yet it is not enough merely to withdraw from society; we must also withdraw 'from such attributes of the mob as are within us'. By the time we reach the middle of life, after all, we have lived quite enough for others; we should at least be able to live 'the tail-end of life' for ourselves. The aim of middle age, in Montaigne's view, should be self-sufficiency.

Like many a self-help guru, however, Montaigne has a paradox at the heart of his project. For the more he searches for himself, the more he eludes his own aim. Straining too consciously after enlightenment is the surest way to miss it. 'Where I seek myself I cannot find myself,' he concedes in one aside – a curious admission, it would seem, for someone whose whole enterprise is predicated on self-examination. But the concession is perhaps not so strange once we notice that most of the time he does not so much enquire directly after his own thoughts as interrogate them indirectly, by way of existing precedents on a given topic. For Montaigne, as a typical Renaissance thinker, these precedents were overwhelmingly classical in origin.

Montaigne's native language, as he remarks on more than one occasion, was Latin. His father found him a tutor who spoke to him only in Latin, and by the time he was a young boy his facility in the language was such that he intimidated all his teachers. And yet, strikingly, as a middle-aged adult he chose to write his essays in the modern French vernacular, tinted with the accent of his native Gascony. Why? The answer lies in the nature of his project. Montaigne wanted to speak to the educated, but not the over-educated, general reader; his essays were designed to 'please [neither] common vulgar minds nor unique and outstanding ones' (1:54). Writing in French, rather than Latin, was a way to 'eke out an existence in the middle region'. Montaigne aspired to appeal not so much to Renaissance Man as to Renaissance Everyman.

The concessions to common taste go only so far, however. The *Essais* are dotted with – indeed, they are almost defined by – classical references, and on almost every page Montaigne has recourse to examples from antiquity. In part, this is because he could count on the shared frame of reference of Renaissance humanism (although he was uncommonly erudite even for those times), a humanism that was equal parts Christian and classical. But it is also because the very nature of his undertaking – and of his understanding of midlife wisdom – was fundamentally classical in character. Above all, Montaigne was a Stoic.

If there is one thinker who defines Montaigne's stoicism – and, by extension, his views on the vanity of the human condition – it is the Roman philosopher Seneca (4 BC–AD 65). Montaigne cites Seneca's so-called *Moral Epistles* (known in Latin as the *Epistulae Morales ad Lucilium*) no fewer than 298 times in the course of his essays, and even when he is not directly citing him the influence of the Roman thinker on Montaigne's attitudes to such subjects as suicide or suffering is all too obvious. While Socrates' life remained the supreme example of the Delphic injunction to 'know thyself', for Montaigne the quest for self-knowledge was always an essentially Senecan undertaking, defined as it was by the cultivation of simplicity and humility. At the heart of this quest was the Stoic relationship to time.

Seneca's most famous single work is no doubt the essay *On the Shortness of Life* (*De brevitate vitae*), written some time around AD 49. Its title is programmatic. As a former tutor to the capricious tyrant Nero, Seneca knew a thing or two about the instability of existence (and indeed the suicide that was ultimately forced upon him confirmed his worst fears about the mutability of fortune). In the second half of his life, Seneca increasingly specialized in writing moral tracts about the ephemerality of life; the philosophy that emerged from them, not surprisingly, was a variation on the Horatian imperative to 'seize the day': *carpe diem*. With the future uncertain, seizing the present becomes all the more urgent.

The implications of this for how we view middle age are striking, since they run counter to the modern orthodoxy of constant renewal. Where a writer such as Goethe, for instance, will advocate perpetual incipience as the best defence against ageing, Seneca insists that it is the intensity of experience in the present moment that really counts, not whether we keep attempting new beginnings. Life is already short enough, he notes in one of his *Moral Epistles*, without shortening it still further through starting time and again. The passing stages of life are to be treated with caution: 'how many steps for how short a climb!'[3] We will never reach the top, in his view, if we keep replacing the steps.

That is not to say, however, that Montaigne uncritically endorses this Senecan view of time. However much their two voices sometimes seem to merge, Montaigne is not as dogmatically uncompromising as standard Stoicism would advise. A brief essay in Book I entitled 'On Constancy' suggests as much: Montaigne sides with Socrates in allowing that fleeing can in fact be as praiseworthy as standing firm, citing the example of the Spartans who, by retreating, lulled their enemies the Persians into breaking rank. The first essay of Book II immediately picks up on the topic by insisting, contrary to Stoic orthodoxy, on 'the inconstancy of our actions' as we age. No one can be true to their younger self all the time.

The essay immediately preceding this (the final essay of Book I) makes the link to middle age explicit. Montaigne's reflections 'on the length of life' insist on the fragility of existence: 'I cannot accept the way we determine the span of our lives,' opens the essay defiantly (1:57). Those who reach the pre-ordained 'three score years and ten' are the exception; in a sixteenth-century France riven by the brutal Wars of Religion, attaining old age was a luxury granted to few. Montaigne's advice is to consider ourselves lucky to have lived as long as we have, since if we have made it to maturity we have in any case enjoyed the best of life. The second half of our existence is a bonus; writing at the age of 47, Montaigne claims that we reach our zenith at 30. Hannibal and Scipio, he cites by way of example, 'live a good half of their lives on the glory achieved in their youth', and his own experience of ageing is hardly more encouraging, marked as it is by diminished vitality and vigour. In an era of gruesome sectarian violence, reaching even middle age was no mean feat.

Montaigne's decision to place this brief essay at the end of Book I lends it a particular significance. Within the broader ecology of the *Essais*, it functions as a pivot to the general concerns of ageing, experience and the passing of time. 'On the length of life' – and thus, Book I – ends with the word 'apprenticeship', a period that Montaigne criticizes as taking up too much space in our brief, fragile lives. Moving beyond such apprenticeship, however, is easier said than done, for maturity, in Montaigne's reading, is perhaps the trickiest phase of all, implying as it does the acceptance of inevitable diminishment. One of the most celebrated ideas associated with the *Essais* is accordingly that 'to philosophize is to learn how to die'. The essay of this name takes its impetus from Montaigne's own life situation (although it begins with a nod to Cicero, from whom he derives the notion): exactly a fortnight after he turned 39 – George Miller Beard's 'year of maximum productivity' – Montaigne tells himself that he 'ought to live at least as long again'. Yet he then questions the wisdom of such reasoning, arguing – against the standard animal instinct for survival at all costs – that cultivating our sense of mortality is a better strategy than repressing it, since 'to practise death is to practise freedom.' This, in turn, determines our sense of middle age, a period designed by nature to 'lead us by the hand down a gentle slope . . . so that we feel no jolt when youth dies in us' (1:20).

Cultivating our sense of mortality is necessary in order to mitigate the brutal reality of ageing. For 'in essence and in truth it is a harsher death than the total extinction of a languishing life as old age dies.' Moving from youth to middle age is worse than moving from old age to death, in Montaigne's view, since one loses so much more: 'it is not so grievous a leap from a wretched existence to non-existence as it is from a sweet existence in full bloom to one full of travail and pain' (1:20). The implication of this is an inversion of the standard midlife advice: rather than coming to terms with middle age in order to accept mortality, we should come to terms with mortality in order to accept middle age. We must concentrate on the end, Montaigne argues in this most stoical of chapters, to mitigate the middle.

If to philosophize is to learn how to die, however, it is also to learn how to live. Montaigne starts writing his essays in middle age because the whole project depends, both explicitly and implicitly, on this existential ambivalence. To be middle-aged is to begin the long, slow descent towards death; but it is also to be in the prime of life. Montaigne can teach us how to age as a Christian Stoic – but he can also teach us, in true Renaissance fashion, how to age as a self-fashioning humanist. How we read Montaigne depends, in short, on how we read ourselves.

II

The first time I encountered Montaigne I was little more than a teenager. Returning from La Réunion in the final year of the twentieth century, I found myself in Vienna, a city that had seemingly changed little since its glory days at the end of the previous century. Across literature and medicine, music and the visual arts, for a brief period around 1900 the Habsburg capital had emerged as the centre of European culture, and such luminaries as Hugo von Hofmannsthal, Arthur Schnitzler, Gustav Mahler and Egon Schiele made the city glitter as never before. One hundred years later, for better or for worse it was still living off its reputation for morbid beauty, carefully cultivating its image as an embalmed empire of the mind. Little surprise, then, that the 'beautiful corpse' of Viennese legend should have produced arguably the defining science of our era: psychoanalysis.

However contested Freud's legacy is today, there is little doubt that the discipline he invented has come not just to diagnose, but to define our narcissistic modernity. In our confessional era of self-help and self-disclosure, the publicly examined life is the only one worth living. Yet Freud – he would be the first to admit – hardly invented the idea of the self; the Freudian version of consciousness merely codified those aspects of the ego that we find unpalatable (and thus 'repress'). The exploration of identity as a constituent element of the modern self goes back to the late Renaissance – and, above all, to Montaigne.

Montaigne essentially invented a form of psychoanalysis three hundred years *avant la lettre*. If his language is different from that of Freud – more humanistic, less scientistic – his aim is the same: to understand why we behave the way we do. From the late sixteenth to the early twentieth century, from the Renaissance to modernity, human instincts and ambitions hardly change. The quantum of wantum, in Samuel Beckett's resonant phrase, cannot vary.[4] Yet there is one very obvious difference between the two thinkers, and it colours the entire nature of their respective voyages of discovery: where Freud analyses others, Montaigne analyses himself. This may seem like hubris, but it is in fact humility, since Montaigne limits himself to the one area in which he can claim unrivalled expertise. As with creative fiction, so with midlife modesty: write about what you know.

The problem with giving this advice to someone barely out of adolescence, of course, is that they know so little. When I began reading Montaigne in wintry Vienna, I had an instinct for self-development, but little else. The *Essais* seemed the perfect vehicle for this, a self-help manual of Early Modernity. Like everything else in life, though, what we read and whether we learn from it is a function of timing. There are books that are best read in late adolescence – J. D. Salinger's *The Catcher in the Rye*, for instance – since they capture the all-consuming quest for authenticity that characterizes those threshold years. But can we really sustain Holden Caulfield's categorization of people as either 'phonies' or 'non-phonies' into middle age? The black-or-white, all-or-nothing nature of adolescence gives way, all being well, to the greying nuances of maturity.

There are also books that require this maturity in the first place. Montaigne's reflections on ageing, on vanity and the virtues of moderation, are not those of a man in the first flush of youth; one cannot respond to them fully without some comparable degree of experience. Another Viennese writer, Stefan Zweig, opens his book on Montaigne (1942) with precisely this claim. Written in the desperation of his Brazilian exile – in the same year in which he would ultimately kill himself – Zweig's last book resonates with the pathos of past time. 'Only a seasoned man who has tested himself can appreciate the true worth of Montaigne,' he writes, 'and I count myself one of them. When at the age of twenty I picked up a copy of the *Essais*, that incomparable book he left us, I must confess I had little idea what to do with it.'[5] Looking back on my own twenty-year-old self as I roamed the streets of Vienna, I realize that I too had little idea what to do with it. Had I done enough living to philosophize about dying? Was I hoping Montaigne's maturity would curb my immaturity? What, in short, did I expect to derive from reading him at so callow an age? But then the question is equally valid, *mutatis mutandis*, for any stage of life: why do we read what we do when we do? Montaigne, as ever, anticipates the answer: 'In youth', he writes, 'I studied in order to show off; later, a little, to make myself wiser; now I do it for amusement, never for profit' (III:3).

Montaigne's parabola of purpose applies, no doubt, to a great many of us. It certainly applied to me. My own 'showing off', thank God, was more to myself than to anyone else, but its underlying aim was clear: to give the impression of being a certain kind of person. Montaigne, ironically, has long been used in this way. There is an iconic picture of François Mitterrand posing, in full presidential pomp, with a copy of the *Essais* open on his lap. If Montaigne himself was modest, Mitterrand preferred the false modesty of conspicuous cultural consumption; Montaigne, we are given to understand, signals maturity and wisdom. The pose is in this regard more revealing than intended, since it tells us not so much that Mitterrand *is* mature and wise as that he wishes to be *seen* this way. At fifty, to adapt Orwell's famous formulation, everyone has the portrait they deserve.[6]

Showing off; becoming wiser; seeking amusement: the changing ways in which we read as we age reflect these changing imperatives. This is even more the case if we think about how we re-read. Just as there are certain books that one really needs to read at a particular age, so there are certain books that one can only really understand upon re-reading. Marcel Proust's *In Search of Lost Time*, absurd though it may sound for a work of fourteen volumes, only fully makes sense the second time around, since the narrator's discovery, in the final volume, of his vocation as a writer underwrites the whole cycle. Something similar could

Mitterand, Montaigne and midlife posing: Gisèle Freund's presidential portrait of François Mitterrand, 1981.

no doubt be said about other cyclical works – Richard Wagner's *Ring*, John Donne's *Corona* sonnets – in which stylistic echoes and refrains refer the end back to the beginning. The *Essais* do not function in this manner (although the sequence is carefully composed, and the final essay 'On Experience' sets a seal on the whole undertaking), but re-reading them in middle age nonetheless brings out the underlying purpose of Montaigne's 'attempts' at self-knowledge: to make himself, in his own words, a little wiser. In youth, one reads to be clever; in maturity, to be true.

Montaigne reflects on this distinction in an essay entitled simply 'On Books' (II:10). In true Socratic fashion, he holds that what matters is not our (almost inevitable) ignorance about a given topic, but our ability to *recognize* this ignorance. Such true ignorance can be attained, paradoxically, only through knowledge – the knowledge that the major classical authorities pass on to us. In Montaigne's view, the supreme sources of such wisdom are Plutarch and Seneca, largely because – unlike their contemporaries Cicero or Caesar – they are less interested in writing beautifully than in writing wisely. For Montaigne the moralist, ethics always trumps aesthetics.

This distinction maps directly on to the experience of ageing as he conceives it. Montaigne adopts the standard orthodoxy of Renaissance poetics – namely, that true poetry must both 'delight' and 'instruct' – as his benchmark not only for literature, but for life. If the terminology is as old as Horace's *Ars poetica*, with its epochal advice to mix the *dulce* with the *utile*, in Montaigne's hands the scales tip very firmly towards utility, towards 'books that use learning not those that trim it up'. As we age, moreover, the balance tips still further; we have less and less need for ostentation, and more and more need for instruction. 'For me, who am only seeking to become more wise not more learned or more eloquent,' Montaigne observes of Cicero's style, 'all those marshallings of Aristotelian logic are irrelevant.'

(Even women, he suggests, should 'change the title *beautiful* for *good* after they have reached thirty'.) In literature as in life, wisdom, not wit, is the core requirement of maturity.

The obvious paradox here is that Montaigne himself indulges in countless marshallings from others. Constant reference to the classics is almost his trademark; barely a page goes by without some passing allusion to previous authorities. Even the advice to avoid citation is itself effectively a citation, looking back as it does to his beloved Seneca: 'For a man (*vir*) . . . to chase after choice extracts and to prop his weakness by the best known and the briefest sayings and to depend upon his memory, is disgraceful; it is time for him to lean on himself.'[7] Seneca's explicit reference to virile maturity (my French edition translates *vir* as 'homme d'un age mûr') drives home the point: by middle age, we should have the courage of our own convictions, not those of others. Yet Montaigne, ironically, attains autonomy precisely by way of others.

It is an irony, it goes without saying, that applies equally to the book you are currently reading. In order to assert the self-sufficiency of middle age, I am leaning on the examples of others, combing the canon of European literature for instructive precedents. The whole structure of the book depends on balancing autonomy with authority, the first-person singular with the third-person plural: what 'they' have written and thought informs how I experience getting older; what I have read and registered determines who 'they' are in the first place. If the book sketches out a canon of midlife literature, it remains, unavoidably, *my* canon. Bibliotherapy requires a bibliography.

Yet this is also the very nature of middle age. Successfully negotiating the middle of life involves finding a balance between independence and indebtedness; we find our own voice, but through other people's words. Obtaining full maturity depends on learning to walk for ourselves – the metaphor is Kant's – but we cannot learn how to do so without being taught by others.

To reach the middle of life, and to be aware of it, is not to forget everything that has come before, but to stop deferring to it. The middle of life, in short, is the moment when we must learn, with their help, to outgrow our mentors.

Such a lesson is nothing if not in the manner of Montaigne. Anyone who reads him must be struck by how often he cites his favourite authors; yet he does so from a deeply personal perspective, having learned to foreground his own thoughts and experiences. 'I want authors to begin with their conclusion' (II:10), he states, and by and large this is what he himself does, adducing his authorities only once he has established his argument. The procedure echoes the advice an older colleague gave me just after I had turned forty: strip out all the references to other critics; make your claim rapidly; be bold. You can no longer be judged on potential, he warned me, so it is what *you* have to say that matters (or indeed does not), not what others have already said more eloquently than you could possibly hope to. Show, in short; don't tell.

Such advice was hopelessly beyond me when I first read Montaigne in Vienna. And rightly so: who wants to be old before their years? If I have any purchase on the wisdom of the *Essais* twenty years later, it is because it is not Montaigne who has changed, but I. It would be foolish, however, to think that I am necessarily the better for it. We age in zigzags, not straight lines, a process Montaigne captures memorably when comparing the first and second editions of his book:

> My first edition dates from fifteen hundred and eighty: I have long since grown old but not one inch wiser. 'I' now and 'I' then are certainly twain, but which 'I' was better? I know nothing about that. If we were always progressing towards improvement, to be old would be a beautiful thing. But it is a drunkard's progress, formless, staggering, like reeds which the wind shakes as it fancies, haphazardly. (III:9)

Montaigne's self-doubt characteristically undercuts the supposedly unchanging ego, which he reconfigures, in proto-Freudian fashion, as unstable and beholden to the vicissitudes of time. Like faces frozen on photographs, the succeeding editions split his ageing self into so many snapshots of identity: 1580, 1588, 1595. We could all undertake similar cross-sections of our own lives – I for my part have staggered formlessly from Vienna in 1998 to Canterbury in 2018, from early adulthood to belated maturity. Such form as our lives can be said to have is imposed retrospectively, not in real time.

If we can only recognize the zigzag when looking backwards, however, it is the act of recognition itself that matters. Understood literally as re-cognition, it is the moment that marks the middle of life. The search for this moment – Aristotle termed it *anagnorisis*, the change from ignorance to knowledge that the hero must undergo in order to fulfil his or her destiny – provides a more positive model for midlife lucidity than the infamous crisis.[8] Our progress may be drunken, but our perception of it, at least, can be sober. Montaigne's term for this sobriety, in the essay that crowns his half-life's work, is 'experience'.

III

Montaigne wrote his final essay, 'On Experience', at what, for the sixteenth century, was the ripe old age of 56. It shows.

What have we – or what should we have – learned by the time we are into the second half of life? In a phrase: to know and to trust ourselves. Montaigne never strays far from the Delphic injunction *nosce te ipsum*, but as he ages it assumes ever greater force, becoming a moral pre-condition for the exercise of judgement. His final essay reasserts the importance of self-understanding, but now suggests that it can be obtained as much through physical observation as through metaphysical speculation. Like Dante at the opening of *The Banquet*, Montaigne begins by citing the opening sentence of Aristotle's *Metaphysics* – 'No desire is more natural than the desire for knowledge' – but then immediately suggests that personal experience can teach us the same lessons as impersonal reason. 'I study myself more than any other subject,' he remarks later in the essay. 'That is my metaphysics, my physics' (III:13).

This empirical bias leads Montaigne to a number of very concrete observations on the indignity of ageing, as he unsparingly tracks the physical and psychological changes wrought by time. Where Freud concentrates on childhood, Montaigne focuses on (late) middle age, meaning that biology and its discontents cannot be avoided. Montaigne suffered horribly from gallstone problems, and a good part of his essay is accordingly taken up by an enumeration of his afflictions: he cannot sleep by day, nor go to bed too soon after eating; he can no longer have sex without falling asleep, nor in any other position than lying down; his stomach is increasingly intolerant, with flatulence and vomiting his constant companions. Homer had his catalogue of ships; Montaigne has his litany of complaints. The ageing essayist is human, all too human.

Montaigne's response to his worsening condition is typically Stoic – 'anyone who is afraid of suffering suffers already of being afraid' – but it is no less pressingly personal for that. Ageing forces apart the mind and the body, leading the former to fight back against the latter with rhetorical trickery and intellectual sleight of hand. One of Montaigne's recurring tactics in this regard is to take what one might term the Achilles approach to ageing. The Homeric hero, the reader will recall, was enlisted by the Greek philosopher Zeno to illustrate one of his famous paradoxes – namely, that no matter how fast Achilles runs he will never catch up with the tortoise, since one can always divide his trajectory in half, then half again, then half again, and so on *ad infinitum*. Montaigne repeatedly does something similar in his deployment of the rhetoric of division: 'now that I have entered the approaches to old age, having long since passed forty ... from now on what I shall be is but half a being', he writes in 'On Presumption' (II:17). By the time he comes to write 'On Experience' some ten years later, the mathematical metaphors have multiplied still further:

> God shows mercy to those from whom he takes away life a little at a time: that is the sole advantage of growing old; the last death which you die will be all the less total and painful; it will only be killing off half a man, or a quarter. Look: here is a tooth which has just fallen out with no effort or anguish: it had come to the natural terminus of its time. That part of my being, as well as several other parts, are already dead: others are half-dead, including those which were, during the vigour of my youth, the most energetic and uppermost. That is how I drip and drain away from myself. What animal-stupidity it would be if my intellect took for the whole of that collapse the last topple of an already advanced decline. I hope that mine will not. (III:13)

At first reading, the slide in this passage from a 'total' man to a half to a quarter seems straightforward: age is cutting up the author slice by slice. Closer examination, however, suggests that something more interesting is going on. Quite aside from the strikingly Freudian slippage from fallen tooth to flaccid penis ('the vigour of my youth'), Montaigne's progressive subdivision evokes an embattled self, attempting ever more desperately to shore up fragments against its ruin but with inevitably diminishing returns. Unlike in Zeno's paradox, however, the point is not to claim that death will never catch up with him, but rather that when it does arrive there will be little left for it to take. As his mathematical rhetoric becomes increasingly military – with his 'intellect' the command centre of a collapsing imperial body – Montaigne's response to moving into and beyond middle age is to abandon ever more of his empire. Strategic self-division forestalls the final reduction to zero.

'On Experience' approaches the ageing self mathematically, then. But it also examines it visually. In its depiction of the changes wrought by the passing of the years, the essay at times becomes almost literally a self-portrait, or at least an ekphrastic attempt at one: 'It is my face which gives the game away first; so do my eyes: all changes in me begin there, appearing rather more grim than they are in practice.' Echoing the previous, penultimate chapter, 'On Physiognomy', Montaigne stumbles across paintings of his younger self and is startled by how much he has changed when seen from the outside: 'I have portraits of myself aged twenty-five and thirty-five. I compare them with my portrait now: in how many ways it is no longer I! How far, far different from them is my present likeness than from what I shall be like in death.'

In our age of instant images, when the shock of coming across a younger version of oneself in a photograph is all too common, the observation is no doubt banal. In the sixteenth century, however, the vertigo of time was experienced differently, since it was both more compressed (people did not live as long) and less ubiquitously visible (people did not constantly see themselves in photographs). If the changing portraits thus function as the physical counterpart to the intellectual alterations that Montaigne observes in the successive editions of his essays, they introduce a new note of mortality. By objectifying himself across the abyss of time – into both subject and object, observer and observed – the essayist gains purchase on the years that have passed. Montaigne's portraits provide early modern proof of Barthes' ostensibly modern claim that photographs are indices of death.

What, though, of life? Montaigne is not merely morbid; he is also vivid. 'You are not dying because you are ill,' he tells us with Seneca; 'you are dying because you are alive' (III:13). Ageing portraits and changing editions are evidence, after all, that the

Montaigne in his thirties.

author is developing as much as he is decaying. His positioning of himself in the middle of life, here and elsewhere, is ultimately part of a strategy designed to emphasize not just his incipient mortality, but his enduring vitality. And indeed he remained vital well into middle age; despite his worsening kidney stones, after ten years of study in his tower Montaigne set off, in 1580, on a journey across the Alps, reaching Rome and the Vatican. His restiveness was part of his capacious understanding of the human condition, an understanding born of experience as well as of erudition. For self-consciousness – Montaigne is one of the first to show this – is not just what makes us humanist; it is also what makes us human. Middle-aged Montaigne, like the rest of us, was half-full as well as half-empty.

Reading the *Essais* while in the middle of life is thus a complex affair. The emotional register, the tonal variety, offers both succour and severity. In this, of course, Montaigne merely

Montaigne in his fifties.

mirrors the ambivalence of middle age, the period in which the comedy of life first fully encounters the tragedy of death. 'My natural style is comedy,' he remarks, 'but one whose form is personal to me,' and this form, as he aged, was increasingly elegiac, a kind of gallstone humour (1:40). Ageing without modern medicine, after all, was no laughing matter, and stoicism of one sort or another was indispensable. As with all ageing artists, such suffering had an inevitable impact on Montaigne's preoccupations – this can be seen, above all, in 'On Experience' – but it had remarkably little impact on his style, which was mature from the moment he withdrew into his library. Being reborn directly into middle age has its advantages.

As readers of Montaigne in the twenty-first century, we can only wonder and wince at what it meant to be middle-aged in the late sixteenth century. The maturity of his style was nothing if not hard-won, forged as it was not only by his hot-housed education in classical culture, but by the brutal reality of life during a civil war. Literary criticism teaches us that the *way* we write about something is as telling as *what* we write about, and even now, more than four centuries later, Montaigne's unfailingly civil, serene manner provides as successful an example as one could hope for of how to master the passing of time through writing. The great lesson of the *Essais* for anyone struggling with middle age is that to master time is to master oneself, to cultivate modesty as the essence of maturity. It all comes down, in short, to keeping a room at the back of the shop. Just a few decades later, an even greater writer would place such questions of style and genre at the very heart of what it means to be middle-aged.

5

Getting On
The Tragicomedy of Middle Age

I

As with so many things in life, one of the simplest but most telling ways to think about middle age is to consider the phrases we use to describe it. Metaphors and euphemisms abound: we move past our 'prime' to being 'over the hill'; we are 'not as young as we used to be' as we reach 'a certain age'. Perhaps the most revealing of these formulations is the notion that we are 'getting on'. The ambiguity of the idiom is astonishing, testament to the elasticity of everyday English in its encompassing of registers at once social, professional and biological. For a while, we get on with each other socially as we get on in our careers professionally; but soon enough we start to get on in years biologically. The phrase seems to age as we do, moving from youthful idealism to middle-aged reality. Like characters in a narrative by Beckett, we can't get on, we must get on, we get on.

Life may abhor such multiplicity, but literature is defined by it. Writing in 1930, the critic William Empson famously identified 'seven types' of ambiguity as the basis for literary language; the richer the ambivalence, the greater the writer.[1] Literature, in this reading, emerges as something like the willed suspension of final meaning. By deferring conclusion, by holding two or more meanings at the same time, the poetic use of language opens a space for indeterminacy. Such a process can be of relevance to any life stage, but it is of particular significance to middle age, defined as it is by the double perspective of past and future. As we start to feel our options narrowing, as we begin to feel our doors closing, the idea of prising open alternative realities through the power of the imagination becomes ever more appealing. The midlife crisis is nothing if not the realization that we don't (yet) want to settle on a final meaning. The unsteadiness is all.

If the greatest writers thrive on such ambiguity, the very greatest of them all is a virtuoso of ambivalence. The power of Shakespeare's language derives in large part from its semantic density. When Macbeth mutters to himself 'Come what come may, time and the hour runs through the roughest day,' the verb 'runs through' the supposedly consoling sentiment like a knife through his utterance. Macbeth tries to steel himself by insisting that the terrible day will pass like any other; the murderous undertone of the verb, however, insists that he, like the rest of us, is impaled on time. Language, in Shakespeare's masterly hands, is forever revealing us to ourselves.

As centuries of critics and schoolteachers have shown, such subtlety suggests the importance of attending carefully to Shakespeare's style. What matters is not just *what* is being said, but *how* it is being said; this is the first lesson of literary criticism. Form, in the fully achieved work of literature, enacts content – such is the modernist orthodoxy. My own late twentieth-century schooling in close reading encouraged a sense that meaning was to be found between the lines, behind the surface, beyond the ostensible significance of a given sentence or statement. The more multiplicity one can find in a text, the better. It is up to the critic to tease out the hidden truth, like a hermeneutic detective.

Sometimes even the cleverest of critics, however, just needs to say what literature is *about*. In the case of Shakespeare's plays, the answer is surely: power. The human condition, as it emerges from his work, is defined by who has power, who wants power and who can get power. Getting on, in all its ambivalence, is a central idea in his drama; between human intercourse (the comedies), political struggle (the history plays) and metaphysical time (the tragedies), the three principal senses of getting on correlate to the three principal categories of play. Underlying these, though, is the idea of *getting*: why and how do we envy and acquire things, why and how do we covet and conquer those around us? As such terms suggest, the emotional impetus for this drive is fundamentally erotic; 'getting', in Shakespearean language, means to get with child. We need to talk, in short, about sex.

Sex in middle age is not the taboo it is in old age. We are comfortable with the idea that middle-aged people have sex, want sex and – who knows? – even enjoy sex. The terms of the idea are different, however, from those of its youthful incarnation. Where sex in early adulthood is all about the glamour of the body, by middle age it is about the glory of the mind. Lust in youth is physiological; by the middle of life, it becomes increasingly psychological. This transition suggests that sex – and our changing vision of it – goes to the very heart of what it means to be middle-aged, defined as it inevitably is by an increasingly defensive attitude towards our slowly decaying bodies. The cliché of seeking a new partner in midlife is not about the promise of better sex so much as about the premise of a better self: we want to prove to ourselves that we can still be attractive. This is why only someone in middle age could have coined the old saying that everything is about sex except sex, which is about something else. For that something else, of course, is power.

With a few exceptions notable largely for their offstage absence (such as Fortinbras in *Hamlet*), what is so striking about Shakespeare's depiction of power is that it is invariably embattled. Power, in the Shakespearean vision of it, is almost always contested power; as Henry IV famously observes, 'uneasy lies the head that wears a crown'. All interpersonal rivalries aside, such regal queasiness is in large part a simple function of time.

As we get older, we are increasingly embattled by age, which is to say by anxiety about our dwindling capacities. Monarchy amplifies such anxiety, but it does not alter it; even those who are not subjects are subject to time.

For Shakespeare as a man of the late sixteenth century, such an anxiety of ageing is overwhelmingly male, a fact that is betrayed not only by his interest in older male figures, but by his recurring concern with questions of virility, generation and succession. Power, in short, is potency. And potency, for the playwright, lies in writing, in the ways in which the author asserts authority. The analogy with physical conception is clear: to be creative is to be procreative, to 'father forth' new beings. Where the modern writer worries about the consequences of *having* children – the pram in the hall as the enemy of art – the Renaissance writer worried about the consequences of *not* having children (which meant above all, of course, male children). Offspring, both textual and sexual, were the ultimate status symbols.

Such a weave of sex, text and power runs through Shakespeare's work like a red-blooded thread. Perhaps its most cogent expression, as it relates to the metaphysics of middle age, is to be found not in the plays but in the sonnets, which begin with a sequence known as the 'procreation sonnets' (1–17). The link between procreation, creation and time is in fact made implicit before the poems even begin, dedicated as they are to their 'onlie begetter', the elusive Mr W. H., wishing him 'all happinesse and . . . eternitie'. By the time of sonnet 7, this link has become explicit:

> Lo, in the orient when the gracious light
> Lifts up his burning head, each under eye
> Doth homage to his new-appearing sight,
> Serving with looks his sacred majesty,
> And having climbed the steep-up heavenly hill,
> Resembling strong youth in his middle age,

> Yet mortal looks adore his beauty still,
> Attending on his golden pilgrimage.
> But when from highmost pitch, with weary car,
> Like feeble age he reeleth from the day,
> The eyes, 'fore duteous, now converted are
> From his low tract, and look another way.
> So thou, thyself out-going in thy noon,
> Unlooked on diest unless thou get a son.[2]

Shakespeare plays here, as only he can, on a small but vividly imagined set of terms. Chief among them is the central image of the sun, which rises steadily through the course of the poem to culminate in the closing pun on 'son'. It is almost as though the whole sonnet were composed as a virtuoso response to a creative writing exercise, or perhaps to a psychiatrist's word-association game: write a poem about the word 'sun'. Shakespeare's anxiety about the importance of (pro)creation – and more broadly, that of the late sixteenth century – emerges more and more as the poem progresses: 'getting' a son (that word again) is the only act that can forestall death, or what in sonnet 2 he terms 'the forty winters [that] besiege thy brow'. The sun goes down, but the son also rises.

Scrutinized more closely, the semantics of the sonnet reveal much about how the Elizabethans conceived ageing. The body language of the poem bristles with defensiveness about the passing of time; the very word 'age' occurs four times – not just in the obvious phrases 'middle age' and 'feeble age', but also in the notions of 'hom*age*' and 'pilgrim*age*' – as though the Shakespearean subconscious were (not very successfully) trying to suppress its anxiety about getting older. Set against this is the emphasis on sight as the dominant sense. Like age, the word 'look' occurs four times, an apt reflection of Shakespeare's obsession with the 'fair youth' to whom so many of the sonnets are addressed. By the time the poem reaches its conclusion, however, the term is taken hostage by the logic of the argument – 'So thou ... unlooked on diest' – and will be released only on pain of procreation. The closing subjunctive 'unless thou get a son' becomes an imperative: have an heir.

That this process of procreation also manifests itself in sexual echoes – both 'highmost pitch' and the final invocation of dying can function as synonyms for orgasm – is only logical. For the poem is all about remaining vigorous even into middle age. The heart of the sonnet lies in the second quartet, anticipating as it does the final fear of 'out-going in thy noon'. Shakespeare picks up here on the classic image of the hill or mountain as a spatial metaphor for ageing; at the top of the 'heavenly hill', middle age still resembles 'strong youth'. The adverbs that follow, however, are telling: '*Yet* mortal looks adore his beauty *still*' strikes that note of defensiveness again, as though this beauty might be snatched away at any moment. 'Middle age' is still the prime of life at this point, but only just. And something strange is happening, in any case, to the whole allegorical force of the sonnet: the rising sun is like an ageing man, who is like a rising son. The circularity of the comparison becomes a tactic, it would seem, to avoid the linearity of time.

One might thus paraphrase the message of the poem in the following way: when getting on, one should get a son. That this, in turn, suggests to the poet's mind the image of the sun is hardly surprising. The sun is one of the most common of all Shakespearean metaphors ('Shall I compare thee to a summer's day?'), and one of the principal reasons for this is that its daily course across the sky lends itself so readily to anthropomorphic echoes of ageing. *A Midsummer Night's Dream*, for instance, is nothing if not an attempt to capture the prime of life – the wedding of Theseus and Hippolyta – and make it last longer in the realm of the imagination (the 'dream' of fairyland). Even its seasonal opposite, *The Winter's Tale*, explicitly associates midsummer with midlife as a function of ephemeral nature, as when

Perdita describes marigold that 'goes to bed with the sun, / And with him rises, weeping. These are flowers / Of middle summer, and I think they are given / To men of middle age' (IV, iv, 105–8). Shakespeare thus establishes a temporal variation on the standard spatial metaphors for middle age as a hill or mountain.[3] This means that the whole structure of sonnet 7 – and it is one that recurs across all the sonnets – pivots on the conjunction 'so' at the start of the final couplet. The ageing of the addressee of the closing lines is like the course of the sun across the heavens; so 'noon', the zenith of the day, represents the prime of life. But it is also the middle of life, with all its attendant anxiety about what comes next.

That this anxiety was felt all the more keenly in the late sixteenth century is self-evident. Montaigne felt ready to retire by his mid-thirties; Shakespeare was about the same age when at his peak in 1600. Up to this point his career as a playwright had been a series of successes; after this zenith at the age of 36, however, his sun started coming down again, as it does for so many ageing actors and writers. This lessening of the light is arguably reflected in the increasing number of collaborations that Shakespeare pursued after he turned forty. As his brand was on the way out, he yoked it to that of such up-and-coming Jacobean playwrights as John Fletcher and Thomas Middleton; he couldn't beat the younger upstarts, so he joined them. The angry, embittered characters of the latter part of his career – Timon, Antony, Lear, Coriolanus, Prospero – surely reflect this reality.

By the time he was 52, Shakespeare was dead. If life expectancy in the early seventeenth century was not quite as different from that of the early twenty-first century as one might think – at least for the educated classes, who could hope, if they made it past their early years, to live well into their sixties – *age* expectancy certainly was. Middle age, quite simply, began earlier. This was not so much biological as cultural: men (and occasionally women) were expected to be mature soldiers and statesmen by their mid-twenties. Shakespeare captures this sense of accelerated ageing in the old shepherd's words in *The Winter's Tale*: 'I would there were no age between ten and three-and-twenty, or that youth would sleep out the rest; for there is nothing in the between but getting wenches with child, wronging the ancientry, stealing, fighting' (III, iii, 58–62). After three-and-twenty, then, boys were expected to be men. Youth was an offence against maturity, to be surpassed as quickly as possible.

The problem with such an emphasis on maturity, however, is that it heightens the sense of mortality. Like so many writers of the early modern period – most obviously, Montaigne – Shakespeare is constantly whispering into our ears *memento mori*. The pathos of Hamlet's description of poor Yorick as a 'fellow of infinite jest' is that he was in fact all too finite, as his skull attests. We are born astride the grave; laughter and tears are two sides of the same loin. Comedy and tragedy stand side by side. Middle age is the period best placed to capture this ambivalence, poised as it is between the comedy of youth (romance, sex, friendship) and the tragedy of old age (diminishment, decay, death). At the zenith of our lives, we are also at the start of our decline; the culmination of comedy – marriage – is the beginning of middle age. It may be helpful to consider, then, what genre best describes the middle of life.

The ageing process follows a kind of pre-determined parabola of genres. As we emerge into adulthood, we see ourselves as leading men and women, *jeunes premiers* as the French call them; the best-looking, most charismatic among us are the romantic heroes, but all of us, no doubt, would like to think of ourselves in this way. By the time we reach middle age, such a role is no longer open to us, even in our imagination. The fire and fight of romantic youth give way to the supposed solidity of realist maturity; the bourgeois ideal of career and marriage is either embraced or evaded, but either way it defines the norm.

The first transition in genre as we age, then, is from romance to realism.

A second transition occurs if we consider the classic Aristotelian categories of lyric, drama and epic. Lyricism is the preserve of the young, since it is predicated on erotic yearning, which means above all on a sense of unfulfilled desire. Middle age, on the other hand, is defined by a sense of *fulfilled* desire, or perhaps more accurately by the realization that such fulfilment can in any case never be as satisfying as one had hoped. The long, slow stretches of midlife ennui lend themselves much more readily to dramatic or epic writing than they do to lyric transports of emotion. The poetry of middle age is not, after all, a phrase that trips off the tongue.

It is the distinction between comedy and tragedy, however, that offers perhaps the greatest purchase on the midlife mentality, and it is here that Shakespeare is so helpful. In a twenty-first century spoiled by instant access to unlimited entertainment, it is hard not to find the comic moments in Shakespearean drama somewhat forced; even a very good performance of *The Comedy of Errors*, I would suggest, contains its quota of dutiful, pre-packaged laughter. Like so many others, I had my fair share of obligatory outings to Stratford-upon-Avon as a schoolboy; like so many others, I bunked off to the pub at the interval, tired of the cross-dressing and ever-so-delightful romantic misunderstandings. Comedy, then, is more a genre description than anything else – and it is a genre that is defined above all by its happy ending. Yet it is also defined by the fact that this ending signals a new beginning, something that is rarely the case in the tragedies. This new beginning, carefully kept offstage, is middle age.

Shakespeare's tragedies, on the other hand, bring middle age centre stage. Of the eleven tragedies listed as such in the First Folio of 1623, only two focus centrally on younger characters (*Romeo and Juliet* and *Hamlet*). The other nine – all, except for the early *Titus Andronicus*, written in the decade before and after 1600, which is to say at the point at which Shakespeare himself was moving into middle age (baptised in 1564, he would die in 1616) – concern themselves with the human as ageing animal. Othello, Macbeth, Julius Caesar, Antony and Cleopatra, Coriolanus, Timon of Athens: all are, at least initially, at the zenith of their lives. The problems that beset them are the problems of middle age, when power and prestige call forth rivalry and resentment. Seen from this point of view, the old adage must be reversed: tragedy is comedy plus time.

The passing of time, the one universal experience for all living beings, is the ultimate Shakespearean subject. Often, of course, it occurs offstage, or has already occurred as the play begins (the aged Lear being the supreme example); but equally often it is discussed directly by one of the characters. What is so striking when this happens is that Shakespeare consistently compares time to a stage – and this in both the comedies and the

Sticking the knife in: Brutus attacking Caesar in the Joseph L. Mankiewicz film of *Julius Caesar* (1953).

tragedies. No doubt the most famous example of the former is the 'seven ages of man' speech in *As You Like It* ('All the world's a stage, and all the men and women merely players'); as for the latter, no passage is more metaphysically resonant than Macbeth's cosmic indifference to his wife's death:

> To-morrow, and to-morrow, and to-morrow
> Creeps in this petty pace from day to day
> To the last syllable of recorded time,
> And all our yesterdays have lighted fools
> The way to dusty death. Out, out, brief candle!
> Life's but a walking shadow, a poor player
> That struts and frets his hour upon the stage,
> And then is heard no more. It is a tale
> Told by an idiot, full of sound and fury,
> Signifying nothing. (v, v, 18–27)

The relevance of Macbeth's mutterings to how we experience midlife ennui is clear: time itself, in the petty pace of middle age, seems to slow down. Characteristic for the midlife mentality is also his double perspective, both backwards and forwards: 'all our yesterdays' point towards the 'last syllable of recorded time'. But it is the analogy of life as a player or tale that alerts us most fully to Shakespeare's own apprehension of middle age. We all see ageing through our own, ever thickening lenses; as a man of the theatre, it is entirely natural for him to experience it as analogous to acting a role in a pre-determined drama. We fret our brief hour upon the stage, and then shuffle off. That this hour is both comic and tragic is in the nature not only of life, but of art, distracting us as it does with promises of meaning that ultimately signify nothing. For Shakespeare, in short, middle age, as a microcosm of life more generally, is necessarily a tragicomedy.

II

It remains a curious fact, however, that there is no iconic midlife role in the Shakespearean canon. Young male actors aspire to play Hamlet; older actors aspire to play Lear. Where is the canonical part for the middle-aged actor, whether male or female? Perhaps there are simply too many: Othello and Iago, Caesar and Brutus, Antony and Cleopatra. Middle age comes in pairs, it would seem, and that may be one of the reasons why ambitious actors seek the limelight elsewhere. Yet such actors, like the rest of us, too readily overlook the fact that Shakespeare is the master of midlife neurosis, of the moment when we stop rushing through life and catch our own race in the mirror – only to realize that we, too, are finite. If Shakespeare teaches us one thing, it is that we too will die.

One of the ways we come to terms with this mortality is to overcome it through art. This is as true for the reader as it is for the writer; classic, supposedly 'timeless' works of literature offer us the possibility of transcending our own historical moment, if only in our imagination. This is also true of how we respond emotionally to created characters; as theorists from Aristotle to Martha Nussbaum have explained, emotion is not only evoked, but expunged, through exposure to art.[4] Perhaps the principal way this happens is through identifying with the protagonists. We feel their pain – or joy, or desire – because we put ourselves in their place; we derive satisfaction from happy endings because we experience vicarious pleasure. We are masters, in short, of self-projection.

Nowhere are there such rich possibilities for self-projection as in the works of Shakespeare, and this is perhaps the very secret of his success. The breadth of the Shakespearean canon lends itself readily to an existential identity game. Ask yourself as honestly as you can: with which character do you most closely identify? Chances are that the answer will vary depending on your age and stage of life – but also on the extent of your self-awareness. When young, we like to think of ourselves as doomed, glamorous figures such as Romeo or Juliet; when older, we perhaps see ourselves as Prospero abjuring his rough magic, or else we sympathize with Lear's paternal predicament. The reality, of course, is that we are often more batty Bottom than romantic Romeo, more long-winded Polonius than austere Lear. But we are unlikely to want to perceive ourselves in these terms. We do, however, tend to choose age-appropriate characters. We have surely all had the experience of watching a film for the first time since adolescence and realizing that we now identify not with the rebellious teenager, but with the long-suffering adult. Maturity, in this sense, is rebellion plus time.

My own answer to the question has certainly evolved with age. As a young man, like every other self-respecting intellectual I wanted to play the Dane; as time has passed, I have come to the reluctant realization, to speak with Eliot's Prufrock, that I am not Prince Hamlet, nor was meant to be. Does this make me an attendant lord? We are all the lead characters in our lives (even if it sometimes doesn't feel that way), but standing on the margins of the action and observing how things unfold also has its advantages. For one thing, it means we can watch ourselves change over time.

Classic works of literature provide a vantage point from which to observe these changes precisely because they do not change, even if we do. To adapt the Heraclitean metaphor: one cannot step into the same river twice not just because the water is constantly flowing, but because one is never the same person when stepping into it. The river of writing that flows alongside us throughout our lives forms a foil for our changing concerns, for the various kinds of getting on that preoccupy us. But it is also ever fuller, ever more replete as we move through the years – not just because we read more, but also because the books we first encounter in childhood grow with us. Such books don't so much gather dust as gather *us*, shaping us into who we are, who we were and who we want to be. To think about our changing relationship to the works that grow with us is to suffer a kind of vertigo, as the years fall away and middle age squints wistfully back at youth. Reading the *Odyssey* with my two young boys, for instance, I am struck not only by the fact that they are drawn – like so many children before them – to the more picaresque episodes involving monsters such as the Cyclops or Scylla and Charybdis, but by the realization that my own perspective has demonstrably altered. At their age, I too craved adventure and encounter; now, I empathize with the middle-aged Odysseus, battle-weary and traumatized after nineteen years away, desperate to get home. Shakespeare's vivid characters, similarly, are as though designed to encourage this vertigo. Here they come now, the ghosts of half a lifetime: Hamlet with his bare bodkin, Cleopatra with her mandragora, Jaques with his seven ages. Spectres of our ageing perspective, how different they seem when perceived from the middle of life rather than from childhood. They say that film stars are always smaller in real life; Shakespearean characters seem bigger to us in midlife, more fully rounded and human. And the reason for this, of course, is that we ourselves are more fully rounded and human.

Literature not only reflects, then, but shapes our incipient maturity, and Shakespeare as no other, if only on account of his ubiquity in the English language (not for nothing are the two books taken as read on BBC Radio 4's *Desert Island Discs* the Complete Shakespeare and the Bible). My own experiences with his work, typical to the extent of cliché, are a case in point. First introduced to his language as an eight-year-old schoolboy, I recall initially puzzling over words such as 'bodkin' or 'mandragora'. My teacher Mr Lewis, a kindly, intelligent man whose principal attribute, in my memory, was that he had a son who revelled in the name of Lewis Lewis, carefully explained the finer points of Elizabethan English to us, but the real appeal was not the content, but the cadence. Knives and narcotics no doubt have a certain cachet for young boys, but it was above all the language in which they were couched that lodged them in my mind. As with all good writing, the rhythm of Shakespeare's blank verse insinuated itself into my consciousness, indeed to some extent it *determined* my consciousness. Having learned a number of the sonnets by heart at such an early age, I cannot now recall a time before I knew how to recite 'Let me not to the marriage of true minds / Admit impediments'. Installed early enough, the furniture of the mind becomes a fixture.

As a middle-aged adult, though, I wonder what a pre-pubescent child could make of such sentiments. What does a schoolboy know of marriage, whether true or false? Clever children think they understand the ideas they are taught, but they understand them only *as* ideas. They learn the theory, but have little access to the practice. The distinction is a crucial one, since it goes to the heart of what ageing – understood in Montaigne's manner as experience – actually means in moral terms. Which is, in essence, that the practice of life comes to repudiate the theory.

Shakespeare, of course, already knows this, even if it takes the rest of us half a lifetime to learn it. His comedies are full of love overcoming pride (*Much Ado about Nothing, All's Well that Ends Well*); his tragedies are full of pride resisting love (*Othello, King Lear*). Experience either does, or does not, teach us the error of our ways. The question of whether we learn anything from life is so often subordinate to the actual business of living that we forget to ask the question in the first place. If part of reaching middle age is a process of stocktaking – have we achieved what we hoped to achieve? Are we happy with our life so far? – then literature, with its role models and salutary figures, can help to define the value of the stocks.

Yet the whole idea of assessing one's achievements from the middle of life remains fraught with danger. How can we be sure we are not being too harsh on ourselves, or too lenient? Where is the transcendental viewpoint from which to make a fair judgement on life so far? The midlife crisis is nothing if not an attempt to force the issue, but the real problem is that the terms of our self-worth age with us. Seen from afar, the various goals that we desire (jobs, promotions, relationships, travel) tease us with the promise of fulfilment; if we are lucky enough to attain them, however, they often come to seem vain and facile, and in any case quickly give way to newly tantalizing goals. We take success for granted, as our due; it is failure that continues to sting. As Nietzsche noted, only that which hurts remains in the memory.[5]

One is tempted to conclude with Oscar Wilde, then, that there are two types of tragedy in midlife: one is not getting what one wants, and the other is getting it. But there we go getting again; acquisition emerges once more as the principal yardstick for middle age. Are there not other models of maturity? The more I reflect on the question, the more I am convinced that growing older is not about accruing ever more power, but rather about failing better with what we already have. Self-assessment requires assessment of what it means to have a 'self'; I don't just want to ask myself whether I have achieved this or that externally approved goal, but also – and far more pressingly – whether I have become, through all this, a 'better', fuller person. This is, of course, equally difficult to answer, but it is at least the right question. If we have the face we deserve at fifty, we have the character we deserve at forty.

Maturity, then, would seem to impose a moral tax, a chronological imperative: use your own experience to help others. Getting on should not be about getting on with your career, but about getting on with other people. The middle, in short, is not only a biological and epistemological category, but a moral one. If the philosopher Aristotle knew this already – in all things, moderation – the playwright Shakespeare, like any good dramatist, leads us to the realization through engineering its opposite. Some of his most memorable characters are extreme personalities – Richard III or Iago, Coriolanus or Titus Andronicus – the very extremity of whom illustrates, by way of contrast, the virtues of moderation. Apemantus castigates the arch-misanthrope Timon in precisely these terms: 'The middle of humanity thou never knewest, but the extremity of both ends' (*Timon* IV, iii, 302–3). Most people, Shakespeare implies, are neither saints nor sinners; most are not arch-misanthropes. 'Extremely good and bad people are both very few in number, and the majority lie in between,' as Socrates states in Plato's *Phaedo*.[6] Remembering this – and reminding others of it – is itself a moral virtue, and it is one that Shakespeare's tragedies highlight by default. Most people, thank God, are somewhere in the middle.

It is vital not to forget this as we slide into, and out of, the middle of life's way. One of the more sobering markers of middle age is the realization that you, now, are in charge. For a while as you get older, you can continue to think that someone else will make the tough decisions, that someone else will be the grown-up in the room – but at some point it becomes irrefutably clear that you are now that grown-up, and that you can no longer shirk those difficult decisions. Imposter syndrome is one thing; immaturity syndrome, quite another. Power, like it or not, passes down the generations, as Shakespeare shows us time and again. Middle age is a moral category not least because of the responsibility it imposes.

Yet this realization can also, quite obviously, be enormously empowering. To look behind the curtain and see that there is no older puppet-master may be terrifying at first, but it also means that the strings are now yours to pull. If life is a stage, to use the Shakespearean metaphor, by middle age we are not only acting in the play, but directing it. Age creeps up on you, but so does agency; even at the most difficult of times – the loss of a parent, the failure of a professional project – we are more in control of our lives in middle age than at any other point. This, too, literature can show us.

As I struggle to master my own sense of being in the middle of life, then, I take solace in the fact that such mastery is possible – but only at the price, paradoxically, of renouncing the urge to all-encompassing 'mastery'. We assert control best when accepting that there are certain things that we cannot – indeed, never will – control. There is no path that leads ever upwards towards the wisdom of old age; we will always remain imperfect, imprecise creatures. Poor, bare, forked animal as thou art, acceptance remains the final stage of middle ageing.

6

Perpetual Incipience
The Midlife Gap Year

I

On 3 September 1786 at three o'clock in the morning, in the southwest German spa town of Karlsbad, a 37-year-old man crept quietly out of bed and into a waiting carriage. Bumping up and down as he went rapidly south – travelling in a post-chaise was nothing if not a rocky ride – Johann Philipp Möller felt the giddy thrill of departure. All summer long he had been planning his escape, and now, finally, here he was, hurtling south towards the Alps as fast as the roads would take him. That he had kept his plans secret only heightened the illicit pleasure; friends and enemies alike would discover what had happened to him only once he was safely on the other side of the mountains. The last thing he wanted was to be overtaken and recalled, as he had been in 1775. This time he was taking no chances. This time he would make it to Italy come what might.

It had been a difficult few years for Möller. Like many a man approaching middle age, he had become increasingly dissatisfied with his circumstances. Success had arrived early, and all too easily; his reputation thus secured, status and stability had become suffocating and repetitive. Professionally, he was stuck; personally, he was bored. Try as he might, he could not stop yearning for something new. Möller was in the throes, in short, of what we would now call a midlife crisis.

If Möller's state of mind detains us more than that of millions of people approaching middle age before and since, it is because he was, in reality, one of the greatest figures in the history of Western culture. Johann Wolfgang von Goethe's adoption of a pseudonym was not only an attempt to escape the crushing burden of fame that preceded him wherever he went; it was an attempt to escape himself. Like Superman stepping into his phone booth, Goethe stepped into his carriage in order to become Clark Kent once again, to shake off the pressure of being the Olympian 'Goethe'. That he also pretended to be ten years younger tells us much about the motivation behind his journey to Italy. Like so many of us who find ourselves *nel mezzo del cammin*, he wanted to begin again.

Why was Goethe so desperate to get to Italy? Why now? Twice before, he had hoped to reach the other side of the Alps; in 1775 he had been recalled before he could get any further than Heidelberg, and in 1779 he had decided not to continue south from Switzerland in order to return to Weimar and his employer, Grand Duke Karl August. Spurred on by such frustrations, Goethe's yearning for the south was given fresh impetus by the drab summer of 1786. As he notes repeatedly in the opening pages of (what would subsequently be published as) *The Italian Journey*, by September he was in dire need of blue skies and warm air. Above all, though, he was suffering from a creative paralysis brought on by his many official duties as Privy Counsellor to the Weimar Court. Goethe, to put it in modern terms, was suffering from writer's block.

His flight south constituted an attempt to revivify himself as he approached middle age. Hurrying over the Alps and down into northern Italy, Goethe noted, in the excited tone of someone setting off on holiday, that anyone coming towards him from the south would consider his breathless reaction to everything he encountered childish. This moment of self-awareness captures the two main emotional impulses of the trip: a yearning for the south, and a desire to turn back the biological clock. When shortly thereafter he arrives in Venice, the sight of the gondolas immediately reminds him of a childhood game he used to play with model boats, and he enjoys a 'long-lost impression of youth'.[1] The fact that he had left his watch behind in Weimar tells its own story: Italy was to be time*less*. The geographical pull of the south to a northerner was also the chronological pull of childhood to middle age.

Goethe's journey may have gone down in history as 'Italian', but the real focus of his interest was Rome. After two brief weeks in Venice – much of which he seemed to spend in the theatre – he hurried south to the eternal city, pausing for barely three hours in Florence. Only once he reached Rome on 1 November could he breathe out and relax; only once he reached Rome could he write to the Grand Duke back in Weimar, safe in the knowledge that this time, at last, he had arrived at his long-anticipated destination. His desire to see the city, he writes, was 'over-ripe'. Just as in Venice, so in Rome Goethe immediately turns to a language of rejuvenation: 'I see all the dreams of my youth coming to life.'[2]

It is hard not to be carried along in his exuberant wake, so obviously thrilled is he to be in the city of his dreams. The early letters ooze excitement, and indeed if there is one adjective that defines them, it is 'new'. In a letter written on the day of his arrival, Goethe uses the word five times in one paragraph, sketching out his 'new thoughts' on his 'new life' in a 'new world'. Dante's *Vita Nuova*, the great dream of middle age, opens up before him tantalizingly. Logically enough, he rapidly starts referring to this new life as a 'rebirth'; he considers the day of his arrival in Rome as a 'second birthday' and wonders whether he can in fact be considered the same person – shades of the philosopher's axe – since he has been 'transformed to the very marrow'.[3] Almost two months after his arrival, on 20 December 1786, he reflects at length on the nature of this transformation:

THE MIDLIFE MIND

> The rebirth which is transforming me from within continues. Though I expected really to learn something here, I never thought I should have to start at the bottom of the school and have to unlearn or completely relearn so much. But now I have realized this and accepted it, I find that the more I give up my old habits of thought, the happier I am. I am like an architect who wanted to erect a tower and began by laying a bad foundation. Before it is too late, he realizes this and deliberately tears down all that he has built so far above ground. He tries to enlarge and improve his design, to make his foundations more secure, and looks forward happily to building something that will last. May Heaven grant that, on my return, the moral effect of having lived in a larger world will be noticeable, for I am convinced that my moral sense is undergoing as great a transformation as my aesthetic.[4]

This passage (in W. H. Auden and Elizabeth Mayer's translation) brings together many of the emotions Goethe felt at the time, as well as many of the reasons why he had decided, at this midpoint in his life, that he had to throw everything up in the air. He is not only learning new things; he is unlearning, and relearning, old ones. The more he destroys his old self, the more he can find a new one. The image of an architect redesigning the foundations of a tower suggests Goethe's characteristic vision of reaching ever upwards – as well as his realization that in order to continue doing so, he must revisit the very fundaments of his existence. But then the passage takes a surprising twist, eliding the moral and aesthetic consequences of his midlife rebuild into a composite sense of what he *would like* this transformation to constitute – namely, a complete overhaul of his sensibility. Between 'rebirth' and 'return', Goethe was determined to emerge from his year in the south with a renewed 'moral sense'.

A letter of five days later, written on Christmas Day 1786, provides a pithier image still for this rebirth. What joy it is, he

Johann Heinrich Wilhelm Tischbein, *Goethe in the Roman Campagna*, 1787, oil on canvas.

writes, to watch a sculptor making a new mould out of plaster, as the limbs of the statue emerge from the cast to take a completely new form. But how did this new form look for Goethe? Although he had his entrances into any number of high-society addresses in Rome, he rapidly sought out the lively community of expatriate German artists and bohemians. He moved in with the painter Johann Heinrich Wilhelm Tischbein – who in due course would paint the famous portrait of the great poet reclining masterfully in front of the Italian *campagna*, the iconography of antiquity stretching out behind his two left feet – and surrounded himself with younger artists who could instruct him in Roman art. That they were younger was not accidental; Goethe was on a gap year *avant la lettre*, flirting with artists' models and living the student life. His account of this period exudes a happy, carefree *joie de vivre*, a mood that would later be captured in the erotic swoon of the *Roman Elegies* (written on his return to Weimar): 'Do I not learn, after all, by tracing the lovely breasts' / Forms, by running my hand down the beautiful hips? / Only then do I grasp the marble aright, I think and compare, / See with a feeling eye, feel with a seeing hand.'[5]

Beyond their obvious *eros*, such lines are energized by Goethe's newfound emphasis on the aesthetics of the eye. Throughout his time in Italy, the poet was drawn to painters and sculptors, to visual artists who enhanced not only his interest in Roman art and architecture, but his sense of wanting to move away from being a mere scribbler of words. One should draw a lot and write a little, he told himself, promptly ignoring his own advice. Overwhelmingly, his interest in Italy was visual, not verbal, so much so that during his second stay in Rome a year later – after having made a return trip south to Naples and Sicily, he would spend the winter of 1787 in the ancient capital – he could claim that he felt not only newly born, but 'newly educated'.[6]

What lay behind this re-education? Italy's status for Goethe as the very essence of the South – as the land where the lemon trees bloom, in the words famously sung by Mignon in *Wilhelm Meister's Apprenticeship* (1795) – owed much, of course, to its mild climate and *dolce vita*. But it also reflected Goethe's lifelong preoccupation with Greek and Roman art, with mythological sculptures and pagan temples, a preoccupation that was schooled in particular by his reading of the father of art history, Johann Joachim Winckelmann. Winckelmann's reflections on the 'noble simplicity and quiet grandeur' of Greek sculpture, as outlined in his seminal *History of Ancient Art* (1764), had been enormously influential in developing the aesthetic tastes of German intellectuals at the end of the eighteenth century, in particular by emphasizing the sheer plasticity and physicality of antique sculpture. Goethe's decision to travel with one painter after another constituted a corresponding attempt to move away from the art of the mind towards that of the body – an attempt, in short, to reinvent himself not only as a man, but as an artist. In all his artistic endeavours, in all his efforts to reinvent himself in Italy as both creator and critic, this meant that one category came to dominate his thinking: the classical.

Goethe's intense engagement with the theory and practice of classical art can be seen, at this pivotal moment in his development, as an aesthetic reflection – or perhaps deflection – of biological reality. At the midpoint of his life, the poet feels the urge to 'seek the midpoint, towards which an irresistible need has been drawing me.'[7] Coming as it does in the very first letter he wrote on arriving in the ancient capital, this striking evocation of a transcendental *Mittelpunkt* – the midpoint of what? – suggests that for Goethe in his late thirties, all roads led to Rome: aesthetic, emotional, psychological, physical. The term recurs, with minor variations, throughout his stay in the city – for here 'one has the impression of reading history from the inside out', as he notes in his final diary entry of 1786.[8] Rome functions for Goethe as the middle of history, as well as that of life.

The psychology of this new classical phase – a phase that set the tone for the second half of Goethe's life, echoing into his subsequent friendship with Friedrich Schiller and their cultivation of a 'classical style' when back in Weimar – pivots on his understanding of time. Perhaps the most explicit statement of Goethe's classical aesthetics in Italy occurs in December 1787, when he identifies 'what one might term the contemporaneity of classical soil. I call this the sensual, spiritual [*sinnlich geistig*] conviction that here greatness was, is, and shall be.'[9] Aside from the conflation of body and mind so typical of Goethe's approach to Roman culture, what is notable here is his view of classical art as mediating between past, present and future – which is to say, as timeless. Yet it was precisely his *over*-awareness of time – a sentiment that we might now summarize under the term 'midlife crisis' – that drove Goethe to Italy in the first place, and that continued to define his newly emerging sense of himself as someone seeking 'solidity': 'I am not here to enjoy myself,' he claims in November 1786, 'but to apply myself to the great things, to learn and to develop, before I turn forty.'[10] His classical turn is a way of conferring what he calls 'ballast' or 'gravity' on his existence – a way of combating time through timelessness.

The works Goethe completed during this period reflect this awareness of time passing. As he settles into his second stay in Rome, a sense of struggling against time comes to characterize his way of thinking. 'Now that age is coming,' he writes, 'I want to attain the attainable and do the doable, since I have long suffered – both deservedly and undeservedly – the fate of Sisyphus and Tantalus.'[11] The quintessentially Goethean verbal nouns – 'the attainable' (*das Erreichbare*), 'the doable' (*das Tunliche*) – are positive inversions of the mythological figures that follow; in order to escape having to suffer like Sisyphus or be tortured like Tantalus, one must redouble one's focus on what can and cannot be achieved in the course of a single life. The two mythological characters are condemned to timelessness (always the cruellest aspect of mythological punishment); Goethe, like the rest of us, is condemned to time. 'I am old enough, and if I still want to do anything, I must not tarry,' he writes just a few days later. 'It comes down not to thinking, but to doing.'[12] Do or die, in the haunting words of Elliott Jaques's midlife patient.

Such doing manifested itself in Goethe's renewed efforts to complete unfinished projects. As he returned to his play *Egmont* – began several years earlier, before he had even moved to Weimar – he remarked that 'I feel quite young again as I write the play.'[13] This feeling notably found its way into not only the play itself, but the final book of Goethe's autobiography *Poetry and Truth*, which he concludes with an extract from *Egmont*: 'As if lashed by invisible spirits, the solar horses of time bolt off with our fate's flimsy wagon, and there is nothing left for us but to calmly and bravely keep hold of the reins and steer the wheels clear of a stone on the right, a precipice on the left.'[14] Middle age, then, becomes the basis for age *tout court*.

While Goethe completed a number of other longstanding projects during this period – including his play on the Italian poet Tasso, which he had begun a decade earlier and which accordingly lends symbolic resonance to his pretence of being ten years younger – he also received the proofs of a four-volume edition of his complete works up to this point. Their arrival led him, unsurprisingly, to reflect on his position at the midpoint of his life, and to divide his career into a past and a future: it is 'an odd feeling that these four delicate volumes, the result of half a lifetime, should seek me out in Rome'.[15] From this distance, and with this lapse in time, Goethe had the impression – one familiar to anyone looking back on something they wrote a long time ago, as we saw with Montaigne's portraits – that he was no longer the person who wrote those works; the constituent elements of the poet's art, like those of the philosopher's axe, had aged and changed.

This feeling emerges, in fact, as the defining sentiment of Goethe's Italian journey. The Nordic traveller believed that he had come to Rome to find 'a supplement to his existence', as he noted in October 1787, yet he slowly realized that he must completely change himself and start all over again.[16] His understanding of ageing was that of incessant evolution. This is brought out neatly by the changing responses to his 'incognito'. The poet in fact refers to his 'half-incognito', since he is aware – no doubt with a certain degree of satisfaction – that people only *pretend* not to know who he is.[17] The great advantage of this, he claims in November 1786, is that people can no longer talk about him, and so they are forced to talk about themselves and their own projects. Yet six months later he encountered a Maltese aristocrat who enquired – not knowing who Goethe was, but realizing that he was German – after the hero of his youth who wrote *Werther*.

Upon hearing Goethe reply that this hero was none other than he, the Maltese stranger was shocked and stuttered that he must have changed a lot; yes, replied Goethe, 'between Weimar and Palermo I have indeed suffered changes.'[18] His anonymity rumbled, Goethe was forced to confront the fact that he had aged.

Here as elsewhere, however, it would be a mistake to think that ageing is necessarily negative. The great lesson of Goethe's Italian journey is that one can learn to embrace the passing of time; in rediscovering his appetite for living – and in discovering a new form of classical aesthetics – the poet made a virtue of necessity, finding a 'midpoint' in both his life and his art. When we describe someone we have not seen for a long time as 'changed', we do not normally mean it as a compliment; yet continuing development, for a writer or artist, is the one true precondition of creativity. The perpetual incipience that characterized Goethe's life and work may be beyond most of us – it was beyond his contemporary William Wordsworth, for instance, who produced little of note once he had finished the first version of *The Prelude* at the age of 35 – but its example can nonetheless serve us well as we grow older. How to be the same while becoming another person is the great challenge of middle age.

II

My own engagement with Goethe began, in earnest, as an undergraduate. I had been lucky enough to hear the name at school, so I was not as gauche as some of my peers with their stumbling attempts to discuss the great *Go-ether*. In fact I felt a frisson of pride, almost of ownership, on learning that the poet came from Frankfurt, since my grandmother's family had come to Britain from Frankfurt as wool merchants in the late nineteenth century. With the advent of the Great War, they had anglicized their name from *Schwan* to Swan, a pleasingly Proustian way of preserving the Jewish cadence while escaping the opprobrium of a nationalistic age. Or so it seemed, at least, to my overheated imagination.

Looking back on the works I read in my earliest years at university – and that I now teach to first- and second-year students – I am struck by how readily they map on to life as seen from the perspective of late adolescence. The *Sturm und Drang* of Goethe's love poems of the 1770s, and not least of his early novel *The Sorrows of Young Werther* (1774), pulses with the all-or-nothing intensity of youth; death or glory, *thanatos* or *eros*, are the only options available. Werther shoots himself not only because he cannot be with his beloved Lotte, but because it is the sort of melodramatic gesture that corresponds to – and in a certain sense justifies – his world view. All that matters to him is *passion*, in its etymological senses of both sentiment and suffering. There is simply too much pathos in his pathetic fallacy; the natural world reflects back to him only what he projects on to it. He has not yet learned to take existence on its own terms.

That the mature Goethe of the late 1780s was clearly embarrassed by Werther's effusiveness tells its own story. It is hardly an exaggeration to say that the whole Italian journey was conceived as an attempt to escape not only the suffocating celebrity that the novel had conferred on him, but the cloying sentimentality of his youth. The move towards an aesthetic of objectivity, as conceptualized through Roman classicism, is nothing if not a reaction against the extreme subjectivity of his earliest work. The tone of greater distance that Goethe cultivated in the 1787 edition of the novel suggests as much; Werther's own voice (as heard through the first-person perspective of the letters that form the bulk of the text) can no longer be allowed to stand unchallenged. The excesses of the young hero Werther – and by extension of the young writer Goethe – are tamed by maturity.

Whether this is a good thing or not is, of course, a matter of taste, but there is little doubt that it reflects the standard narrative of how temperament develops over the course of a life

– from passion to reason, from intensity to experience. Middle age, one might say, is supposed to temper temper. It is worth asking, however, whether this narrative corresponds to the continuing unfolding of creativity that manifests itself in the greatest artists – or whether the greatness of those artists who manage to continue creating into middle age consists precisely in finding ways to resist such a slackening of intensity. Goethe provides a compelling case study not only on account of his obvious artistic significance, but because of the dramatic caesura in his life represented by the Italian journey. Rather than doing what so many of us do – continuing to drift while feeling vaguely dissatisfied – he took a decision, against no little opposition and in great secrecy, to do something about it. The path of least resistance certainly did not lead over the Alps, and yet that is the way he went.

In Goethe's case, the development of temperament that we call maturity can be neatly illustrated by contrasting two of his best-known poems. The first, 'Prometheus', was written in the early 1770s:

> Cover thy spacious heavens, Zeus,
> With clouds of mist,
> And, like the boy who lops
> The thistles' heads,
> Disport with oaks and mountain-peaks,
> Yet thou must leave
> My earth still standing;
> My cottage too, which was not raised by thee;
> Leave me my hearth,
> Whose kindly glow
> By thee is envied.
>
> I know nought poorer
> Under the sun, than ye gods!
> Ye nourish painfully,

Perpetual Incipience

With sacrifices
And votive prayers,
Your majesty:
Ye would e'en starve,
If children and beggars
Were not trusting fools.

While yet a child
And ignorant of life,
I turned my wandering gaze
Up tow'rd the sun, as if with him
There were an ear to hear my wailings,
A heart, like mine,
To feel compassion for distress.

Who help'd me
Against the Titans' insolence?
Who rescued me from certain death,
From slavery?
Didst thou not do all this thyself,
My sacred glowing heart?
And glowedst, young and good,
Deceived with grateful thanks
To yonder slumbering one?

I honour thee! and why?
Hast thou e'er lighten'd the sorrows
Of the heavy laden?
Hast thou e'er dried up the tears
Of the anguish-stricken?
Was I not fashion'd to be a man
By omnipotent Time,
And by eternal Fate,
Masters of me and thee?

THE MIDLIFE MIND

> Didst thou e'er fancy
> That life I should learn to hate,
> And fly to deserts,
> Because not all
> My blossoming dreams grew ripe?
> Here sit I, forming mortals
> After my image;
> A race resembling me,
> To suffer, to weep,
> To enjoy, to be glad,
> And thee to scorn,
> As I![19]

Written when Goethe was in his early twenties, 'Prometheus' is typical of the *Sturm und Drang* of his youth, full-throated and fiery in its defiance of the tyrannical gods. Its very syntax and punctuation reflect this confrontational attitude, driven as it is by bold imperatives – 'Cover thy spacious heavens, Zeus, / With clouds of mist' – and exclamation marks. From challenging the gods it moves downwards to the egotistical Titan, hubristically positioning himself as rival to their divine powers of creation: 'Here sit I, forming mortals / After my image'. By the end of the poem, the arrogation of power could not be clearer, as Prometheus concludes with the injunctive to humanity to scorn the gods 'as I', the closing pronoun the very epitome of ego. As a model of the defiant subjectivity of youth, it could hardly be more egocentric.

Only ten years later, the mature Goethe presents the relationship between man and the gods very differently:

> When the All-holy
> Father Eternal,
> With indifferent hand,
> From clouds rolling o'er us,

Perpetual Incipience

Sows his benignant
Lightnings around us,
Humbly I kiss the
Hem of his garment,
Filled with the awe of
A true-hearted child.

For with Gods must
Never a mortal
Measure himself.
If he mounts upwards,
Till his head
Touch the star-spangled heavens,
His unstable feet
Feel no ground beneath them;
Winds and wild storm-clouds
Make him their plaything; –

Or if, with sturdy,
Firm-jointed bones, he
Treads the solid, unwavering
Floor of the earth; yet
Reaches he not
Commonest oaks, nor
E'en with the vine may
Measure his greatness.

What doth distinguish
Gods from us mortals?
That they before them
See waves without number,
One infinite stream;
But we, short-sighted,
One wavelet uplifts us,

> One wavelet o'erwhelms us
> In fathomless night.
>
> A little ring
> Encircles our life here;
> And race after race are
> Constantly added,
> To lengthen the chain
> Of Being forever.[20]

First drafted in 1780, 'The Limits of Man' gently repudiates the Promethean arrogance of the earlier poem. The individual perspective has given way to that of the collective, the first-person singular to the first-person plural. Goethe now conceives of himself merely as part of the great 'chain of Being' – a term that the founder of the history of ideas, Arthur Lovejoy, would make famous in his book of that title published in 1936 – as part of the 'little ring' that encircles our life.[21] Humans constitute only one small wave in the sea, whereas the gods see infinite numbers of waves stretching out before them. To get older is to realize, in true Socratic fashion, how little we know. Where the Promethean youth railed against the very notion of having limits, the mature poet acknowledges and celebrates them. Like Dirty Harry in the 1970s, a middle-aged man's gotta know his limitations.

The acceptance of mortality represented by this progression is, as we have already seen, the defining aspect of middle age. It is not only Goethe for whom the bell tolls; as we grow older, the resistance to inductive arguments about mortality that we subconsciously entertain when young – just because everyone else has aged and died, why should I? – becomes irrefutably untenable. Early middle age is the point at which the mirror becomes a *memento mori*. What purchase can literature offer on this mirror? It is not only the reader who cannot look into the same mirror twice; the writer is equally fated to view the evolution of his work from an ever-shifting perspective, as we saw with Montaigne. If literature is like a mirror, it is because it does not, in itself, change – it is the person looking into it who changes. This is why it forms the ideal companion and therapist. Great works do not judge us or censure us, they merely listen and evolve with us as we bring our changing concerns to them. It is an oft-cited cliché that what defines the classics is their timelessness, but this is not quite right; it is their time*li*ness, their ability to reflect our ever-altering emotions, that keeps them fresh. My own encounters with Goethe – from eager undergraduate to earnest postgraduate, from stumbling lecturer to seasoned professor – have evolved with experience into something very different from their callow beginnings. The work of art may be the death mask of its conception, as the critic Walter Benjamin famously claimed, but it is also the midwife of the reader's rebirth.

What are the consequences of such a rebirth? Goethe's most explicit exploration of this question is to be found in his novel *Elective Affinities* (1809), the very first sentence of which draws attention to the hero's middle age: 'Edward – so we shall call a wealthy nobleman in the prime of life – had been spending several hours of a fine April morning in his nursery garden.'[22] The phrasing immediately calls into question the authenticity of the cliché 'in the prime of life' [*im besten Mannesalter*], foregrounding the essential arbitrariness of how narrative constructs characters. What does it mean to be a man 'at the best age'? What shall we call such a creature? The whole story unfolds, in a sense, from this first parenthetical statement: the cliché alerts us to the inevitable temptation of the younger woman Ottilie, and of Edward's 'chemical' attraction to her that will form the chief metaphor of the novel. Middle age becomes a kind of self-perpetuating fiction.

In Goethe's own case, this fiction emerges most vividly from the project that accompanied him for sixty years, and that would ultimately form one of the great masterpieces of world literature: *Faust* (1808/1832). From the early 1770s to the early 1830s, from youth to old age, the various incarnations of his hero preoccupied Goethe throughout his adult life; as such, when seen from the perspective of its author *Faust* represents nothing so much as a reckoning with the existential scandal of ageing. Certainly, other works came and went, some of them directly a consequence of middle age: the erotic revivification of new-won enthusiasm in the *Roman Elegies* (1795), the emotional complications of long-term relationships in *Elective Affinities*. Yet no other work aged with the author in quite the same way.

When I first read *Faust*, like everyone else I thought it was a story about a deal with the Devil. The relationship between Faust and Mephistopheles is, of course, at the heart of the plot (although in Goethe's version of the legend it is, importantly, not a *pact* but a 'wager', and one that has been anticipated – and thus ultimately forestalled – by a preliminary wager in the prologue between God and Mephistopheles). Yet as I settle ever more uncomfortably into middle age, it strikes me that the motif of the 'deal with the Devil' is merely a plot device, a mechanism to enable the exploration of the real subject matter of the play: ageing.

What Faust yearns for, above all, is to be young again. Energy, innocence, enthusiasm: as the play opens, the desiccated old scholar can lay claim to none of these qualities. Having worked his way through all the principal disciplines available in the Middle Ages – from theology to jurisprudence, from philosophy to medicine – Faust still feels no wiser in the real terms of human emotion, which is why he turns to the dark arts in search of succour. He has experience; now he wants *experiences*. Faust turns to Mephistopheles in the way that a man in a midlife crisis buys himself a new car; he seeks adventure. His tour through Classical antiquity in the second part of the play – complete with the ultimate trophy mistress in the form of Helen of Troy – represents an attempt to (over-)compensate for everything he feels he missed out on when he was younger. That is why he is so confident that he will never say the fated words 'stay, you are so beautiful' (the words that would condemn him to an eternity of damnation); no single moment, he believes, can ever bring supreme satisfaction. It is not sex he desires so much as rejuvenation. If Mephistopheles is a pimp, he is selling time.

What is so striking for our purposes is that this is also the promise, and indeed the premise, of literature. Mephistopheles the magician is Goethe the author, rewinding the ageing process and flashing backwards and forwards as it suits him. Art enables what time disables: unfettered movement among past, present and future. In the cinema, in particular, with its essentially infinite powers of special effects, we are so used to seeing this that we barely notice it any more. Yet Mephistopheles has his special effects, too, whisking Faust between the centuries and conjuring up historical encounters at will. It is no coincidence that F. W. Murnau's film version of *Faust* in 1926 was one of the most expensive films ever made up to that point, exerting a decisive influence on the evolution of early, Expressionist cinema. As the years melt away from Faust's body and face, as he flies thrillingly through the skies, what we are seeing is the power not just of Mephistopheles to turn back time, but that of art.

From the vantage point of middle age, however, it is not always clear how best to deploy this power. We tend to think of the middle of life as characterized by its transitional nature; if youth lives in the future tense and old age in the past, then middle age exists in the continuous present, the Aristotelian 'midpoint' of time. Yet the intermediate position this suggests is in fact illusory, since the middle-aged person *knows* youth, but can only *imagine* old age. This simple difference, obvious though it is on reflection, is in fact crucial, since it means that we give

Special affects: Mephisto (Emil Jannings) revivifying Faust (Gösta Ekman) in F. W. Murnau's *Faust: A German Folktale* (1926).

priority – in art as in life – to what has already been experienced, which is to say to the past. It is surely for this reason that the art of middle age tends to the elegy of what has been lost – Thomas Mann's *Death in Venice* (1912), in which the ageing artist Aschenbach lusts after the beautiful boy Tadzio, provides the paradigmatic example in German literature – rather than to the anticipation of what is to come.

The greatest artists and thinkers, however, manage to turn this tendency on its head by making middle age the basis for self-renewal. Dante's metaphysics, Montaigne's self-fashioning and Shakespeare's tragedies all make maturity out of mortality, insisting that the human condition in the middle of life is as much about believing in the future as about bemoaning the past. If Goethe belongs in this company, it is precisely because he is *not* Faust, because he manages to learn from his hero's failures. Where Faust cannot forgo Gretchen – thereby condemning her to her fate – Goethe comes to cultivate, in his later work, an ethic of 'renunciation' (*Entsagung*), understood as a kind of middle-aged counterpart to the all-consuming desire of his youth. *Not* doing things becomes a way of doing them better; self-denial becomes the basis for self-renewal.

In our age of instant gratification, such a path is not for everyone. We have to find our own way to move forwards: for some this means amusing themselves, for others it means improving themselves. But we all have to move forwards. It is the constant hope for something better that makes life possible; if you are in any way creative, indeed, it is what makes life tenable. I am struck, for instance, by my own almost pathological preoccupation with moving on, with 'looking forward' to the project to come rather than backwards to the projects completed. Edward Said observes in his memoir *Out of Place* (1999) that he has no sense of cumulative achievement,[23] and I for my part feel the same way; my views about whatever I have achieved are constantly open to renegotiation. Well-meaning friends tell me that I should try to enjoy such success as I have had, but they are missing the point. It is not that I feel bad about my previous work, merely that it no longer really interests me. Perpetual incipience comes at a price; with every new book one starts again at zero.

But perhaps this is a healthy way to view life. Time may be an arrow – the great lesson of *Faust* is that we should not even *try* to stop it – but there is no reason why we shouldn't change its target from time to time. The mistake as we reach middle age is to think that we, or the activities to which we dedicate ourselves, are now 'set'. Maturity may be mortal, but it need not be fatal. We can always start off in a new direction, be it over the Alps or under new management. The past is a foreign country, but so is the future, and I for one want to move there. Something of this sentiment surely animates all productive, creative activities; we need to think that the most interesting project is the one we are working on now, since we need to think that the future will be at least as good as, if not better than, the past. As we move up the mountain of life, in short, the view narrows, but it also broadens. We may be halfway up the hill, but we are *only* halfway up the hill.

III

The second half of Goethe's hill was no less spectacular than the first. With his new, 'classical' aesthetic he undertook – and, just as importantly, completed – many an important work, including *Elective Affinities, West-Eastern Divan* (1819), *Wilhelm Meister's Journeyman Years* (1821) and, ultimately, *Faust*. The period following his return from Italy was marked by numerous new personal as well as professional projects, not least marriage to (the scandalously low-born) Christiane Vulpius and friendship with Schiller. The midlife crisis of the Italian journey gave way to the great flowering of Weimar classicism. Middle age was now maturity.

Goethe's Olympian status by this point was such that this maturity was also, more broadly, that of German culture. Throughout the eighteenth century the Germans had been plagued by an inferiority complex vis-à-vis French 'civilization', which they regarded enviously as the cradle of free thought and Enlightenment. With Goethe as their figurehead, German speakers now had a literature of international standing, as crystallized by the poet's much-mythologized meeting with Napoleon in 1808 (Goethe's own record of which, interestingly, foregrounds the emperor's remark that for a sixty-year-old, he is 'well preserved').[24] Even if it did not yet exist as a nation – arguably *because* it did not yet exist as a nation – Germany now had a culture of its own, the pursuit of which would define much of the nineteenth century on the eastern side of the Rhine.

However much he was identified with one quasi-national culture, though, what is striking about Goethe in the second half of his life is how *inter*national his interests became. In his midsixties he began writing love poems in the style of the Persian poet Hafiz; by the time he turned eighty he was advocating *Weltliteratur*, 'world literature', as a model for modernity. It was not just that German culture was not enough; Europe itself could no longer hold him. The great lesson of Goethe's exemplary biography, in this as in other regards, is that middle age can – and perhaps should – be the point at which we redouble our efforts to learn new things, to continue developing ourselves 'inwardly and outwardly', as he wrote to Schiller.[25] Curiosity remains the greatest currency.

The exchange rate of this currency fluctuates, however, as we get older. The standard arc of ideology, from youthful progressivism to ageing conservatism, points to middle age as the most uncertain of life's stages. Should we turn inwards to our own culture, or outwards to those of others? Should we double down on what we already know, or take new risks in search of what we don't? Should we stick, in short, or should we twist? Goethe embodies this dilemma, but in a characteristically creative, productive manner. On the one hand he is the patron saint of everyone who favours taking new risks, twisting his way over the Alps to a newly revived sense of his own creativity; but on the other hand he does so, paradoxically, via a profoundly conservative turn, finding in Classical antiquity the 'ballast' that he requires to anchor his new aesthetics. Goethe twists, then, in order to stick.

By the time he was an old man, this double movement had become the poker tell of his style. Its most expansive example is his celebrated coinage of the term *Weltliteratur*. Talking to his amanuensis Johann Peter Eckermann in 1827, the 78-year-old poet claims that 'national literature is now rather an unmeaning term; the epoch of world literature is at hand, and everyone must strive to hasten its approach.'[26] His understanding of the concept is seemingly inclusive and democratic, ascribing no particular precedence to any one language or nation. Yet world literature is a pantheism with very personal gods – and for

Goethe, these gods are to be found above all in antiquity. 'While we value what is foreign,' he observes, 'we must not bind ourselves to some particular thing, and regard it as a model. We must not give this value to the Chinese, or the Serbian, or Calderon, or the *Nibelungen*; but, if we really want a pattern, we must always return to the ancient Greeks, in whose works the beauty of mankind is constantly represented.' Timelessness has a time after all; the modern world is to be judged against the predetermined criteria of the ancient world. *Weltliteratur* is more classical than classless.

As he aged, then, Goethe became both more inclusive and more exclusive, both more progressive and more regressive. Is that not true of most of us? My own conception of world literature, I have come to realize, is closer to Goethe's than I would care to admit. We all have the weaknesses of our strengths, and mine, no doubt, is an abiding sense that European culture remains exemplary, however much I try to educate myself in other traditions. When I was younger, to be 'European' was to aspire to the most cosmopolitan of educations; a mere twenty years later it is considered in certain critical circles an elitist, retrograde condition, a relic of the nineteenth century like syphilis or bad teeth. Where Goethe lived in the noontime of Continental confidence, Europe has now entered the evening of its old age.

It goes without saying that many of the criticisms levelled at the presuppositions behind 'European' culture are fully justified. If Europe has become a cipher for everything it excludes, rather than everything it includes, it is because modernity, as Europe constructed it, was built on slavery and exploitation; capitalism was driven by the colonies. However exploitative it may have been, though, Europe in the nineteenth century was comfortable in its own skin. To return to the secure middle age of the continent is to realize that its culture can still help us to navigate our own, insecure middle age. In the words of the old joke in response to a request for directions: I wouldn't start from here. But for better or for worse we can *only* start from here, just as we can only understand midlife from the perspective of our accumulated experiences. If we have the weaknesses of our strengths, we have the prejudices of our convictions.

Reflecting in this manner on changing cultural preferences helps us to realize that this is precisely what middle age is: accumulated prejudice. We can and must try to surpass our own presuppositions, but we will always be starting from somewhere; immaculate re-conception, in midlife as in cultural history, is impossible. Seen from Europe, the world is necessarily pre-judged as the 'Other'. For Goethe, Classical antiquity as he discovered it during his Italian journey – and crucially, as he *experienced* it – remained the gold standard for all forms of beauty thereafter; maturity, for him, meant looking not only beyond his native European culture, but behind it (such is the essence of *Faust Part Two*, a kind of virtual-reality time machine in which the eponymous hero travels at great length through classical culture). The 'midpoint' of classicism served as an anchor for the rest of Goethe's life not just because his mature style emerged during this middle period, but because the very idea of having a midpoint became a model for his mature aesthetics. Like it or not, by the time we reach the middle of our lives we all have a midpoint.

It is surely better, then, to be aware of our midlife prejudices, rather than to pretend that we don't have any. Self-awareness – of the kind that literature, with its blend of reason and emotion, argument and affect, is ideally placed to encourage – is the first step towards moving beyond the self. As we reach the middle of our lives, we should ask ourselves what we have taken for granted up to now, and how we might move beyond such presumptions in the second half of our time on Earth. Our lives may not be as exemplary as that of Goethe, but his questions can nonetheless be ours, too. What do you now see differently compared to twenty years ago? What projects remain incomplete, and how has your perception of them changed with the passing of time? What, in short, is the essence of your own mature aesthetics? However we answer these questions, the great lesson of Goethe's life and work for anyone struggling with middle age is that doing nothing is not an option. If to begin is to be born, to begin again and again is to be middle-aged.

7

Realism and Reality
The 'Middle Years'

I

Growing up in the military ensures a very particular kind of childhood. In an age in which we are all supposed to be classless and confessional, the army remains a bastion of hierarchy and repression. Officers, and their wives and children, are intensely aware of their place in the pecking order; like a caricature of the middle classes, middle-ranking officers aspire to one thing above all, namely to move upwards. The snobbery this occasions filters down into all aspects of life. One of the recurring refrains of my childhood was my father's half-joking admonition that something – or more often someone – was not 'officer-like'. Asked to define precisely what this meant, he would no doubt have pointed to such things as bearing, accent, education and above all a certain tact and reserve. His sisters, my gushing aunts, were always suspiciously voluble, with their girlish gossip and garish red hair; that he married into a family of taciturn farmers, the very epitome of strong-but-silent country folk, suggested as much. Certainly my father paid stiff-upper-lip service to the idea of emotion, but it was a very English kind of emotion; when I turned twelve he told me hugging was no longer appropriate, and that a manly handshake was henceforth the accepted greeting. Airing and sharing of any sort was considered suspect, as codified in the 'don't ask, don't tell' approach to gay soldiers that was for many years the de facto policy of the British military. In this as in so many other matters, the sin was not so much to *be* gay, it seemed, as to *talk* about being gay. Talking, sharing, feeling: an officer simply didn't do such things.

We all grow up thinking of our parents as models of adulthood. They say that we look to reproduce our parents' relationship in our own, that we seek out a partner who is like our mother or father. But our parents also serve as our models of middle age. Without realizing it, we absorb our earliest lessons in what it means to be mature from our mother and father. If grandparents are always already old, parents are always already middle-aged. From my father I learned distance, sangfroid, self-confidence; from my mother, love and self-sacrifice, but also a certain embattled Englishness, reinforced by the constant moving around between postings in Germany and Austria. The English abroad famously become more English, not less so, as though distance does not so much dilute as distil the national character. To be European, to be *Continental*, was traditionally considered an unfortunate condition akin to being born poor or in the 'wrong' sort of family: such people were admirable, to be sure, but best avoided lest the condition prove contagious. In the infamous phrase attributed to Cecil Rhodes, to be born English was to win first prize in the lottery of life. Something of this self-image still hovered, unstated, in military families at the end of the twentieth century.

To say that such attitudes represented a vestigial Victorianism is merely to state the obvious. Etiolated imperialism was the precondition of my childhood, and the muscular Christianity of boarding school was nothing if not a legacy of nineteenth-century pedagogy. But these attitudes were also, it seems to me now as an adult, the reason why I turned to literature and culture, and they are the reason why literature and culture can help us all as we struggle into middle age. I discovered the life of the mind in part because my parents did not; I embraced 'Europe' in part because my parents kept it at a distance.

Literature and culture offer us a way out of what we are and into what we are not.

This possibility of becoming someone else is always defined, however, against our inherited sense of identity. Such cognitive dissonance is typical of middle age; we have become the people we are going to be, but we are also, as the saying goes, slowly turning into our parents. Whether I like it or not, a part of me will always think that being mature means being 'officer-like'; whether I like it or not, a part of me will always be 'Victorian'. What does this mean for my understanding of middle age?

Above all, I fear, it means that I can never be grown-up *enough*, never serious enough to deserve the epithet 'mature'. The Victorian age, the vestigial values of which still echoed into my childhood and education, presented itself as the great age of sobriety, a self-image that started with the empress herself. In fact, Queen Victoria's life divides rather neatly into two halves: in 1861, when she was only 42 – my own age as I type these lines – her beloved husband, Albert, died, leaving her a widow in mourning for forty years, until her death in 1901. The heyday of British imperialism defined itself, for that reason if for no other, by its gravity and sense of mortality. The heyday of British imperialism defined itself as middle-aged.

To be middle-aged in the nineteenth century was to affect high moral seriousness. As Stefan Zweig remarks in his elegiac autobiography *The World of Yesterday* (1942), in the twentieth century everyone wanted to be younger, but in the nineteenth century everyone wanted to be older.

> The newspapers recommended preparations which hastened the growth of the beard, and twenty-four and twenty-five-year-old doctors, who had just finished their examinations, wore mighty beards and gold spectacles even if their eyes did not need them, so that they could make an impression of 'experience' upon their first patients.[1]

Prince Albert in 1859, at the age of forty.

Male middle age was the default setting to which all aspired, as immortalized in a thousand formal photographs: all those big moustaches and mournful eyes, all those starchy shirts and even starchier men. Childhood ended early; adolescence hadn't yet been invented; maturity was the only currency that counted. It was as though the Victorians were born middle-aged.

Such a description is of course a caricature, as any number of Dickensian street urchins attest. But it is the image the Victorians wanted to give of themselves, or at least the one they felt they were supposed to give of themselves: 'men wore long black frock coats and walked at a leisurely pace, and whenever possible acquired a slight *embonpoint*, in order to personify the desired sedateness.'[2] Smiling in photographs, as my grandfather used to say, just makes you look silly. And silliness, light-heartedness – youthfulness – was the cardinal sin for a century so heavily invested in its own sense of moral purpose. God may have been an Englishman, but he was a mature, midlife Englishman.

It is no accident, then, that the term 'middle age' first came into general currency in the late nineteenth century. The Victorian era gave us racial prejudice, Christmas kitsch and middle age: not, one might think, the holiest of trinities. Yet all three functioned, in their differing ways, as tokens of 'progress', that great god of the nineteenth century, since all three were signs of a newly empowered middle class. For women in particular, the emergence of middle age as a recognized demographic category announced that there was life beyond the menopause; in the manner of their queen, women beyond childbearing age began increasingly asserting their freedom and independence. The 'new woman' of the turn of the century was also the new *middle-aged* woman; on the other side of the Atlantic the very term 'middle age' emerged almost exactly as Victoria herself reached the middle of her life. As Patricia Cohen has shown, women's magazines from the 1860s onwards began celebrating, in the words of one *Harper's Bazaar* column of 1889, 'women who number anywhere from forty to sixty years'. A *Cosmopolitan* essay of 1903, similarly, hailed 'The Woman of Fifty' as someone who had attained 'mastery' of life, noting in particular that – unlike at the start of the 1800s – she was no longer 'expected to retire from the game'. By the beginning of the twentieth century, then, middle age was feminized, politicized and – not least – monetized.[3]

At the start of the *nineteenth* century, however, the gender roles remained resolutely unreconstructed. Women existed either as (younger) objects of nature or as (older) objects of nurture; rarely did they get the chance to attain middle age on their own terms. While an exceptional figure such as Mary Shelley could write, in the mid-1820s, that 'I am in the condition of an aged person at the age of twenty-six,' her privileged position within a circle of intellectuals – as well as her unusually tragic situation – was hardly representative of the average woman.[4] Far more common in this late Romantic era was the male anxiety of affluence, as exemplified by William Hazlitt's *Liber Amoris*. Published anonymously in 1823, the book tells the story of what was effectively Hazlitt's own midlife crisis, as the 42-year-old, newly divorced critic becomes ever more infatuated with the daughter of his lodging-house landlord in Regency London. To his infuriation, the pretty young lady leads him on, but becomes evasive when he presses his case; it turns out, to the narrator's if not to the reader's surprise, that she has been playing several men off against each other. The book is subtitled 'The New Pygmalion', but the sculpture that Hazlitt longed to bring to life remains resolutely unresponsive.

The story of middle-aged men chasing after (much) younger women is hardly new, and neither is the sense of embittered entitlement with which Hazlitt seeks to justify himself. More striking, in many regards, is the fact that the nineteen-year-old Sarah Walker resisted his advances; in an era of such inequality between the sexes, the attentions of a famous, educated gentleman more than twenty years her senior must have been of no little consequence. The constellation, in any case, is typical to the point of cliché: middle-aged, upper-middle-class man sets his cap at teenaged, lower-middle-class woman. The resentment Hazlitt's narrative exudes is that of surprise that it doesn't end the usual way – and that of being made to look a fool. Then, as now, middle-aged man tended to get what middle-aged man tended to want.

It would be all too easy to give many more examples of this kind of imbalance between the sexes, the classes and the ages. The nineteenth century was nothing if not dominated by 'a multitude of middle-aged men', in the words of perhaps the most Victorian of all novels, the programmatically entitled *Middlemarch* (1871).[5] But then we remember that *Middlemarch* was, of course, written by a woman, and that this was in fact the great period of the female novelist; from Jane Austen to the Brontë sisters, from Elizabeth Gaskell to George Eliot, the nineteenth century was not exactly short of major women writers. It is all the more striking, then, that even these highly successful female authors should have concentrated, time and again, on a very male vision of middle age.

The logic of this vision almost has the force of a syllogism: middle age is the default setting for power; men are more powerful than women; therefore only men can be middle-aged. Perhaps the supreme exploration of this logic in all of nineteenth-century literature is the relationship between Dorothea and Casaubon in *Middlemarch*. Virginia Woolf famously remarked that *Middlemarch* is one of the 'few English novels written for grown-up people', and as it begins the reader is duly lured into the young Dorothea's longing for (what she perceives as) intellectual adulthood. Her interest in the middle-aged scholar Casaubon, 'over five-and-forty' and 'a good seven-and-twenty years' older than Dorothea, is presented as the yearning of female adolescence for male maturity; to marry him, she tells herself, would be 'like marrying Pascal'.[6] That this inferiority complex is meant as a recommendation, and not as a warning, tells us everything we need to know about her state of mind. The young Dorothea means to penetrate the 'provinces of masculine knowledge'.[7]

It comes as no surprise to anyone but Dorothea that this proves impossible, and that Casaubon remains a distant, selfish prig. Eliot herself seems to tire of the desiccated vicar, wishing more for her heroine than indenture to a living ghost. How to rid herself of this truculent priest? Reader, she buries him: Eliot kills off Casaubon by fast-forwarding his middle age into an accelerated senescence. His doleful influence continues, however, from beyond the grave, when the codicil to his will forbids

Dorothea from marrying the vivid young firebrand Ladislaw, thus generating the narrative tension that drives the rest of the novel. Even in death, middle-aged man sets the rules.

Eliot would not be the novelist she is, however, if she gave us only this external view of Casaubon. In the golden era of free indirect speech that characterized the great Realist novels of the mid-nineteenth century, Eliot was an absolute mistress of the form. Having led the reader to see things primarily through Dorothea's eyes, she then flips the perspective and allows us access to Casaubon's consciousness. Indeed, she even explicitly reflects on our customary obsession with youth, insisting that Dorothea's is not the only possible point of view on their marriage and protesting 'against all our interest, all our effort at understanding being given to the young skins that look blooming in spite of trouble: for these too will get faded, and will know the older and more eating griefs which we are helping to neglect'.[8] Here, as elsewhere, Eliot argues for a universal narrative suffrage, irrespective of gender or age.

What is so helpful about this technique for our purposes is that it enables Eliot to judge without being judgemental, to condemn characters through their own consciousness. She gives Casaubon just enough hope to hang himself with, allowing that he is 'spiritually a-hungered like the rest of us' but then having him reflect on how Providence had furnished him with 'the wife he needed, [since] a wife, a modest young lady, with the purely appreciative, unambitious abilities of her sex, is sure to think her husband's mind powerful'.[9] Strikingly, Eliot even frames Casaubon's decision to get married in terms of his desire to 'leave behind him that copy of himself which seemed so urgently required of a man – to the sonneteers of the sixteenth century'.[10] To Casaubon, at least, the Shakespearean imperative to 'get a son' (discussed in Chapter Five) remains alive well into the nineteenth century. That Eliot refuses him this satisfaction tells its own story.

For by this point in the narrative it has, of course, become abundantly clear that Dorothea is miscast as Casaubon's wife. She is precisely not the submissive worshipper with whom he had hoped 'to adorn the remaining quadrant of his course'.[11] Eliot conjures Casaubon in order to condemn him, and through him the whole caste of middle-aged male intellectuals who obsessively aspire to the 'key to all mythologies'. He is a warning figure, a ghost story for the middle-aged male ego tempted to take a much younger mistress while burrowing ever deeper into futile vanity projects. There but for the grace of self-awareness go all of us. I for one am glad that I read *Middlemarch* only as a mature adult, since I'm not sure I would have seen this so clearly had I read it as a teenager; I'm not sure I would have been capable, as Daniel Deronda tells Gwendolen Harleth in Eliot's final novel, of 'enjoying my own middlingness'.[12] Through a combination of luck and instinct, we find the books we need *when* we need them, whenever and wherever they were originally written; bibliotherapy, in this regard, is timeless and ahistorical. If the sixteenth century can counsel the nineteenth century, then the nineteenth century can surely help the twenty-first.

Middlemarch is the major novel of middleness in the Victorian era in part because of its extreme complexity. The tangled narrative webs and sheer length of Eliot's finely tuned prose reflect the intractability of midlife existence, where the seeming stasis of stability belies the many minor tremors and micro-movements bubbling beneath the surface. The blockbuster novels of the mid-nineteenth century are in many ways the perfect medium to convey the incremental inching of middle age; the nineteenth-century mania for Realism is the rage of maturity at seeing its own face in the mirror. Perhaps that is why adultery is such a recurring theme of the period; from Emily Brontë's *Wuthering Heights* (1847) to Gustave Flaubert's *Madame Bovary* (1857), from Leo Tolstoy's *Anna Karenina* (1878) to Theodor Fontane's *Effi Briest* (1895), bored female protagonists assert what little agency they can find. The emergence of a distinctly feminine conception of middle age in the nineteenth century begins, in this manner, with self-assertion beyond the bonds of bourgeois marriage. Adultery, at this point, is the female version of the male midlife crisis.

Beyond these major novels of the period, there are also a number of minor poems and novellas that explore what it is like to be in the middle of life at the end of the nineteenth century. In his *Wessex Poems* of 1898, for instance, Thomas Hardy included one brief piece entitled 'Middle-age Enthusiasms'; typically enough, it is more middle-aged than enthusiastic, concluding each of its four stanzas with a bathetic recognition of the irrevocability of time. The final verse captures the combination of presence and absence, enthusiasm and ephemerality, that animates the poet's vision of the midlife mind:

> 'So sweet the place,' we said,
> 'Its tacit tales so dear,
> Our thoughts, when breath has sped,
> Will meet and mingle here!' ...
> 'Words!' mused we. 'Passed the mortal door,
> Our thoughts will reach this nook no more.'[13]

The closing couplet, in particular, encapsulates Hardy's sense of being haunted by mortality: the place may be 'sweet', but time is bitter. Ending with a syntax of negation – and reverting once again to the image of the threshold employed by both Dante and Montaigne – this is middle age in a minor key.

Perhaps no text of this period is more instructive of the midlife mentality, however, than Henry James's brief story 'The Middle Years'. Written in 1893 – the year James turned fifty – it is a slight, somewhat melodramatic tale about a 52-year-old writer named Dencombe, who retreats to a hotel on the English south coast to protect his fragile health. There he encounters a young doctor, Hugh, who turns out to be a fervent admirer of his work – so much so that the doctor neglects the dying countess who intends to leave him a fortune, thus forgoing the promised inheritance. Reduced to the bare bones of its plot in this manner, the story barely transcends the melodrama of a thousand Victorian serializations.

Yet James is hardly a purveyor of penny dreadfuls. As ever in his writing, it is the quality of the consciousness that retains our interest, and here he deftly explores the anxiety of the ageing author. His portrait of the artist as a middle-aged man obviously reflects his own anxiety, but it also raises broader questions for us all about how we come to terms with our sense of self as its centre of balance shifts ever further towards the past. In his major novels, James is often viewed as the very epitome of over-refinement, his exquisitely balanced sentences circling imperiously back on themselves as they track the subtleties of their own thought processes. This can make his style seem *too* mature, an always already late style that makes few concessions to the reader's attention span. What becomes clear in 'The Middle Years', however, is that to reach this consummate late stage the artist had to go through a middle phase riddled with doubt and uncertainty. Such a phase surely applies, *mutatis mutandis*, to us all.

James's convalescent begins by reflecting on the idea of 'getting better'. But better than what? Strolling in the sea air on a fine April morning, he is starting to *feel* better, but he will 'never again, as at one or two great moments of the past, be better than himself'.[14] The crisis of his middle years, then, is to be one of self-transcendence, or rather of the sudden realization that the possibility of self-transcendence is now foreclosed to him. He may be getting on but he is not, in any fuller sense of the term, getting better. In Elliott Jaques's terms, he has not merely reached the crest of the hill; he is now over it. In Dencombe's case – and of course also in that of James – this realization relates above all to his work, since we soon learn that his new book, entitled 'The Middle Years', has just appeared. This is thus a story both *of* and *about* the midlife crisis.

Dencombe's crisis is prompted above all by his sense of dissatisfaction with his own limitations. It is not so much the feeling that he has not done everything he could that torments him, but rather the realization that he *has* done everything he could – and yet still it is not enough. Only now does he feel that he has gathered sufficient experience to produce true art; but *now*, at the age of 52, he fears it is too late. A single existence is too brief, he laments: 'to fructify, to use the material, one must have a second age, an extension.'[15] The writer's crisis is not just a reaction to the sudden arrival of middle age, but also one to the fear that he is already well beyond it. In this regard, Dencombe presents a – typically Jamesian – variation on the standard form of the midlife crisis; unlike so many of us, he actually *wants* to be in the middle of life.

The irony, of course, is that James's fears would prove unfounded. He *did* get to have a productive second age, culminating in one of the most celebrated of all literary late styles. *The Ambassadors, The Wings of the Dove* and *The Golden Bowl*, to cite just the three major novels, were all written between 1902 and 1904, when James was about sixty. Reading James the author against Dencombe the character in this manner suggests that there is light at the end of the middle, that life narrows in our forties but broadens out again as we emerge into our late fifties. That this seems to have happened for James at precisely this point in his life merely confirms the statistics; the graph of happiness starts climbing again on the far side of the U-bend. The best plumber for unblocking this bend is not psychoanalysis, it would seem, but experience.

What James's story also brings out, however, is that middle age is not only U-shaped, but you-shaped. For all its common concerns across classes, genders and generations, middle age is a bespoke affair. The anxiety we feel about being in the middle

Realism and Reality

of life's way – or even about being beyond it – is both universal and individual; such is the lesson of literature. Through feeling and fiction, through the empathy of the imagination, we can adopt someone else's perspective on ageing, but we all, necessarily, have our own. Writing ten years after James, Rainer Maria Rilke implored God to grant us 'our own death' – but we must also cultivate our own middle age.[16] For James, appropriately enough, the middle years are unambiguously those of a writer.

Within the terms of his story, moreover, these middle years are not only you-shaped – they are also Hugh-shaped. The doctor's name identifies him as a placeholder for Dencombe's younger self, framed, with only slight variations in pronunciation, as both question and answer: Knock knock. Who's there? Doctor Who? Doctor You. The self-projection holds true not only because Hugh is half the age of the ailing writer, but, crucially, because he is a *reader*. When Dencombe first sees Dr Hugh with his patient, the countess, he imagines a little melodrama whereby the countess's young female companion is hoping to win the affection of the doctor in order to gain access to his supposed inheritance. But he also sees that the doctor has a book open on his lap – a book that is in fact, he comes to realize, an advance copy of his own work, 'The Middle Years'. Addressing the author himself, then, we might say that a younger Hugh is reading the older you.

This effect of an existential *mise-en-abîme* is compounded by Dencombe's description of the cover of Dr Hugh's book as 'alluringly red'. For this could also be taken to mean, it becomes clear, alluringly *read*. The doctor is to form Dencombe's ideal reader, ministering to his crumbling sense of self-esteem by rejecting a financial fortune in favour of his fictional treasure. Dencombe is particularly gratified when the doctor tells him that his latest book is the best thing he has done yet – for that little word *yet* opens up a 'grand avenue of the future', and it is precisely this avenue that Dencombe feels closing down in front of him.[17]

There remains something uncanny, however, about the almost preternatural symmetry of the encounter; after all, to meet your own doppelgänger – which is essentially what we can take the doctor to be for Dencombe, albeit in rejuvenated form – traditionally betokens death. But such is the logic of the story: 'it isn't till we *are* old that we begin to tell ourselves that we're not.'[18]

As so often in James's work, then, the true pathos of the prose resides in the past conditional, in everything we *might* have done. Unlike in his later work, though, James's middle years force the realization not so much that he is too old as that he will never be young enough. Dencombe despairs when he thinks of what he could have done, but Dr Hugh gently corrects him: 'What people "could have done" is mainly what they've in fact done.'[19] We all hold ourselves hostage to the counterfactual, and it can be a particularly bitter mood when applied to the past – why did I not do this or that, rather than what I actually did? The reality, though, is that this kind of existential *esprit de l'escalier* brings nothing but bitterness, since we live, necessarily, in the indicative. Subjunctives and conditionals have very little purchase in the world of the real, as opposed to that of fiction. In the words of the wise Mary Garth in *Middlemarch*: 'Might, could, would – they are contemptible auxiliaries.'[20]

Middle age is about realizing this. We may feel that doors are shutting and alternative paths are closing off, but if we have not taken them, it is in all likelihood because they were never right for us in the first place. Kafka's parable 'Before the Law' captures this memorably: after a lifetime of waiting in front of the gate, the man from the country learns, just before he dies, that this particular gate was only ever meant for him.[21] Better to realize that in the middle of life, when there is still time to accept it and come to terms with our choices. Such, at least, is the conclusion of James's 'middle years': 'A second chance – *that's* the delusion. There never was to be but one. We work in the dark – we do what we can – we give what we have.'[22] Renouncing this delusion and rejecting its implications is the great challenge of midlife psychology. The Realism of literature, in short, is the realism of middle age.

II

Another way of saying this is that middle age imposes what we might call a tyranny of the real. The romantic delusions of youth – that we will be different from our parents, that we will change the world and not succumb to the lure of career and ambition – give way to the realpolitik of maturity. Little by little, we accommodate ourselves to the messiness of adult life, to the many minor compromises that constitute our incremental negotiation with reality. First to go are those grandiose daydreams that were never really possible in the first place: becoming prime minister or president, playing centre forward for the national football team. Saying goodbye to such ambitions is easy enough, since we never pursued them properly anyway. Harder to renounce are the possible possibilities (to adapt Rumsfeld's 'known unknowns'), the personal and professional goals to which we cling precisely because they may yet just be attainable: getting that dream job, publishing that half-written novel. Partial fulfilment is more tantalizing, because more promising, than no fulfilment at all.

Making such accommodations requires a readjustment of our self-image. If this readjustment is in many ways the very essence of middle age, it points to the structural difficulties in defining the concept. For one thing, the incremental nature of ageing makes it difficult to pinpoint the precise moment at which we become 'middle-aged'; the Sorites paradox in philosophy, which asks at what point an accumulation of grains of sand becomes a pile, might equally be applied to our accumulation of years. We don't really notice the changes in our own faces because we see ourselves every day; it is only when we see photographs of our younger selves – like Montaigne with his various portraits – that we are shocked into acknowledging the passing of time. Still, physical changes do happen, and they help to orientate us as we age.

Psychologically, the process is much more complex. Do we alter as we grow older, veering off in new directions, or do we simply follow the established train tracks of our temperaments ever further down the line? Do we *change* or do we *continue*? There are perhaps two basic categories of character in this regard: those who noticeably evolve (either 'mellowing' as they relax into their own ageing skin, or conversely becoming much more radical), and those who become ever more set in their ways (either culminating in supreme versions of themselves, or fossilizing into caricatures of their earlier avatars). No doubt we all have a foot in both camps, depending on mood and circumstances. And no doubt we are not our own best judges. I for one may feel I have mellowed, becoming less quick to judge others as I realize that people are mostly doing what they can (to echo the Jamesian formulation). But perhaps this is simply a further form of self-delusion.

For that's the thing about maturity: it's all about the stories we tell ourselves. Self-image is a narrative, and we are at once story, storyteller and reader. The most significant aspect of this narrative, from a stylistic point of view, is that we now find ourselves *in medias res*; from being a spectator looking in on the action from outside, we are now in the thick of it. Until my mid-thirties, I had what is surely a very common sense that the true source of power and knowledge was elsewhere, that meaning and fulfilment lay somehow always in the future. But being in the prime of life – being *aware* that you are in the prime of life – means realizing that you, more often than not, are now that source. It is inevitable that this changes how we view it.

For human nature ascribes mystery and glamour to the unknown. Without evidence to the contrary, we tend to assume,

Realism and Reality

as we are growing up, that those in positions of authority over us – at school, at work, in government – have access to some secret store of knowledge that enables them to make decisions with confidence. And, of course, in a way they do: it's called experience. As we acquire more of this experience ourselves, however, we begin to realize that there *is* no transcendental store of knowledge, no external frame of reference by which to orientate our lives. By the time we reach maturity, we realize that Nietzsche was right: God is dead, and we have to make the decisions in his place. To be middle-aged is to look behind the curtain of power and see that everyone is making it up as they go along.

I often ponder this paradox as I sit in meetings. Ten or fifteen years ago, before I had any real say in such matters, I thought it must be empowering to be involved in the decision-making processes, to be the one adjudicating on the affairs of the day. Now that I increasingly am that person, I find myself staring out of the window at the grey sky outside and wondering when the meeting will end, impatiently waiting for my favourite professional acronym: AOB. And all the while, I am less sure than ever of my right to sit there in judgement on others, be they colleagues or students. As the other members of the committee turn their faces towards me in expectation of an opinion, as I hear myself summoning however much accumulated authority I can find, I am reminded just how much of life is essentially a confidence trick.

Such confidence was the superpower of the nineteenth century. Britannia ruled the waves – which meant, in practice, that male middle age ruled the waves. It is no coincidence, for instance, that Joseph Conrad's image for reaching the middle of life was that of becoming captain of a ship; his novel *The Shadow-Line*, published in 1916, looks back to the time of his first command in the 1880s – 'the magic word "Command"' – as a symbolic crossing of the threshold from youth to maturity.[23] Time itself, in the Whiggish view of history that dominated the late nineteenth century, had reached a world-encompassing maturity. 'Victorian Whig historians could write with confidence about the onward march of liberty,' as Stefan Collini notes, 'because they were essentially at ease with their present.'[24] From our twenty-first-century vantage point, it is easy to ridicule the sense of certainty that characterizes the Victorian era; stealing other people's countries under cover of a *mission civilisatrice* is not, to put it mildly, what we would now consider an acceptable motive for self-esteem. However misplaced, though, this colonial self-confidence was enormously empowering. If we can put aside the condescension of posterity, there is much to be learned from the nineteenth-century conception of middle age – not least, that it need not be a source of shame or embarrassment. In our profoundly immature era, a little extra maturity would hardly go amiss.

The literature of the nineteenth century offers this sense of maturity to a fault – not just because we can excerpt characters from it to illustrate either the assurance or the anxiety of middle age, but because it is in the very nature of realist prose to have confidence in reality. The genre reflects the culture that produces it, and Europe at the time saw itself as the centre of the world. The very metaphors of centre and periphery that dominate the imperial age suggest the extent to which the Victorians unquestioningly placed themselves in the middle of life's way; the discovery of other cultures merely reinforced their own sense of supposed superiority. The more they learned, the less – it seems – they doubted themselves.

For anyone lost on their own life's way, then, a dose of Victorian self-confidence can do wonders. It requires care, however; take too much and the bad faith that underlies it becomes overpowering. The salient distinction in this regard is between aesthetics and ethics. Despite the obvious links between them, literature can remain contemporary even when its moral universe is dated. It is the difference, ontologically speaking, between what we learn from fiction and what we learn from history. Realism depicts the real, it delineates the real – but it does not define the real. Art does not exhaust experience, nor, *pace* Nietzsche, does it justify it; it is simply a product of it. What art can do, however, is *shape* experience. We may envisage adultery differently because we have read *Madame Bovary*; we may imagine middle age otherwise because we fear turning into Casaubon. In the middle of life's way, literature can tell us which path (not) to take.

Perhaps the principal way it does this is by offering us changing identities. Persuading the reader to identify with its characters is arguably the secret to the novel's success, and this is particularly true of the realist mode of narration that typifies the Victorian era. One of the many advantages of narrative fiction is its psychological suppleness. With its characteristic use of free indirect discourse, the realist novel invites the reader to adopt the perspective of the protagonist, encouraging empathy and emotional imagination. But it also, crucially, allows for a perspective outside this single consciousness: it is not *direct* discourse. Such sleight of hand is crucial, since it allows us to identify, as we age, not only with individual characters, but with numerous characters simultaneously. By middle age, we have been more than one person; perhaps more to the point, we now *realize* that we have been more than one person. To cite just a few of my own archetypes, I have been a son, a brother, a student, a lover, a teacher, a critic, a husband, a father. I have lived in various languages and various countries; I have succeeded in some ventures and failed in others. This range of experience allows me to identify, to varying degrees, with all these roles and more, in a manner foreclosed to the monomania of youth. Maturity is not so much about finding yourself as about finding your selves. By middle age, we all contain multitudes.

Narrative literature is perfectly placed to explore these changing identities. If James captures the split personality of the middle years by dividing himself into the older Dencombe and the younger Hugh, his pithiest description of the psychology behind the division occurs elsewhere, in a story pointedly presented as 'The Diary of a Man of Fifty': 'Everything reminds me of something else, and yet of itself at the same time; my imagination makes a great circuit and comes back to the starting-point.'[25] Anyone who has reached this age will surely recognize the epistemology; experiences are no longer new so much as renewed, variations on a familiar refrain. Every encounter, every thought, is now shadowed by the past, by previous iterations that echo and encumber the unmediated moment. The flicker of later acquaintances recalls the flame of earlier ones – perhaps that is why we make fewer and fewer new friends as we grow older. Shared history becomes ever more important. The middle of life is like Plato's cave: what we see, ever more as we get older, is our own past projected on to the present.

The task of literature, of course, is to *re*-present, which is what famously motivated Plato's suspicion of it in the first place. And in some ways, indeed, he was right to be suspicious; literature may offer important insights into the human condition, but it is also – especially in the hands of overeducated critics and scholars – an echo chamber unto itself. Literature, in this regard, is both truth and trap. The more we read, the more we learn, but the more we are also reminded of other re-presentations of the world. The 'great circuit' of the middle-aged imagination risks becoming a closed circuit, endlessly circling comparisons of one text or passage with another, endlessly deferring authentically *new* meaning. '"Like" and "like" and "like" – but what is the thing that lies beneath the semblance of the thing?': Virginia Woolf's description of the 'waves' of consciousness serves as a warning against the midlife tendency to refer every new experience back to some previous avatar.[26] We must look forward as well as back.

Realism as it emerged in the nineteenth century provides perhaps the most flexible model for doing so yet invented.

Realism and Reality

Not only are contemporary art forms such as the novel and the television series direct descendants of it, but so too is the way we live our lives. The 'narratives' we invent for ourselves, the stories we tell ourselves (and indeed others) about our aspirations and achievements, are unthinkable without the realist model of narration; we are heroes of our own fiction, and our self-image is realist, if not realistic. As Hayden White showed in his classic study *Metahistory* (1973), the way we understand history – and, by extension, our own story – is a legacy of nineteenth-century narrative prose; we are engaged in a constant battle to reinforce our sense of verisimilitude vis-à-vis our past and future development.[27] By middle age, we are firmly 'emplotted' in our autobiographies, simultaneously both author and reader of our own lives. Reading back over what we have experienced so far, we project ourselves forwards by inventing plausible scenarios for self-realization and then trying to live up to them. This is as true financially and professionally as it is culturally and artistically; to be in the middle of life's way is to be in the middle of life's story. The reality of ageing requires realism, in both the lower- and upper-case senses of the term.

What emerges from considering middle age in these terms as a narrative construct, then, is just how much it underpins our contemporary world. Modernity itself is middle-aged, at least in its Western incarnation; the imperial self-confidence of the nineteenth century continues to manifest itself in all the middle-aged men and women who run things. Equally important, however, is *narrative* self-confidence, the notion that we can continue to control our lives as we grow older. Realist – and 'realistic' – narration gives us a sense, however illusory, of being in charge, of being in command of the intractable messiness of life. And we need such justification ever more as we get older, since life, unlike literature, is never complete or fully formed. Narrative literature has a beginning, a middle and an end, whereas life is only ever experienced *in medias res*. We live in real time, and it is always running out. For better or for worse, middle age pivots on this paradox; at the precise point in our lives when we have the greatest power, we begin to fear that power slipping away. Perhaps that, too, is what my father meant by being officer-like: being middle-aged.

8

'The Years that Walk Between' Midlife Conversion

I

I first encountered Radiohead in the early 1990s, when they were just another Oxford band with terrible haircuts and moody stares. Jumping up and down to their crunching guitars, I heard little to suggest that this particular group was any different from the countless others scratching around in student dives the length of the Cowley Road, angry young men straining for self-expression. Well, maybe I did; their early hit 'Creep' already hinted at an ability to speak to the disaffected, to marshal misery as a valid emotional response to late twentieth-century culture. And Thom Yorke's soaring, keening voice was always pretty extraordinary. In those early years, though, their music was as generic as those haircuts, curtains of guitars interspersed with sporadic shocks of peroxide lyricism.

Their second record, the breakthrough album *The Bends* (1995), took this tortured sincerity to new extremes. All questions and laments, all pressure and uncertainty, for millions of listeners it uncannily captured the vertigo of early adulthood. The narrative address, the emotional appeal, was direct and unadulterated in a manner that would prove unique in Radiohead's long career. We had all, it seemed, come up too quickly for adult air.

It was only with OK *Computer* (1997), however, that Radiohead actually attained adulthood. With the release of their third, epoch-making album, they emerged as the minstrels of millennial angst, troubadours of a turn-of-the-century *tristesse* that seemed to define an entire generation. At an age when their contemporaries were pursuing City careers and company lives, success afforded Radiohead, and by extension all those who followed them, a degree of critical distance on the aspirational yuppies and 'Gucci little piggies' heading inexorably to London. The lesson for a boy from Oxford was clear: culture – music, literature, art – could be an alternative to career. The secret was to take it seriously enough.

Writing from the safe distance of middle age, it is hard to recapture precisely how gauche one is – or, at least, I was – at twenty. Everything matters so much, because everything matters so little: clothes, clubs, lifestyle choices, the narcissism of so many minuscule, middle-class differences. And music, above all music. Understood as an extension of one's identity – which in my case was something like that of a self-appointed arbiter of authenticity – as an adolescent it mattered more than anything else to have the 'right' taste in bands. To be credible, a band had to *mean it*, an expression that essentially meant being prepared to make the right sort of countercultural noises about integrity and not 'selling out'. Then, as now, highly stylized nihilism was the privilege of youth.

All this makes it astonishing that Radiohead, unlike almost every other serious band of their generation, should have continued to produce such challenging yet commercially successful music. The combination of worldwide sales with worldwide acclaim is a rare one indeed. Audiences normally want more of the same, yet Radiohead have somehow reached middle age in a state of perpetual incipience, constantly regenerating their work as both artists and activists. The haircuts have changed, but the hunger for experimentation has remained. Can we all say the same?

My twenty-year-old self may or may not have seen his forty-year-old counterpart – married, mortgaged and middle-aged

– as a disappointment. My forty-year-old self is certainly embarrassed, at times, by his predecessor. But then experimentation is itself subject to change; what counts as edgy at twenty is unlikely to feel the same way at forty, and if it does, you are probably trying too hard, like ageing men wearing leather jackets and Converse shoes in an attempt to signify that they are still, underneath it all, on the side of the adolescent angels. Cool, that great currency of youth, is subject to chronological inflation: the older you get, the less it is worth, if only because the necessary self-absorption is unsustainable into mature adulthood. Children, if nothing else, see to that. But maturity is also a question of the discipline and focus required to be a successful adult, qualities that were simply not a part of my younger years. Perhaps, indeed, their absence was what defined those years: two characteristics in search of an author, they were waiting for me on the other side of adolescence. The metamorphosis of maturity was a moral process, that is to say – but it was also an intellectual process, crystallized into all those major works I took with me to La Réunion. The trigger for this transfiguration, strange though it may seem, was the lead single on OK Computer, 'Paranoid Android'.

'Paranoid Android' is surely one of the greatest single songs of the past thirty years. Its epic sweep and noble grandeur, its tonal shifts from tender vulnerability to brutal, lacerating anger, leave you reeling every time you hear it. In a little over six minutes – unusually long for a rock song, let alone one released as a commercially viable single – the mood is by turns lyrical and livid, haunted and haunting. The song progresses through three main sections before reaching its ultimate crescendo: a lilting, liquid introduction, which explodes into a raging torrent of guitars, which then rains gently down again in a polyphonic descant. To my ears – and the accompanying lyrics about yuppies networking and being first against the wall suggest as much – it is like moving on fast-forward through life, death and the afterlife, or hell, purgatory and paradise. A malign comedy, perhaps, for the consumerist, attention-deficit age.

It was another literary analogy, however, that had the longest-lasting effect on me. Puzzling over the album, I read all the reviews I could find, and in one of them, someone somewhere suggested that 'Paranoid Android' was *The Waste Land* of the turn of the millennium. I was dimly aware of T. S. Eliot and of the enduring significance of his great poem, but I had never sat down and worked my way carefully through it. Thinking about it now, I can see that it's actually a pretty good comparison; the length and ambition, the paranoia and obsession with death, and above all the unsettling shifts between moods and perspectives – Yorke sings of the unborn voices he hears in his head; Eliot originally wanted to call his poem 'He do the police in different voices' – all bespeak a shared attempt to articulate the malaise of modernity as a doomed, demotic sublime. At the time, however, I was mostly just stunned by the realization that popular music could point beyond itself to ever more intricate forms of artistic expression. In effect, I had discovered literature.

It is hardly an exaggeration to say that my life has never been the same since. It is not just that my adult life has been centrally concerned with the understanding and interpretation of words, true though this is; more fundamentally, my whole conception of what it means to be an adult has been inextricably bound up with the discovery of literature as the most capacious and self-reflexive of art forms. Being a mature human being has always meant, in my view, trying to be as subtle and self-aware as possible – which has meant trying to learn from those far more subtle and self-aware than I myself can ever hope to be. *Du gleichst dem Geist, den du begreifst*, as the Earth Spirit tells Faust; 'you are what you understand,' one might paraphrase somewhat lamely.[1] To discover this with such irrefutable, irrevocable force at the age of twenty was a life-defining experience, little short of a Damascene moment. I was converted to the life of the mind.

Am I making too much out of this one moment? One of the markers of middle age is that you start to reflect on how you got there, on how you ended up as the kind of settled, responsible adult who used to seem so unfathomably confident and wise. We all have our own versions of this narrative, and we are all unreliable narrators, tempted not so much to romanticize the past as to ascribe meaning to its inherently contingent contents. It's not that I don't trust my memory, but rather that I don't trust myself not to overemphasize certain aspects of it, those pivotal moments that turned me – so the teleology of retrospect would have us believe – into the person I have become. My sense of self, in this regard, is a cognitive fiction, a story I tell myself to make sense out of the fact that I am now a professor of literature, a husband, a father and so on. Somewhere along the line, I seem to want to believe, there must have been a big bang that got me going. Or was it all incremental?

Moments of conversion are, by definition, exceedingly rare, occurring only once or twice in any given lifetime. Adolescence in its broadest sense is one such period, as we metamorphose slowly from childhood into puberty. Yet middle age, too, has its own rites of passage, and nowhere are they given more symbolic force than in the idea of literal, rather than metaphorical, conversion. Since antiquity, the precedent for such midlife transformation has always been, of course, the story of Saul turning into Paul.

Within the Christian tradition – Islam, too, is said to have started with Muhammad's famous revelation from the Angel Gabriel at the age of forty, making Muslims the true believers in the transformative power of the midlife crisis – the classic response to this precedent is that of St Augustine, who recounts in his *Confessions* (written c. AD 400) how at the age of 31 he discovered God. Prompted by a child's voice to 'take up and read' – *tolle lege!* – he opened the Bible at random and came across Paul's *Epistle to the Romans*, more specifically the section describing the 'transformation of believers' from the law of

The Damascene moment: Caravaggio, *The Conversion of St Paul*, c. 1600, oil on wood.

Moses to the grace of God.[2] Augustine, taking this as a sign to change his ways, was baptized the following year.

A secular version of Augustine's famous imperative applied to me, one might say, at the age of twenty. Taking up Eliot, I took up the grace of literature and the life of the mind. Eliot himself, however, who had been steeped in the humanist tradition from his earliest years next to the Mississippi in St Louis, followed something closer to the Augustinian model of midlife conversion. Emerging from his training in philosophy at Harvard and Oxford, in the pre-First World War years the young American poet had 'modernized himself on his own' (to cite Ezra Pound's famous letter of 1915 to the editor of *Poetry* magazine, Harriet Monroe) – by rejecting the vestigial nineteenth-century cadences of the 'Georgian' poets and turning instead to French symbolists such as Jules Laforgue and Paul Verlaine.[3] Pound recommended publication of Eliot's major early poem 'The Love Song of J. Alfred Prufrock', and its scandalously modern diction propelled the writer into notoriety in London literary circles of the immediate post-war years. Following a number of further minor poems and essays, Eliot's rapidly growing reputation as both poet and critic was sealed on publication, in the autumn of 1922, of his modernist masterpiece *The Waste Land*, a work that would prove to be the single most important poem of the twentieth century. By any reckoning, Eliot now mattered.

All was not well, however, in Eliot's empire. For one thing, his ill-advised marriage to the unstable governess Vivienne Haigh-Wood was rapidly unravelling, proving a constant source of guilt and recrimination. In his work, too, he was increasingly unsure of himself, wrestling with the inevitable – but far from straightforward – question of what to do next. He had pushed as far he could in the direction of post-war despair over Europe's epic bloodletting: 'death had undone so many,' to cite his Dantean description of the crowds flowing over London Bridge. After such carnage, what forgiveness? Psychologically drained by his job as a bank clerk ('the prospect of working there for the rest of my life is abominable to me,' he told Pound in 1922), and physically repelled by his own wife, in 1923 Eliot wrote to one correspondent that 'I have not even time to go to a dentist or to have my hair cut ... I am worn out. I cannot go on.'[4] In his mid-thirties, he was facing burnout.

Eliot's answer to his midlife problems was to change everything: religion, nationality and style. In 1927 – the year, strikingly, in which he turned 39, the very year of 'maximum productiveness' according to George Miller Beard – he embraced the double whammy of Englishness: he was baptized into the Anglican Church, and he became a British citizen. Famously, he could now proclaim himself 'Anglo-Catholic in religion, a classicist in literature, and a royalist in politics'.[5] One must be wary, however, of seeing too clear-cut a division between Eliot's successive phases. For one thing, he was always already middle-aged; as early as his mid-twenties, after all, 'Prufrock' was growing old and wearing the bottoms of his trousers rolled. More broadly, the conversion model of middle age risks oversimplification, since it tempts us into thinking of midlife as a punctual moment, a precisely identifiable time and place. Moments of midlife conversion, of changing path in the middle of life's way, may seem like sudden caesurae, epiphanies in the interstices between one way of living and the next. Yet whatever the mythography of revelation may suggest – Saul falling to his knees as he hears the voice of 'Jesus whom thou persecutest', Augustine hearing the child's voice telling him to read the Bible – such psychological upheavals do not happen overnight. They are the result, rather, of years of subterranean movement, of 'roots that clutch' at our semi-conscious, semi-articulated sense of dissatisfaction with our slowly unfolding lives.

In Eliot's case, these roots stretched back many years. If his East Coast, Unitarian upbringing predisposed him to the cultivation of conscience and personal responsibility, his native temperament was undoubtedly the most important factor in his emerging sensibility. For Eliot was drawn, above all, to the calling of the martyr. Tortured, ascetic, self-abnegating martyr figures abound in his early poetry. Indeed, both his major early works, 'Prufrock' and *The Waste Land*, ventriloquize martyrdom: 'The Love Song of St Sebastian' (1914) points towards the former; 'The Death of Saint Narcissus' (1912/13) anticipates the latter. St Sebastian, in the early Eliot's telling, 'would come in a shirt of hair' and 'flog myself until I bleed'; Narcissus, meanwhile, becomes 'a dancer to God / Because his flesh was in love with the burning arrows'.[6] Self-sacrifice had always appealed to Eliot – largely, one suspects, because it's all about the self.

Posing as an anchorite afforded Eliot a sense of metaphysical drama, then, long before he actually embraced the Church. But this pose was also driven by a very physical sense of drama, namely his estrangement from the great love of his life, Emily Hale. They had met at Harvard in 1913; by 1914, Eliot had declared his feelings to her, before promptly leaving for Europe. Following fifty years of speculation, the correspondence between Eliot and Hale, sealed until 2020, has now finally been opened, allowing us to confirm the intensity of these feelings.[7] Out of reach on the other side of the Atlantic, Emily served as the model for a lifetime of frozen, unreachable female figures in Eliot's poetry. She became his ethereal Beatrice, his 'eternal feminine'; by the mid-1920s, the contrast with the all too flesh-and-blood presence of Vivienne must have made her absence all the more compelling. Divine love, as Eliot was starting to imagine it, had the otherworldly face of lost love, a disembodied ideal on the other side of the ocean. As Eliot would later write in 'Burnt Norton' (1936): 'What might have been is an abstraction / Remaining a perpetual possibility / Only in a world of speculation.'[8]

The contrast between Emily and Vivienne, between New World and Old, was sharpened still further by the sense of a cultural caesura. For Eliot, of course, the New World was now the old; England (and, more broadly, Europe) was his adult environment. Friends noticed, in the mid-1920s, that he was becoming ever more affectedly 'English', dressing like a City gent and losing his transatlantic drawl. Of all his many masks and poses, this was perhaps the final and longest-lasting one: if America represented his childhood, England was his middle age. Converting to the Anglican Church would set the seal on his maturity, as he saw it, and lay the tracks for the work to come, all the way

The mask of midlife respectability: T. S. Eliot in his mid-thirties, 1926.

to *Four Quartets* and beyond. By his late thirties, in short, Eliot had become a middle-aged, churchgoing Englishman.

Eliot's road to respectability is in many ways a classic tale of midlife regression. As we settle into adulthood, so the cliché runs, we become ever more conservative, ever more aware of history and our place in it. Tradition starts to weigh more heavily on the individual talent. Yet Eliot's case is more complex and interesting than this superficial reading suggests. For him, as no doubt for many of us, middle age was a mask behind which the anarchy and uncertainty of youth continued to compel his carefully policed emotions. Behind success lurks the fear of failure; behind the mature adult reading poetry, there remains the raging adolescent listening to Radiohead. On the outside, Eliot had become the very emblem of the Establishment; on the inside, he remained the wary outsider, more New England in his instincts than Old England. The more he settled into superficial respectability, the more his emotions were driven into the depths of his poetry. 'I feel that he has taken the veil,' Virginia Woolf wrote of him in 1923, a comment that is as perceptive with regards to his impending conversion as it is suggestive of the extent to which religious belief, for the modernist poet, was simply another kind of mask.[9] The brittleness of such masks would be epitomized by Eliot's major transitional work of this period, *The Hollow Men*.

Written in the years immediately following publication of *The Waste Land*, *The Hollow Men* is the product of Eliot's attempts to 'settle down and get at something better which is tormenting me by its elusiveness in my brain'.[10] First published as a whole in 1925, the poem testifies both to his sense of feeling lost in his work and marriage and to his concomitant sense of religion as a possible means of salvation. Looking back in 1936, Eliot described the poem as blasphemous – 'blasphemy because it is despair, it stands for the lowest point I ever reached in my sordid domestic affairs' – and the term aptly evokes the metaphysical melodrama behind the mask.[11] From the title and opening lines onwards, *The Hollow Men* explores the sense of emptiness that Eliot experienced in his mid-thirties:

> We are the hollow men
> We are the stuffed men
> Leaning together
> Headpiece filled with straw. Alas![12]

The image of the stuffed guy evokes the gunpowder plot of 1605, suggesting that sacrifice – the ceremonial immolation of Guy Fawkes – may be necessary for renewal. 'Death's other kingdom' accordingly emerges as the focus and refrain of the poem, both in this first part and throughout the five sections. It is almost as though Eliot *wants* to deaden himself, the better to re-emerge on the other side. 'Death's twilight kingdom / [is] The hope only/ Of empty men', he suggests in the penultimate section; the hollowness behind the mask is cultivated like a chrysalis, a pupa presaging rebirth.

If the hollow mask thus represents one image of the emptiness of middle age, the machine represents another. By his mid-thirties, Eliot had become every inch the company man, first as a bank clerk working for Lloyds and then, from September 1925, as a publisher with Faber & Gwyer. Despite his avowed antipathy towards the daily grind of clerical work, he needed the routine and structure it afforded him, in part because it provided a distraction from his more personal feelings of guilt and failure, as he explained in a letter of 1925:

> In the last ten years – gradually, but deliberately – I have made myself into a machine. I have done it deliberately – in order to endure, in order not to feel – but it has killed V[ivenne] ... Is it true that sometimes one can only live by another's dying?[13]

Common to both images of adulthood – the mask and the machine – is Eliot's attempt to suppress all feeling. Against this backdrop, the move towards conversion in the 1920s reads differently, not so much as an endorsement of Anglo-Catholic dogma as a way to corral 'undisciplined squads of emotion'.[14] To use his own terms: Eliot's embrace of Christianity functions as an 'objective correlative' to his poetry, as a way to formalize the 'escape from personality' that he had outlined aesthetically in his early essays.[15] The final section of *The Hollow Men* is telling in this regard, dramatizing the incipient convert's groping attempts at self-mastery. On the left-hand side of the page, the stuttering ejaculations of desire ('Between the desire / And the spasm / Between the potency / And the existence / ... Falls the shadow'); on the right-hand side, the sober refrain of renunciation ('For Thine is the Kingdom'). By the closing lines of the poem, one of the most famous anticlimaxes in all literature crowns the self-imposed celibacy 'Not with a bang but a whimper'.

Yet might this whimper also be that of (re)birth? The impression of being 'in between' that resonates in the closing section of *The Hollow Men* emerges in a much more affirmative manner in *Ash Wednesday* (1930), the first major sequence to be written after Eliot's conversion. The hesitant repetitions of 'between' are now triumphant iterations of 'because': 'Because I do not hope to turn again', begins Eliot, citing the medieval Italian poet Guido Cavalcanti, 'I rejoice that things are as they are and / I renounce the blessèd face'.[16] The language is the Goethean idiom of renunciation, but in the service of something greater. Certainly this has biographical resonance, too; as Eliot wrote to his brother in 1929, 'I have begun life three times: at 22, at 28, and again at 40; I hope I shall not have to do so again, because I am growing tired.'[17] So many rebirths take their toll.

Yet, as Eliot remarked to numerous interlocutors, this rhetoric of rebirth also had a very clear and specific avatar, namely Dante's *Vita Nuova*. Dante was perhaps the single most important precursor for Eliot, and indeed his influence can be mapped, very broadly speaking, on to the three main phases of Eliot's work: from the inferno of *The Waste Land*, through the purgatory of *The Hollow Men* and *Ash Wednesday*, to the paradise of *Four Quartets*. By the end of his midlife purgatory, Eliot was groping towards a new life as a fully baptized Christian; the celebrations of Christian love in the *Vita Nuova* accordingly assume particular significance. Eliot's description of *Ash Wednesday* as 'merely an attempt to do the verse of the *Vita Nuova* in English' becomes clearer when he identifies Dante's book as 'a work of capital importance for the discipline of the emotions'.[18] *Ash Wednesday* represents an attempt to apply this discipline to modern life. As Eliot writes in an essay on Dante, for all its emphasis on courtly love the *Vita Nuova* is in this sense 'antiromantic': we have to 'look to *death* for what life cannot give'.[19] At the age of forty, Eliot is not so much in the middle of life's way as in the middle of death's way.

'Antiromantic', then, is a very good summary of Eliot's late thirties and early forties. Rejecting the messy imprecisions of marriage, he moved towards the Church; rejecting the adventurousness of his American childhood, he embraced the respectability of English middle age. What is so telling in terms of our broader narrative of middle age is not only that he underwent a midlife crisis in the form of religious conversion, but that he became ever more self-consciously aware of what he terms, in *Ash Wednesday*, section IV, 'the years that walk between'. Time, in short, emerged as Eliot's major topic. By the time of the *Four Quartets*, it had become the very essence of his art.

II

Eliot was hardly the only significant poet of the modernist period to undergo a midlife conversion. In English literature, the most obvious point of reference is no doubt W. H. Auden, who started going to church when he moved to New York in 1939, and formally declared himself a Christian in 1940. A more pertinent, if lesser-known comparison can also be found outside the English-speaking world, in the form of the German poet and man of letters Rudolf Alexander Schröder (1878–1962). Schröder shared Eliot's increasingly conservative sensibilities, so much so that he was an obvious choice to translate his work into German (in 1939 Schröder rendered the play *Murder in the Cathedral*, for instance, as *Mord im Dom*). What he also shared with Eliot, however, was a similar story of midlife conversion to Christianity, and in 1930 he published a collection of 'spiritual poems' entitled simply *Mitte des Lebens*. By the fourth decade of the twentieth century, the whole generation of modernists was reaching middle age.

'The Years that Walk Between'

It is worth reflecting on what this means for our understanding of the midlife mind. We are so used to thinking of modernism as an aesthetic of youth and innovation that we baulk at the idea of its ageing, as though this could mean only a retrograde, reactionary calcification into classicism. But what if this classicism were another name for middle age – and middle age another name for the discovery of time? Eliot's example teaches us that time – its passing, but also its presence – is the great obsession of the midlife mind. This is true not only of the conversion period itself, understood as a manifestation of what Jung calls 'the religious outlook' that naturally emerges in the second half of one's thirties, but of its subsequent reverberations. 'Midlife' is not just the crisis, but the decades of consolidation that follow it. Time present and time past are both perhaps present in time mature.

Eliot developed, in fact, a persistent interest in the idea of maturity. Unsurprisingly, around the time of his conversion he was particularly exercised by the question of what it means to develop and change, and he wrote to William Force Stead – the man who would baptize him – in the following terms:

> One may change one's ideas, sentiments and point of view from time to time; one would be rather atrophied if one did not; but change of mind is a very different thing from repudiation. Certainly I am 'dissatisfied' with everything I have done, but that also is a very different thing. I do not see why one should 'repudiate' anything that one has written provided that one continues to believe that the thing written was a sincere expression at the time of writing. One might as well repudiate infancy and childhood.[20]

Eliot's distinction between 'change' and 'repudiation' has important implications for the way we conceptualize middle age. While change is inevitable, indeed desirable, repudiation is a category error, since it is based on the assumption of continuity between the mind of the past and that of the present. As we age, we naturally start looking back to our childhood more and more – 'I find that as one gets on in middle life the strength of early associations, and the intensity of early impressions, becomes more evident,' notes Eliot in a letter of August 1930 – but this also means that we become ever more aware of the distance we have travelled.[21] The trick is to acknowledge this distance, and to accept the change. In Eliot's view, *sincerity* is the key criterion for creativity; but it is a sincerity that is incessantly recalibrated as we age. If we constantly feel dissatisfied with what we write and produce – I for one certainly do, always aware that every book could be better – it is because we judge what we used to be against what we are now. One might as well repudiate time.

The category of the 'middle' emerges out of this distinction not only as an increased self-consciousness about time, then, but as an epistemological implement for prising open the question of how we change. Across the course of the 1930s and '40s, Eliot applied the implement both to his own writing and to that of others. In an essay of 1940 on W. B. Yeats, he attempts to codify the choices facing the ageing artist:

> It is difficult and unwise to generalize about ways of composition – so many men, so many ways – but it is my experience that towards middle age a man has three choices: to stop writing altogether, to repeat himself with perhaps an increasing skill of virtuosity, or by taking thought to adapt himself to middle age and find a different way of working.[22]

The three types of maturity that Eliot ascribes to writers correspond, broadly speaking, to the three choices facing all of us as we age: less, more, or new life? Eliot, clearly, favours the latter model, describing Yeats as 'pre-eminently the poet of middle age' precisely because (unlike Shakespeare, in Eliot's telling) he becomes a very different kind of poet as he ages.

The middle-aged Yeats even gives Eliot cause to reassess his celebrated doctrine of impersonality, which he first outlined in 1919: writing in 1940, Eliot now claims that 'there are two forms of impersonality: that which is natural to the mere skilful craftsman, and that which is more and more achieved by the maturing artist.'[23] In ageing, Eliot suggests, Yeats managed to retain the particularity of his experience, but make of it a general symbol – thereby exemplifying what Eliot calls the 'Character of the Artist: a kind of moral, as well as intellectual, excellence'. Maturing as a poet, in short, means maturing as a man.

In Eliot's view, then, evolution – and not repudiation – is an essential criterion of artistic greatness:

> In theory, there is no reason why a poet's inspiration or material should fail, in middle age or at any time before senility. For a man who is capable of experience finds himself in a different world in every decade of his life; as he sees it with different eyes, the material of his art is constantly renewed. But in fact, very few poets have shown this capacity of adaptation to the years. It requires, indeed, an exceptional honesty and courage to face the change.[24]

If sincerity was the key prerequisite for artistic achievement in 1927, by 1940 it is *honesty* that has come to the fore. Are we keeping up with our own evolution? Are we being true to our current selves, and not merely imitating our past incarnations? One of the attendant dangers of middle age, Eliot warns, is the 'insincere mimicry of . . . earlier work'; but how do we move beyond this? Perhaps this is one definition of midlife genius – 'one of the greatest capacities' of which, Eliot writes of Joyce in 1949, 'is the power of development.'[25] Artists who keep developing – writers such as Yeats or Joyce, or musicians such as Radiohead – are for this reason much to be admired, even if we may demur from their direction of travel.

Given his well-attested views on the importance of continuing development, it is all the more striking that Eliot should have come to see being in the 'middle' in largely negative terms. In the same year that he made his statement about Yeats – he was in his early fifties at this point – Eliot coined the term 'middle style' in a letter to his friend John Hayward: 'I think the thing is to start in a sort of middle style, the kind one can go on with indefinitely, and let it develop (as it will) into the Personal Idiom in the course of becoming a habit.'[26] If middle style here is damned as a faint phase – serviceable, but hardly sublime – in Eliot's own writing of this period it is simply damned:

> So here I am, in the middle way, having had twenty years –
> Twenty years largely wasted, the years of *l'entre deux guerres* –
> Trying to learn to use words, and every attempt
> Is a wholly new start, and a different kind of failure
> Because one has only learnt to get the better of words
> For the thing one no longer has to say, or the way in which
> One is no longer disposed to say it.[27]

Writing in 1940, Eliot here brings together several senses of being in the middle. The awkward, somewhat pedestrian style of much of 'East Coker' – a good number of contemporary critics deemed these and other such passages in *Four Quartets* to be more prose than poetry – is central to the sentiment; Eliot is unable to move beyond (his perception of) his own inadequacy. In the darkest days of the war, he weaponizes middle age into a fear of failure, self-consciously positioning himself and Pound as part of a 'middle generation' of poets (Yeats representing the older guard, Auden and Stephen Spender the younger) neither fully developed nor radically new.[28] He conceives 'the middle way' accordingly as a series of abortive attempts to begin again, a perpetually thwarted incipience that is strikingly similar to the language of his critical statements on Yeats or Joyce

– with the difference that his own sense of arrested development reads like a photographic negative of their (supposedly) positive evolution. Failure seems to be the only way forwards.

In a passage excised from the published text of a lecture *On Poetry* (1947), Eliot raises this sense of failure into a manifesto for middle age:

> As one goes on, writing verse, into middle age, one can only do well by becoming more and more conscious of one's limitations: of what one can do well, and what one cannot do; learning to use one's abilities to the best and to avoid overstraining oneself where weakest. And I think that some of what I have said about the practice of poetry is applicable to the greatest and most general profession of all – that of marriage ... Every moment is a new problem, and you cannot succeed ... unless you approach the new poem, or familiar husband or wife, with a feeling that there is a great deal for you to learn.[29]

For Eliot, then, literature offers a template for middle age more generally. Humility – Montaigne's midlife modesty – remains the defining virtue; in relationships as in writing, we must accept what we cannot do, as well as emphasize what we can. Middle age amounts to the cultivation of less, not more. The sentiment is proto-Beckettian, albeit a Beckett hedged with typically Eliotic caginess.

Such caginess was both personal and political. In the passage from 'East Coker' cited above, for instance, Eliot makes middle age sound almost like old age, not least because the phrase 'here I am, in the middle way' echoes the beginning of his earlier poem 'Gerontion' (1920): 'Here I am, an old man in a dry month.' The 'twenty years largely wasted' – the twenty years that Dante defines in the *Banquet* as the period of maturity, the twenty years that Eliot identifies, in his essay on Yeats, as the standard span for each new school of poetry – correspond precisely to the passage of time between the earlier and the later poem, only plotted in reverse. Like F. Scott Fitzgerald's Benjamin Button, Eliot seems to have lived life backwards, from the premature senescence of his neurotic youth, through tired middle age, to the rejuvenated levity of his second marriage in 1957.

Yet these twenty years also hold, of course, a broader historical significance, in as much as they correspond to the years between the wars. Eliot's numerous variations on the Dantean refrain 'in the middle of life's way' carry this political resonance, too: where being in the middle personally implies a sense of threat and loss – 'not only in the middle of life's way / But all the way, in a dark wood, in a bramble, / On the edge of a grimpen, where there is no secure foothold, / And menaced by monsters' – politically it holds out the promise of compromise and communication. Comments Eliot made in the late 1920s, around the time of his conversion, suggest that he would have gladly reconceived the public sphere as 'a middle way', in terms both of national politics ('In a period of debility like our own, few men have the energy to follow the middle way in government') and of international relations:[30]

> Britain is the bridge between Latin culture and Germanic culture in both of which she shares. But Britain is not only the bridge, the middle way, between two parts of Western Europe; she is, or should be... not only European but the connection between Europe and the rest of the world.[31]

Putting aside the somewhat questionable identification of Britain as the missing link between different parts of Europe – surely as much wish-fulfilment then as it is now – what is striking is the changing nature of the idea of being in the middle. In the private sphere, 'the middle way' is a dark wood or bramble; in the public sphere, it is a bridge or connection. It all depends what you are in the middle *of*.

For Eliot as for other writers, then, middle age amounts to a canvas on to which one projects one's own anxiety. But this is equally true of literature itself, and of the choices one makes when reading as well as when writing. I certainly don't read Eliot now the way I did twenty years ago (to take his own, Dantean frame of comparison); but I would be 'rather atrophied' if I did. Given his obsession with intellectual evolution, given the way the twenty years between 'Gerontion' and *Four Quartets* map on to my own trajectory between discovering him in late adolescence and writing about him in early middle age, Eliot functions for me as a test case for my own development. No doubt we all have such tutelary figures, intellectual exemplars that for whatever reason have accompanied us throughout our adult lives, be they writers or musicians, thinkers or artists. Re-reading Eliot in my forties, I am struck not only by how much he helped to form my taste – from an early interest in Dante and the French symbolist poets to a predilection for poetry *tout court* – but by how different that taste now feels. For the great modernist technique of allusion and intertextuality works only if one is oneself allusive and intertextual. At twenty, references to authors of whom one has never heard are educational; at forty, the same references to authors one has now read are existential, resonating with the lived experience of intellectual exchange. The mature mind is simply so much *thicker* than the immature mind; the shock of the initial encounter may have dissipated, but layers of midlife meaning have accrued around it. By middle age, in short, we have become our own tradition, allusive to the intertexts of our lives.

Yet what Eliot also shows, conversely, is just how hard it can be to continue developing as we age. The path from adolescence to maturity is one thing; the path beyond it, quite another. Eliot's conversion to Christianity in the late 1920s lent his early middle age an aura of success, the enthusiasm of an active decision that allowed him to embrace his early forties with all the zeal of the

"THAT IS THE GREAT GRIMPEN MIRE."

Sidney Paget, 'The Grimpen Mire' of middle age, from the November 1901 issue of *The Strand*, the magazine that serialized Arthur Conan Doyle's *The Hound of the Baskervilles*.

converted. Yet this active enthusiasm gave way to a more passive sense of resignation as he moved into his fifties, with the middle way becoming like the Grimpen Mire in *The Hound of the Baskervilles*, cited in 'East Coker': 'A false step yonder means death to man or beast.'[32] What Eliot's example teaches us, in short, is that reaching midlife – whether in the form of crisis or conversion – is only the start; the hard part is sustaining it. For instruction in this most difficult of arts, we can now turn to a very different kind of writer.

9

Lessons in Lessness
Midlife Minimalism

I

Work, sleep, repeat. Work, sleep, repeat. By the onset of middle age, repetitive strain syndrome is an existential condition. Anyone who has reached their forties will find the formula all too familiar; however exciting our jobs may be, however happy our families may make us, a certain amount of ennui is inevitable as we grow older. There is no getting away from the fact, mathematically speaking, that the longer we live the more we repeat ourselves. Challenges that once motivated us – pursuing our own projects, managing those of others – begin to feel stale and hollow; the slow puncture of pointlessness deflates our every activity. We talk a lot about staying fit in our forties – but what about staying focused? The trouble with the rat race, as Dorothy Parker didn't quite say, is that even if you win you're still middle-aged.

The standard response to this problem is to run even faster. But what if the real answer is to run more slowly? Movement – the metaphor of the 'race' – defines our imagined lives, but there is of course an alternative model: stasis. We spend so much time trying to do things that we rarely try to *un*do them. Yet doing less – or rather, undoing more – is one way of coming to terms with the view from the summit described by Elliott Jaques's patient. Undo or die; minimalism can mitigate the midlife crisis.

Of all the authors who have accompanied us on our journey through the middle of life's way, of all the artists of ageing, none is as rigorously self-undoing as Samuel Beckett. We think of Beckett as the chronicler of confusion, the laureate of waifs and strays; we may even think of him, if we know his work well, as moving from the early maximalism of the 1930s to the late minimalism of the 1970s and '80s. What we rarely think about, however, is the extent to which his entire aesthetics depends, in a very direct sense, on the idea of being *nel mezzo del cammin*. Can Beckett help us to reconceive what it means to be middle-aged?

Almost everyone first encounters Beckett's work through *Waiting for Godot*, the iconic post-war drama that is probably the single most influential play of the twentieth century. We teach it in our schools to teenagers, and indeed it has a certain intuitive appeal to the adolescent mind, since the absurdity of the dialogue, the buffoonery of the characters and the sheer irreverence towards established modes of knowledge and authority all chime with the restlessness of youth. Yet this most undramatic of dramas is also the play *par excellence* of midlife stasis, with its two protagonists stuck in the middle of a journey that was never going anywhere in the first place. Resolution remains forever out of reach; in the words of one of the most famous of all first-night reviews, nothing happens, twice. *Waiting for Godot* captures, with unflinching precision, the tragicomedy of middle age.

Considered more broadly, such tragicomedy describes one of the greatest middle periods in literary history. In the pre-war years of the 1930s, Beckett had been an ambitious, evasive young man, defined more by what he hoped to become than by what he actually was. Two years as a tutor of English at the École Normale Supérieure in Paris – where he fell under the spell of James Joyce, who was at that point writing what would become his great late work, *Finnegans Wake* (1939) – were followed by a year as lecturer in French at Trinity College Dublin, his alma mater of the 1920s. He lasted just one year as an academic, however, and gave up his post in 1931 to spend the rest of the decade moving between London and Paris, with a hiatus of six significant months in 1936–7 travelling round the art galleries of Nazi Germany. During this decade Beckett published his first books, both critical and creative – including *Proust* (1931), *More Pricks than Kicks* (1934) and *Murphy* (1938) – but they sold very poorly and were ignored by critics. Submitting himself to psychoanalysis and turning his back on his native Ireland, the impoverished author struggled through his *Wanderjahre* of the 1930s.

If the war functioned as a natural caesura for Beckett, as for his entire generation, it was only in its aftermath that he reached the full maturity of his middle years. His great moment of

Nothing happening, twice. The premiere of *En attendant Godot* (1953).

conversion – one is tempted to call it a self-conversion or even 'animadversion', a decisive instant of self-censure – has been much mythologized, not least by the author himself. Having spent the war hiding in the South of France, contributing to the Resistance whenever he could, in the summer of 1945 Beckett returned to visit his ageing mother outside Dublin. Sitting in her bedroom, watching the light fall across her altered face, he had a sudden revelation: he had been going about writing entirely the wrong way. Rather than trying to maximize his resources – whether in terms of vocabulary, syntax or range of reference – he should be trying to *minimize* them. 'Joyce had gone as far as one could in the direction of knowing more,' Beckett told his biographer James Knowlson; 'I realised that my own way lay in impoverishment, in lack of knowledge and in taking away, in subtracting rather than adding.'[1] Less was henceforth to be more.

This midlife revelation famously recurs, transmuted into art, in one of Beckett's own favourite works, *Krapp's Last Tape* (1958). Written from middle age (Beckett was about fifty) but projected to the end of life, the play depicts an old man listening to recordings of his voice as a younger man. The description of the revelation becomes an archetype – or perhaps a parody – of the Romantic moment of artistic inspiration (reminiscent, for instance, of Rilke's claim to have heard the opening of the first *Duino Elegy* whispered to him by the wind on a cliff overlooking the Adriatic):

> Spiritually a year of profound gloom and indulgence until that memorable night in March at the end of the jetty, in the howling wind, never to be forgotten, when suddenly I saw the whole thing. The vision, at last. This fancy is what I have chiefly to record this evening, against the day when my work will be done and perhaps no place left in my memory, warm or cold, for the miracle that ... (hesitates) ... for the fire that set it alight.[2]

What is so striking about this pivotal moment in Beckett's life and work is not just that it re-emerges from the private into the public sphere, but that it fits so neatly into our broader narrative of midlife conversion. For in the summer of 1945, Beckett was 39 – precisely the age that George Miller Beard identified as the middle of life, and precisely the age at which T. S. Eliot was baptized into the Church of England. Despite his lifelong struggle against cant and cliché, then, in this if in no other regard Beckett himself is a cliché. That he intuits as much is suggested by the way he subsequently rewrote the scene of his visit to his mother, gently mocking Romantic notions of divine inspiration by positioning himself in a raging storm at the end of a jetty.

The great difference between Beckett's midlife 'conversion' and that of countless writers before him, however, was that his was not religious but epistemological. To reach the middle of life, for Beckett, was to realize that the accumulation of knowledge – the linear model by which most of us not only live our lives but conceive them, understanding ourselves as progressively adding to our store of insight and experience as we grow older – is unsustainable, since it can never be enough. He undertook, rather, to invert the Sorites paradox of ageing, undoing the accumulated pile of knowledge by taking away the grains of sand one by one. The question was no longer at what point does a pile *become* a pile, but at what point does it *stop* being a pile? Beckett's focus, from this point onwards, was to be on man as a 'non-knower'.[3]

The principal consequence of the midlife crisis of 1945 – and its enduring contribution to Beckett's mature work – was thus what one might term a 'fidelity to failure'. The phrase occurs in the 'Three Dialogues with Georges Duthuit', an art critic and editor (as well, not least, as Henri Matisse's son-in-law) whom Beckett befriended in Paris in the late 1940s.[4] The correspondence between the two – the brief 'dialogues' precipitated out of it – is one of the great documents of Beckett's midlife aesthetics, and indeed one of the major reasons why his letters must surely rank alongside those of Keats and Heinrich von Kleist in the pantheon of posterity. One of his earliest letters to Duthuit, written from Dublin in the summer of 1948, combines his views on his writing, on his mother, on his sense of getting older and on his syntax of negation into a plangent portrait of the artist as a middle-aged man:

> Here I have difficulty in believing that it has ever happened to me, that it may happen to me again, to write. In the old days, I used to make up for that, used to rejoice in it if you like, by talking in abundance, in this city of talkers. Not these days … 'Ange plein de beauté connaissez-vous les rides, Et la peur de vieillir et ce hideux torment, De lire … ?' … Do you know the cry common to those in purgatory? Io fui. I went with my mother to church last Sunday, a distant church, so that she could find the pillar behind which my father would hide his noddings-off, in the evening, his physical restlessness, his portly man's refusal to kneel … I keep watching my mother's eyes, never so blue, so stupefied, so heartrending, eyes of an endless childhood, eyes of old age. Let us get there rather earlier, while there are still refusals we can make. I think these are the first eyes I have seen. I have no wish to see any others, I have all I need for loving and weeping, I know now what is going to close, and open inside me, but without seeing anything, there is no more seeing.[5]

The personal and the literary, the physical and the metaphysical, are conflated here into a moving sketch of the 42-year-old author's state of mind. A lifelong reader of Dante – he studied him at university and cites him throughout his work – Beckett has a purgatorial vision of midlife: *nel mezzo del cammin* becomes *io fui* ('I was'), the present a continuous past haunted by a foreclosed future of 'no more seeing'. He also cites Baudelaire to evoke 'la peur de vieillir' (the fear of growing old) as the animating impulse behind the letter – but it is a fear that he characteristically embraces, juxtaposing his middle-aged perspective with his mother's 'eyes of old age'. Indeed, he would even have us rush through midlife straight to the end: 'Let us get there rather earlier, while there are still refusals we can make.' Ageing itself now depends on *not* doing and *not* knowing.

This idea of 'refusal' constitutes a typically Beckettian response to the challenge of middle age. If it emerges elsewhere as one of the key terms of his language of negation, here it echoes his long-dead father's 'refusal to kneel', a phrase that in turn sends us back to Dante.[6] In the third canto of the *Inferno*, Dante coins the phrase *il gran rifiuto* to describe those who refuse to commit to any given cause, who remain neutral to a fault. Beckett picks up on the term in a further letter to Duthuit written in March 1949, during a passage in which he discusses the painting technique of his friend Bram van Velde:

> We have waited a long time for an artist who is brave enough, is at ease enough with the great tornadoes of intuition, to grasp that the break with the outside world entails the break with the inside world, that there are no replacement relations for naïve relations, that what are called outside and inside are one and the same. I am not saying that he makes no attempt to reconnect. What matters is that he does not succeed. His painting is, if you will, the impossibility of reconnecting. There is, if you like, refusal and refusal to accept refusal. That perhaps is what makes this painting possible. For my part, it is the gran rifiuto that interests me, not the heroic wrigglings to which we owe this splendid thing.[7]

That Beckett is equally referring to his own work here becomes clear by the end of the letter, when he states that 'I who hardly ever talk about myself talk about little else.' When translated into the medium of literature, the painter's refusal to commit to 'naïve relations' becomes a refusal to write *about* (as Beckett himself phrases it), an insistence on the purely intransitive nature of language that foregrounds the 'impossibility of reconnecting' words with things, inside with outside. When compressed into the brief 'dialogue' about Van Velde, this link between art and failure assumes almost epigrammatic status: 'to be an artist is to fail, as no other dare fail.'[8]

What becomes clear from juxtaposing these two letters, then – and there are others that say very similar things – is the extent to which this 'great refusal' was motivated by Beckett's midlife malaise. Time and again in his letters, Beckett links the idea of 'lessening' himself to the passing of time, repeatedly using what he terms 'the regulation twenty years ago' as the measure of middle age (Eliot, we recall, used exactly the same period of time to define his own middle years in the period between the wars). Beckett's creative force is enhanced, paradoxically, by its attenuation: 'Is my strength ebbing away? Fine, it will make its miserable way into my legs a bit less. Anything that lessens me, starting with my precious memories, makes access to it easier.'[9]

What, though, of Beckett's work? What of his writing itself, rather than his writing *about* writing? It is no coincidence that he should have come into an unprecedented period of creativity in his early forties, exactly at the time his mother, stricken with Parkinson's, was slowly dying. The letter cited above is ample enough evidence of the link between Beckett's filial feelings and his simultaneous inability and compulsion to write. Yet if this double movement – 'the expression that there is nothing to express, nothing with which to express, nothing from which to express, no power to express, no desire to express, together with the obligation to express' – exploded into a 'frenzy of writing' between May 1947 and January 1950, it was also because he quite literally found a new set of words in which to express himself: French.[10] Beckett's midlife conversion was not just epistemological – it was also linguistic.

It is hard to overstate how much the post-war change of language altered Beckett's aesthetics. In the 1930s he had toyed with the idea of writing in various languages, not least German, and indeed there is one particularly powerful letter in that language in which he describes how 'language appears to me like a veil which one has to tear apart in order to get to those things (or the nothingness) lying behind it.'[11] Such sentiments anticipate the post-war shift into French, which commentators have conceived, time and again, as a way of escaping the overbearing influence of Joyce's exuberant English. Certainly it marked an attempt to write 'without style', or at least to assay a new, pared-down style, stripped of ornament and extravagance.

More broadly, however, it was also a response to Beckett's midlife epiphany in his mother's bedroom. Embracing France was a way of abjuring Ireland; committing himself to the new language of his maturity was a way of exiling himself from the old language of his childhood. If such distance, paradoxically, was the prerequisite for returning to childhood, it was this very distance that gave his new writing such force. This sense of pulling oneself up by one's own bootstraps, of trying to escape oneself through oneself, resonates in what emerged at this point as the standard Beckettian 'plot', namely the thwarted journey. The major works written between 1947 and 1950 – the three volumes of the trilogy (*Molloy*, *Malone Dies* and *The Unnamable*) and *Waiting for Godot* – all share some version of this basic structure: no one gets anywhere. Yet this very immobility, in true Beckettian fashion, becomes its own mobility. The opening words of *Godot*, 'Nothing to be done,' can be read both passively in a tone of fatalism and actively in a tone of assertion. In the words of Kafka that will haunt twentieth-century poetics: our task is to do the negative.[12]

The prose trilogy accordingly effects a *reductio ad absurdum*, from Molloy trying to remember how he got to his mother's room to the unnameable narrator stuck in his pot, a mere voice in a vase. The sequence develops as a parody of Cartesianism, with protagonists who are incapable of properly gauging the split between mind and body that age is imposing upon them. Molloy, limping around a forest on crutches, provides a first example, echoing both Dante and Descartes. He comes to a crossroads in the middle of the woods, but is incapable of following Descartes' advice (in the 'morale par provision' of the *Discourse on Method*) to keep going in a straight line, since the crutches make him paddle round in circles. And yet still he feels the imperative to push on. Equally, the detective sent to find him, Moran, sets out blindly without knowing where he is going, circling back, by the end of his narrative, to the beginning of his own report, only this time negated ('It is midnight. The rain is beating on the windows. It was not midnight. It was not raining').[13] The whole charade becomes an act of narrative will.

Viewed in these terms, the trilogy can be understood as an attempt to negotiate the narrative impasse of middle age. Once we have reached the zenith of our lives, how do we keep going? Must we simply keep going? 'I don't know, I'll never know, in the silence you don't know, you must go on, I can't go on, I'll go on': the famous closing words of *The Unnamable*, echoing in innumerable variations across the work of this period, summarize the Beckettian approach to midlife gridlock.[14] To go on is the only way to get on, in the sense both of making progress and of ageing. For all his evident mastery of language and literature, Beckett's real genius resides in his dogged determination to continue, to raise repetition to the level of existential fiat.

Translated into the terms of his technique, one of the principal consequences of this determination was a recurring emphasis on verb tenses. Beckett's work of the late 1940s and early 1950s is characterized by what one might term the purgatorial present. Time and again his prose and plays are narrated in a present tense – as in the closing words of the trilogy cited above – that both perpetuates and postpones the moment at which the present becomes the future. That this reflects the standard Beckettian plot of this period is, of course, no accident; caught between the remembered past of childhood and the anticipated future of senescence, middle age is stuck in a perpetual purgatory: 'My life, my life, now I speak of it as something over, now as of a joke which still goes on, and it is neither, for at the same time it is over and it goes on, and is there any tense for that?'[15] Molloy's hesitations are not only those of middle age; they are, more specifically, those of the middle-aged writer.

Reduced to a bare minimum of disembodied consciousness, the voice in *The Unnamable* functions in this regard as an allegory of the author, exploring what he can and cannot ascertain within his circumscribed circumstances. In the typical Beckettian manner, the voice is a *perpetuum immobile*, existing only inasmuch as it narrates its own futility. If the older Beckett was 'damned to fame' – the telling title of Knowlson's biography – the midlife Beckett was condemned to the present, searching vainly for a way forwards. His heightened awareness of tense merely emphasizes this sense of being islanded in his own consciousness. To elucidate one point, the voice tells us,

> I would need a stick or pole, and the means of plying it ... I could also do, incidentally, with future and conditional participles. Then I would dart it, like a javelin, straight before me and know, by the sound made, whether that which hems me round, and blots out my world, is the old void, or a plenum.[16]

The playful reference here to the first-century BC poet and philosopher Lucretius and his celebrated proof, in Book One of *De rerum natura*, of the infinity of the universe – a spear launched into space would either bounce back or continue, proving either way that something is there – evokes the vertigo of the perpetual present, looming out into the darkness of future and conditional possibilities.[17] In the middle of life's way, the author is exploring just how far the path goes.

How far did it go? The outer edges of Beckett's middle period can perhaps be located in *How It Is*, first published in French in 1961. With money inherited after his mother's death – this, too, no doubt a marker of middle age – Beckett had bought an unassuming house in the village of Ussy-sur-Marne, an hour or so from the noise and clamour of Paris. In December 1958 (he was now in his early fifties), Beckett began to write what would become *How It Is*, conceiving it as a concentration of the style and voice of the earlier trilogy. Not only plot, but now punctuation has disappeared, leaving only an unnamed character crawling aimlessly in the mud, 'panting' from speech bubble to speech bubble. The present tense has become a tense present, a purgatory reduced to infernal extremes; all that remains is 'this solitude when the voice recounts it sole means of living it'.[18]

The original French version of the novel, significantly, was entitled *Comment c'est*, an untranslatable pun that can also be heard as the imperative *Commencez* (or perhaps the infinitive *Commencer*). The possibility of beginning – and of beginning again – thus haunts the present, if only as a distant echo; Beckett's voice sketches out 'two possible formulations therefore the present and that other beginning where the present ends'.[19] Yet this possibility exists only as an auditory hallucination in which past, present and future coalesce into a single voice: 'or then that all begins and then the life you'll have the tormentor you'll have the journey you'll make the victim you'll have the two lives the three lives the life you had the life you have the life you'll have'.[20]

Compared to the earlier texts of the trilogy, Beckett's narrator seems to have regressed. If he is stuck in the middle, he is also stuck in the mud. As with so much of Beckett's work, the allegorical reading is irresistible: it is the human condition to flail around blindly, ignorant both of where we have come from and where we are going. But the psychological reading is equally important. We are both subject and object of life's forces, both 'tormentor' and 'victim' (the original French terms *bourreau* and *victime* betray their Baudelairean heritage in the nineteenth-century poet's famous claim to be both 'la plaie et le couteau ... et la victime et le bourreau').[21] In the muddle of life's way, we torment ourselves by recalling the past and hoping for the future.

Here, then, Beckett outlines something like the ground zero of the midlife journey. Flailing in the infernal mud, his narrator seems condemned to an eternity of stasis, subject to brute forces beyond his control. As a vision of middle age, it is pitiless. But it is also revelatory; it reveals to us who we are meant to be, if only we have the courage to pursue this vision. 'I seemed to see myself ageing as swiftly as a day-fly,' Beckett writes in *Molloy*. 'And what I saw was more like a crumbling, a frenzied collapsing of all that had always protected me from all I was condemned to be.'[22] As we sink ever further into middle age, what Beckett encourages us to do, counter-intuitively, is to accelerate this crumbling, to undo the walls that we have spent the first half of our life building up, in order to gain access to our true, our inner nature. This takes courage, of course, and the kind of unblinking rigour that few of us possess. Yet it is only by acknowledging how it is that we can begin again: *Comment c'est* is *Commencer*. In the words traditionally attributed to Beckett: 'when you're in the shit up to your neck, there's nothing left to do but sing.'

II

I first read Beckett's trilogy in my late twenties on a post-Christmas family trip to Naples. My father-in-law was in a terrible temper for the whole week (hardly an uncommon occurrence, but particularly uncomfortable when we were stuck in a small, noisy hostel with him). As we walked around the city's various museums, he barely allowed us to stop even for coffee, hurrying us through the narrow alleyways of the Spanish Quarter in a constant state of dissatisfaction. A glorious Caravaggio exhibition at the Capodimonte was memorable mainly for the long queues and even longer faces; Pompeii mainly for the foul weather and fouler moods. Even the boat trip to Capri did little to lighten the atmosphere, the sullen water lurching us backwards and forwards like a long-suffering pathetic fallacy fighting back. A success the trip was not.

Between paternal thunderclaps, snatches of Beckett's prose parted the clouds. Every truth has its stopcock, every toxin its eager antidote, and the restive, questioning rhythms of *The Unnamable* kept me sane in the Christmas chaos. The relationship between the time and place in which we read a book and its significance for us is one of the great unexplored subjects of modern literature, largely because it is so difficult to universalize on the basis of personal experience. And yet it is fundamental to how we perceive art, often in ways that are only semi-conscious. We may be well disposed, for instance, towards works that we associate, even after the event, with something demanding and desirable; we may be ill disposed towards works that we associate with complacency and self-satisfaction. That I view Beckett's trilogy through the prism of my memories of Naples is utterly contingent – others will have different geographical associations, most obviously with Dublin – but it is also central to how I respond to it. To say that our perception of art is subjective is to say that it is subject to circumstances often entirely out of our control.

The shafts of sunlight that Beckett shone, having no alternative, on the Neapolitan New Year look very different from the distance of middle age. In my twenties, I was ever on the lookout for moments of insight, for fragments of fugitive beauty that I hoped would somehow advance me in my quest for meaning. My copy of the trilogy, replete with triumphant annotations where I saw significance suddenly swimming into focus, testifies to this approach, all swooping circles and double marks in the margins. And there is no doubt that Beckett's prose lends itself to this kind of reading, defined as it is by lengthy, murky passages interspersed with sudden moments of clarity, shining out of the gloom like 'so many vent-holes in the cask of secrets'.[23]

Re-reading the trilogy in my forties, though, what strikes me is the way Beckett rejects the very possibility of such meaning or advancement, remaining forever focused on stasis rather than movement. Molloy goes round in circles, Moran never finds him, Malone dies, the unnameable voice remains in his vase: they are all defined by their inability to get anywhere. Such moments of lyricism as occur are almost incidental, not to say accidental; they are that which befalls us (*accidere*), visitations of grace entirely out of our control. Having realized this in his midlife revelation in his mother's bedroom, Beckett seems to have concluded that it was better to cultivate this abrogation of agency, rather than to fight it. The grace of stasis is the best we can hope for.

Such midlife modesty has considerable intuitive appeal, in part because it is a question as much of ethics as of aesthetics. I defy anyone to read Beckett – and indeed to read *about* Beckett – and not be impressed by his example of artistic and moral integrity. He was no saint – his numerous affairs, if nothing else, give the lie to this idea – but he was unusually sensitive to the sufferings, both physical and metaphysical, of the poor, bare, forked animal that is the human being. And his prose is so supple, his sentences so beautifully turned, that it is hard not to become addicted to his austere aesthetics. Lessness is moreish.

The problem, though, is that impotence of this order is all too potent. What happens when undoing becomes in turn a new kind of doing, when unwriting becomes a new kind of writing? Beckett himself, tellingly, intuited the problem: 'but I'm starting to write,' he concludes abruptly after one particularly sustained disquisition on 'the language of the no'.[24] After finishing the trilogy he began to feel the need to push beyond mere negation: 'I see myself moving away from ideas of poverty and bareness. They are still superlatives.'[25] The logic of lessness, in this regard, is self-undoing.

It is important, then, to understand the limits of the Beckettian *via negativa* as a model for middle age. These limits are certainly aesthetic – one can celebrate failure only so far before it becomes its own kind of success; one can 'undo' language only so much before it simply falls into silence – but they are also moral. For the great danger of midlife minimalism is that of inverted pride, of feeling that one has attained some privileged insight into the human condition. Where others get fatter, one tells oneself, I get thinner; where others want more, I want less. Where they go low – one is tempted to think with Michelle Obama – I go high.

Such exceptionalism is perhaps the most insidious form of arrogance, and it is one to which intellectuals are particularly prone. As we age, we take great care to appear austere, ascetic and 'humble', all the while wearing such humility as a badge of honour. Eliot captures this arrogance memorably in *Murder in the Cathedral* through the figure of the fourth tempter. Archbishop Becket can resist the first three tempters without any great effort, since they offer merely material or worldly pleasures. The fourth, however, shrewdly identifies his weak spot: pride. Becket *wants* to be a martyr, to show that he is right: 'The last temptation is the greatest treason: / To do the right deed for the wrong reason.'[26]

Midlife minimalism, analogously – throwing everything away, rejecting everything achieved, starting again – risks encouraging the right approach to ageing for the wrong reason. Fetishized for its own sake, negation turns into narcissism, the superiority complex of consciously cultivated inferiority. Selflessness becomes selfishness, as we start heralding our own humility; faux-failure emerges as the shabby chic of aesthetics, a mere pose that requires the cultivation of chic in the first place. Lessness is easier said than undone.

Navel-gazing, in short, is the besetting sin of the midlife mind. Self-consciousness, self-negation, self-pity: the common prefix speaks for itself. Even writing about it risks another level of narcissistic regression, a further twist of the screwdriver of self-obsession. There is something faintly preposterous about middle-aged intellectuals telling others that all the things they cherish – success, status, children – are not worth having, or are at least better undone than done. The distinction is not just semantic; the two senses of 'undone' – not *yet* done, and done but now *un*done – are the two slopes of youth and (Beckettian) middle age. To fail to distinguish between them is to insult those who have not yet had the chance to achieve anything, much less undo it.

How, then, can we adopt midlife minimalism without becoming beholden to it? How are we to resist the fourth tempter? Perhaps the best defence is to remember that we do not get older alone. We age with those around us, and we owe it to them not to undo everything we have done together. Beckett's poetics of subtraction may seem a noble model of aesthetics, but if it diminishes others as well as the self, then it is a questionable model of ethics. Literature is not life, however much certain theorists may argue otherwise, and people can get along – and can get older – just fine without it. We should not make the mistake of extrapolating too far from our own special interests.

Perhaps we should apply the logic of lessness, then, to the literature of lessness. All things in moderation, including moderation; minimalism is best administered in small doses. Few of us can celebrate failure as Beckett could, because few of us have known the success Joyce did. If poverty and bareness 'are still superlatives', we may do better, in midlife, to cultivate comparatives, to think of middle age as not about being the old*est*, but being old*er* – older, of course, than ourselves. Learning from

Beckett's example does not mean copying Beckett's example, but rather using it to reflect on which aspects of our lives should be amplified, and which attenuated. The great lesson of his post-war period is not, ultimately, that he found a means to reduce everything – style, syntax and even sentiment – to a bare minimum, but that he found his own path through the middle of life's way. What we can learn from Samuel Beckett's life and work, in short, is that to reach middle age is to try again, to fail again – and to fail, if not better, then at least older.

10

From the Prime of Life to Old Age
How to Survive the Menopause

I

It is often said that the generation born immediately after the Second World War drew first place in the lottery of life. The baby boomers had it all – security, prosperity, opportunity – and they have not been shy in making the most of it. The twenty-first century, with all its privileges and prejudices, has been shaped in their image. Before this post-war generation could take over the world, however, the most immediate beneficiaries of the ceasefire were their parents, the lucky survivors who found themselves, as hostilities ended, inheriting a new world of possibilities. Having been in the middle of death's way, they were now in the middle of life's way, free to reshape a world that wanted nothing more than to forget what had just happened. Suffering, starvation, occupation: these were to be things of the past, a bad dream of a bygone era. To be middle-aged in the late 1940s was to be in charge of the future.

Assuming, that is, that one was a man. Despite all the changes in gender relations brought about by the two world wars, midlife fulfilment – in personal, professional and creative terms – was still largely limited to one half of the human race. And yet progress there had been. Just as the First World War had led to political enfranchisement for women – in 1918 in Britain for women over thirty (full equality followed in 1928), in 1919 in the United States – so the Second World War had led to professional enfranchisement. As the men went off to fight, women had come into the workforce in unprecedented numbers. Even France, the most recalcitrant of Western countries with regard to gender parity, had finally relented, and women had voted for the first time in April 1945. With the total victory of the Allies, with peace stretching invitingly into what would become the *trentes glorieuses* of the 1940s–'70s, progress seemed assured not only economically, but socially. The era of equal opportunities had begun.

It hardly needs stating, though, that mentalities do not change overnight. Men continued – and, of course, continue – to dominate professional, political and professorial discourse; the life of the mind, to take just this one example, has historically been overwhelmingly male, simply because men have willed it so. Middle age, with all its advantages and disadvantages, offers a microcosm of this history; as this book has shown, for better or for worse it is largely male writers and thinkers who have determined what it means to be midlife. In a sense, then, we must now reconsider everything we have learned so far, or at least turn it around and view it from a female perspective. What does it mean not only to be a middle-aged woman, but to engage, as a middle-aged woman, with centuries of male hegemony? What does it mean to develop a middle age of one's own?

One way to ask this question is to pose it retrospectively. Where Virginia Woolf famously pondered the fate of Shakespeare's notional sister Judith – she ends up killing herself, but returning as a ghost to exhort today's women to assert themselves – we might ask what would have happened to Dante's notional sister on finding herself *nel mezzo del cammin*.[1] Would Virgil have chaperoned her safely through the dark forest of middle age? Would she have found her path through the circles and cornices of midlife? The brutal reality is that Dantea could never have consciously found herself in the middle of life's way, for the simple reason that she was never allowed her own way in the first place. Within the conventions of courtly love, the range of roles open to women was strictly limited; the reason Beatrice appears only on the threshold of paradise is that she never fully existed to begin with. If her psychology seems underdeveloped, it is because when Dante first met her she *was* underdeveloped; she was only nine. The fact that he would see her only once more in his lifetime suggests that Beatrice was more metaphysical abstraction than physical reality, more idea than individual. The woman of the Middle Ages could not have a middle age because she remained a distant object, not a vivid, embodied subject. She was treated, in short, like a child, kept offstage not only in the divine, but in the human comedy. Women were not allowed to grow up, let alone grow old.

Claiming the right to age, then, was an important step in the emancipation of female subjectivity. This process gathered steam, as we have seen, over the course of the nineteenth century, as industrialization changed both the relations between the sexes and the amount of time available to post-menopausal women (at least, to those of sufficient means). Increased agency – and increased adultery – was the inevitable result of these changes; the 'new woman' was also the newly middle-aged woman. This female discovery of middle age still took place, however, within the terms dictated by men, and within the bourgeois institutions of family and marriage dominated by men. It was not until the twentieth century that Western woman began to gain agency over her ageing.

In the optimism of the post-war period, one woman played a crucial role in defining how this agency might look. As the war ended, Simone de Beauvoir (1908–1986) was in her late thirties. Before the war she had enjoyed the most classical of French educations – *normalienne, agrégée*, she was second in the university rankings only to Jean-Paul Sartre, the man who would become her life companion – and had taught at a series of prestigious *lycées*. By the late 1940s she was beginning to publish her first novels and to formulate, in essays such as *Pour une morale de l'ambiguïté* ('The Ethics of Ambiguity'; 1947), the existentialist views with which she and Sartre would become synonymous. She was also, more pointedly, beginning to think about what it meant to be a woman.

The study that would make Beauvoir famous was written in her late thirties – at almost exactly the age, that is, that Eliot was converting to Anglo-Catholicism and Beckett to French minimalism, George Miller Beard's mythical 39. This is no mere biographical coincidence. Much of what Beauvoir writes about the subordination of women as 'the second sex' is driven by her sense of starting to age, of starting to move away from the normative position of the 'desirable' young woman. *The Second Sex* is written from the perspective of the second age – and, like almost everything else, this age has been largely determined by the perception of men. To paraphrase Beauvoir's most famous sentence: one is not born, but rather becomes, a middle-aged woman.

Beauvoir's sense of herself at the time of writing *The Second Sex* (1949) can be reconstructed from her autobiography. The second of four volumes, *The Prime of Life* (1960), covers the war years under German occupation. She concludes this volume with a coda describing her enduring fear of death; this is to be the note that echoes into the third volume, *Force of Circumstance* (1963), the book that follows her transition into middle age. Mortality begins to manifest itself; in the opening pages, she recalls losing a tooth in a bicycle accident and deciding not to replace it with a false one. 'What was the point? . . . I was old, I was thirty-six.'[2] As the book – and Beauvoir's recalled life – progresses, this sense of ageing becomes the recurring refrain of her memory: 'Forty. Forty-one. Old age was growing inside me'; 'at forty-four, I was relegated to the land of the shades.'[3] By the time of her epilogue, de Beauvoir could write that 'since 1944, the most important, most irreparable thing that has happened to me is that . . . I have grown old.'[4] Her subsequent study *Old Age* (1970) is the inevitable culmination of decades of self-observation.

Beyond the basic physiological fact of ageing – and the basic psychological fact of feeling increasingly marginalized by ageing, as the countdown from her mid-thirties onwards suggests – the more interesting question is how Beauvoir's sense of moving into midlife affects her work. How does biology determine biography? In the early pages of *Force of Circumstance*, she strikes a positive, almost triumphant note about her stage of life, noting in her introduction that 'the point was no longer to educate but to fulfil myself,' and claiming a little later that she felt she had now 'reconciled – in a fleeting illusion – the contradictory privileges of youth and age'.[5] By the summer of 1946, however, she was suffering anxiety attacks brought on, she suggests, not just by the lingering effects of the war; rather, 'these crises were a last revolt before resigning myself to age and the end that follows it.' Tellingly, these midlife crises are also explicitly linked to the anxiety of authorship – which is to say, to a feeling of writer's block. Beauvoir at this point was struggling to achieve 'what I had always demanded of writing up till then: the feeling of risking and at the same time of transcending myself, an almost religious joy'.[6] The self-determination that she demands from life – the ability to write one's own life that is the very essence of existentialism – is imperilled by her fear of ageing. Biology blocks biography.

The writer's block of middle age was of particular concern to Beauvoir, it becomes clear, because it threatened the entire edifice of her philosophy – a philosophy that was based, crucially, on perpetual becoming. Stasis is anathema to existentialism: 'those who are condemned to stagnation are often pronounced happy on the pretext that happiness consists in being at rest,' she writes in the introduction to *The Second Sex*. 'This notion we reject, for our perspective is that of existentialist ethics.'[7] It is important to understand that Beauvoir's view of midlife was as much existentialist as feminist – or rather, that her feminism was itself a form of existentialism. If 'existence precedes essence', to cite the classical Sartrean formulation, then ageing is the prototypical topic of existential philosophy. From *The Prime of Life* to *Old Age*, understanding how we get older is the very stuff of existentialism. To be, we have to become.

As Beauvoir saw it, this is particularly true for women. 'Woman is not a completed reality,' she claims early in *The Second Sex*, 'but rather a becoming, and it is in her becoming that she should be compared with man.'[8] Women, she suggests, are not allowed to attain full maturity in the manner of men, since that would imply a degree of autonomy foreclosed to them. Beauvoir thus decided to live like a man, or rather not like a 'lady': rejecting her bourgeois Catholic upbringing, she refused to have children so that she could concentrate on her work; she lived in an open relationship with Sartre – pointedly not a 'marriage' – and she took lovers as she pleased. In a country with such traditional views on the roles of the sexes as post-war France, her behaviour – or rather, her insistence on talking openly about her behaviour – blazed a trail for free-thinking women across the West.

For all her affirmation of the emancipated female condition, however, Beauvoir's conceptualization of middle age emerges in particular out of her relationships with men. Her brand of feminism was not of the kind that disavows the opposite gender; she sought, rather, to assert herself as a woman by acting as a man – and there is no more 'male' way of mitigating the midlife crisis than seeking out a new partner. Beyond her lifelong intellectual companionship with Sartre – who famously nicknamed her *castor* by translating 'beaver' back into French – Beauvoir understood both of her two most significant sexual relationships as ways of taming time. When her liaison with the American novelist Nelson Algren reached its end, Beauvoir feigned indifference, but was quickly overtaken by self-pity:

> 'Well, that's that,' I said to myself; and I no longer even thought about my happiness with Algren ... My age and the

> circumstances of my life left little room, it seemed to me, for a new love. My body, perhaps as the result of deeply ingrained pride, adapts easily; it made no demands. But there was something in me that would not submit to such indifference. 'I'll never sleep again warmed by another's body.' Never: what a knell! When the realization of these facts penetrated me, I felt myself sinking into death . . . I suddenly found myself on the other side of a line, though there was no one moment when I had crossed it.[9]

While Beauvoir resists, at this point, the sense of ageing as physical loss, she strikingly succumbs to it as psychological void. Descartes digs his claws in; triggered by regret at the end of the relationship, Beauvoir's mind ages before her body, reversing the standard Cartesian split by which the body ages before the mind ('inside I still feel twenty'). The ageing philosopher is now no longer in the middle of life's way; she is beyond it, on 'the other side' of the divide.

In response to this midlife crisis, Beauvoir did what men have always done: she took a new, much younger lover. Claude Lanzmann, in his mid-twenties when they met, was some seventeen years Beauvoir's junior, a fact that played no small role in her attraction to him: 'Lanzmann's presence beside me freed me from my age. First, it did away with my anxiety attacks . . . And then, his participation revived my interest in everything.'[10] Beyond reversing the usual cliché of male middle age lusting after female youth, Beauvoir's encounter with Lanzmann brings out an under-discussed aspect of middle age, namely what we might call a quantity theory of curiosity. Even for someone as voracious in her appetites as Simone de Beauvoir, there is only so much life that can be lived, only so many countries that can be visited and political positions discussed. By her early forties, she felt she was no longer having 'new' experiences: 'I was more concerned with controlling, deepening, completing my earlier

From the Prime of Life to Old Age

experiences.'[11] For the younger Lanzmann, however, most of what he was experiencing was still new to him, and that meant he could function as a proxy for his lover's attempts to renew herself, to begin again. Through his eyes, Beauvoir's curiosity, which had become 'temperate', once again became red-hot. 'I was not yet ripe for old age,' she wrote later; 'he hid its approach from me.'[12] The *castor* had become a 'cougar'.

The origin of that term – used to describe a middle-aged woman in a relationship with a younger man – is uncertain, but it is generally agreed that it emerged in Canada in the 1980s. Although the grounds for it were laid by the late nineteenth-century codification of middle age as a newly female category, it is only recently that the cougar has become a staple of popular culture – which is another way of saying that it is only recently that popular culture has come to accept the idea of midlife female sexuality as anything other than emasculated by marriage. For men, of course, there has always been a term for those interested in younger women: 'men'. But the logic, until very recently, has never been reciprocal.

There is, no doubt, a single-word reason for this longstanding taboo: menopause. Millennia of male dominance have dictated that women apparently lose all sexual currency as they reach middle age; beyond the childbearing years – male-run societies have long supposed – women have little interest in sex. If Beauvoir took a particular interest in the menopause, then, it was not only because it is a quintessentially female experience, but because it represented a test case for her existentialist ethics, the point at which woman stops being a 'woman'. For the menopausal woman in fact constitutes not a second, but a *third* sex: 'while they are not males, they are no longer females.'[13] The midlife mind is also the midlife gender.

Historically speaking, this third sex has barely existed. In early modernity, the seven ages of man were just that, and woman was lucky if she had three ages, as in Hans Baldung's allegorical painting from the 1540s. What is striking in Baldung's picture, in any case, is what is *not* there. Between the young woman of about twenty and the old woman of about sixty, there is no representation of the middle years of life, of the middle-aged woman of about forty. The three possible models of femininity, it would seem, are infancy, fertility and senescence; there is no room for what Dante would call *gioventute*, for midlife maturity. Female middle age, to put it in evolutionary terms, is the missing link.

Given such historical precedents, it is no wonder that Beauvoir's exploration of what it means to be a middle-aged woman (in Chapter Twenty of *The Second Sex*) begins with the claim that 'the individual life history of woman – because she is still bound up in her female functions – depends in much greater degree than that of man upon her physiological destiny.' The curve of this destiny, Beauvoir contends, differs radically – or perhaps, changing etymologies, *hysterically* – between the genders:

> Whereas man grows old gradually, woman is suddenly deprived of her femininity; she is still relatively young when she loses the erotic attractiveness and the fertility which, in the view of society and in her own, provide the justification of her existence and her opportunity for happiness. With no future, she still has about one half of her adult life to live.[14]

There is much to be said about this passage from a feminist perspective – not least about the elision 'in the view of society and in her own', which begs the question of whether women really define themselves exclusively through the male gaze – but the underlying point is clear: for men, ageing is a slow process; for women, it is a sudden puncture.

That this puncture is as much psychological as physiological is only seemingly a paradox. The menopausal woman anticipates, and thus integrates, society's view of her, experiencing in

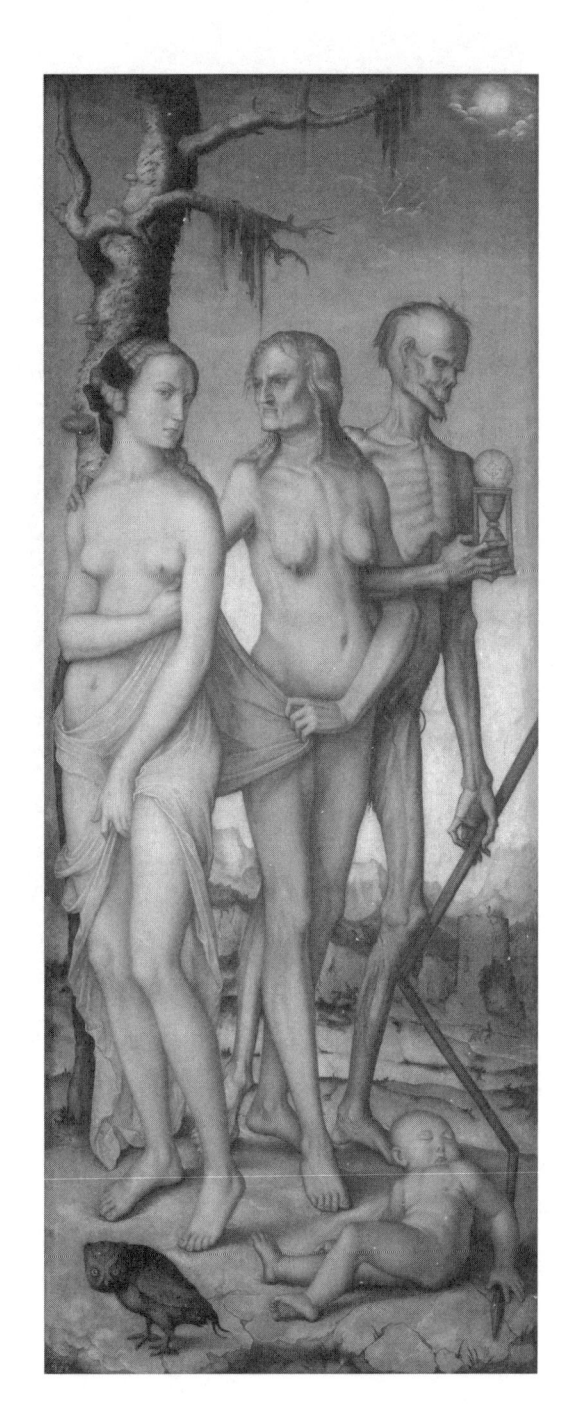

The missing link:
Hans Baldung,
The Ages of Woman and Death, 1541–4,
oil on panel.

'This old woman reflected in the mirror': Simone de Beauvoir, 1965.

particular a 'feeling of depersonalization': 'this cannot be *I*, this old woman reflected in the mirror!'[15] While it is not obvious why this reaction should manifest itself only in women – men, too, can surely experience the cognitive jet lag of feeling outstripped by their appearance – the difference lies, perhaps, in the way age creeps up on us. For men, the sense of reaching middle age comes largely from within, from their own impression of having reached a certain stage in life; for women, it comes – at least partially – from without, from what others tell them and make them feel (isn't it time you settled down, dressed your age, had children?). Middle age, for woman, functions in this regard as the image of an image, her own *re*-construction of how others have *pre*-constructed the idea for her. To live midlife on her own terms, she must turn her back on the mirror of society – just as Beauvoir does in the photograph reproduced here.

How, then, does the mirror image of woman change as she reaches middle age? If her mental value arguably obtains more than ever, her *instrumental* value diminishes, since reproduction is no longer her (at least potential) purpose. 'I stand in front of the mirror,' the *femme rompue* or 'woman destroyed' tells herself: 'How ugly I am! How unlovely my body is!'[16] Men can, of course, tell themselves similar things – Beauvoir's friend the anthropologist Michel Leiris opens his midlife memoir *Manhood* (1939) with a long litany of his physical failings at 'the age of thirty-four, life's midpoint' – but it does not affect their (perception of) social identity in the same way.[17] Perhaps this is why, for women reaching middle age, production sometimes comes to take the place of reproduction: 'It is often at the menopause that woman decides to take brush or pen in hand to compensate for the defects in her existence.'[18]

If Beauvoir is dismissive of such midlife attempts at creativity – remarking waspishly that they will never be more than 'amateurish' – it is not difficult to understand why. Her own perspective on creative middle age was hard-won, forged in the furnace of decades of casual misogyny and institutional sexism. The epilogue to *Force of Circumstance* exemplifies the issue; couched as a response to all those malicious (male) critics who claimed that it was actually Sartre who wrote her books, it rapidly becomes a meditation on the 'pox of time'. For a female writer, as Beauvoir sees it, the most uncomfortable part of this pox is middle age:

> In France, if you are a writer, to be a woman is simply to provide a stick to be beaten with. Especially at the age I was when my first books were published. If you are a very young woman they indulge you, with an amused wink. If you are old, they bow respectfully. But lose the first bloom of youth and dare to speak before acquiring the respectable patina of age: the whole pack is at your heels![19]

With neither the glamour of youth nor the grace of old age, the midlife woman has no defence against the unkindness of strangers. Condescension and resentment, envy and antagonism: such, according to Beauvoir, is the lot of the middle-aged *female* writer. What, though, of the middle-aged female *writer*?

The shift in emphasis offers a way through the impasse. For if living happens in the future and the past – 'I have lived stretched out towards the future,' Beauvoir notes near the end of *Force of Circumstance*, 'and now I am recapitulating, looking back over the past. It's as though the present somehow got left out'[20] – writing recuperates this absent present, concentrating our attention precisely on what we are in the middle of thinking and typing. Writing, as an act of creation, ensures our continuing becoming, asserting vivid existence over moribund essence. Such was also the message of Colette, one of Beauvoir's major predecessors as a strong female voice, who wrote her midlife novel *Break of Day* (1928) after divorcing and falling in love again in her mid-fifties. The salient point for both women is that the writer 'has the good fortune to be able to escape his own petrifaction'.[21]

Such good fortune comes, however, at the cost of gender-specific experience (as the male pronoun in the English translation suggests). In order to transcend what Beauvoir calls the 'immanence' of the female condition, she asserts the universal expenditure of time. She masters midlife not only by becoming ageless – such is the implication of understanding writing as a perpetual present – but by becoming sexless, asserting herself not as a woman but as an author. The notion of the menopausal 'third sex' is reclaimed as an epistemological advantage; neither man nor woman, she is now simply creator. Liberated from the sexual objectification of her youth, middle-aged woman is free to become middle-aged human.

Menopause, as Beauvoir views it, thus asserts something of a paradox: by reducing woman to her body, it liberates her from it. The problem with this solution is that it minimizes the specifically female experience of middle age, suggesting that the disembodied 'writer' can function, in effect, as a neutral, un-gendered category. Perhaps this perspective is in itself not undesirable, but it exerts a strikingly unequal pressure on the two sexes. Unlike women, middle-aged men do not forgo their specifically male experience of middle age – which means that they remain, in practice, the 'first' sex. Neutrality is in the eye of the beholder.

If there is tension in Beauvoir's approach to middle age, then, it is the tension that underlies all of her work, namely the relationship between the individual and the universal. As a writer, she insisted on a deeply personal perspective; as a woman, she sought to generalize this perspective into that of the female condition. As an existentialist, Beauvoir insisted on the primacy of personal experience; as a philosopher, she sought to understand this experience as typical of the human condition. Her whole life project was contingent on understanding herself as a sovereign individual – and yet age forced her, like the rest of us, to recognize the limits of her sovereignty. Writing about women at the pivotal midlife moment took her out of her self-obsession – 'it is both strange and stimulating to discover suddenly, after forty, an aspect of the world that has been staring you in the face all the time which somehow you have never noticed' – but it also forced her to confront her ageing self *as* a woman.[22] Above all, getting older obliged her to abrogate the one thing she had spent her life cultivating: control.

By the time she was in her fifties, Beauvoir had begun to fear, as no doubt we all do, being 'buried by those coming after'.[23] The death of friends and contemporaries – Albert Camus in 1960, Maurice Merleau-Ponty in 1961 – made her feel increasingly exposed: 'This life I'm living isn't mine any more, I thought ... I had no control over it at all. I was merely an impotent onlooker watching the play of alien forces: history, time, and death.'[24] To an existentialist, this sense of passivity is extremely hard to accept, since it is the very essence of existentialism to insist on individual agency: we are what we make of ourselves. The problem, of course, is that by the second half of our lives we are starting to be *un*made by all those external forces that we had previously sought to shape. The sovereign becomes the alien.

The particularity of the midlife perspective in this regard – unlike that of old age, as analysed by Beauvoir in her later study of that name – is that it allows, indeed encourages, hesitation. We are still in control – more so, arguably, than ever before – but we feel this control beginning to slip away from us. We still have a future, but we are starting to feel its finitude. Beauvoir's hesitation in this regard is crystallized in one extraordinary passage in her autobiography, in which she admits that she has always had the secret fantasy that her life was being recorded on a giant tape recorder, and that one day she would play back the whole of her past. This is not so much Beckett's 'last tape' as Beauvoir's midlife tape: 'I don't quite know whether I am a child playing at being a grown-up or an ageing woman remembering her childhood.'[25] The element of fantasy – the imagined tape recorder, the idea of 'playing at' being middle-aged – suggests the extent to which midlife is a conceptual construct, a continuum (or 'spool', to use the Beckettian term) along which one may choose to position oneself at differing places at differing times. The conceit of the tape recorder, more specifically, offers a simulacrum of control that mirrors that of autobiography; at the age of 'almost fifty', Beauvoir wants both to ask the questions and to give the answers. If she can no longer write the future, she can at least write the past.

Midlife, then, is what we make of it: such might be the existentialist view of middle age. But midlife is also what we take of it: such might be the feminist view of middle age. It is not for others – men – to decide how one should feel about getting older; if woman has ever been determined 'by the manner in which her body and her relation to the world are modified through the action of others than herself', then Beauvoir suggests an alternative model of female agency, one that insists on experiencing ageing as a subject, rather than as an object.[26] Her own development into a supremely productive female writer represents a prime example of how to make midlife – and reflections *on* midlife – a microcosm of life more generally. For Simone de Beauvoir, as for women throughout history, the crucial thing is to be able to age on her own terms. The 'third sex' in the second age offers first principles.

II

What does it mean to be happy in the middle of life? How do we even measure this? It is not just that our goals and sense of self change as we get older; our very way of assessing our well-being changes, as achievements that would once have satisfied us no longer seem sufficient. The graph of life may be U-shaped, but it is far from clear how we calibrate that graph in the first place. Happiness has so many variables – health, family, friends, a sense of purpose – that a quantitative, one-size-fits-all approach can take us only so far. We need models for how it feels from the inside.

It is precisely in this regard that literature plays such an important role. The paradox of art is that fictional, invented characters can represent us more fully than factual, flesh-and-blood people. The flesh and the blood can feel more real on paper than in person, since we also have access to the brain. However much of a falsification it necessarily is, fiction helps us to peer behind the curtain of consciousness, providing an unparalleled experience of virtual reality. This means that it can also, by extension, provide an experience of virtual maturity.

Few works provide this perspective as fully as Beauvoir's major novel, *The Mandarins*. Written in her early forties and published to great critical acclaim in 1954 (it won that year's Goncourt Prize), it follows the life and loves of a group of Paris intellectuals as they negotiate the changing politics – ideological and sexual – of the post-war era. The novel's status as a *roman-à-clef* – disputed by the author, as is so often the case, but self-evident nonetheless – was not the least factor in its commercial success. The elder intellectual Robert Dubreuilh is an obvious double for Sartre; his wife, Anne, presented in the novel as a psychotherapist, functions as the Beauvoir figure. With his pugnacious temperament and position as editor of the journal *L'Espoir* (modelled on *Combat*), the slightly younger Henri Perron inevitably evokes Camus. Together they argue over art and politics, travel, fall in and out of love, and sleep with each other's friends and children – indulging in all the Paris privileges, in short, of middle-class middle age.

Whether you find *The Mandarins* appealing as a model of the good midlife will depend on your taste and temperament, but what is indisputable is how much more fully embodied it is than Beauvoir's own recollections. Art, in this sense, trumps autobiography; imagined middle age is more vivid than recalled middle age. It is not at all obvious that this should be the case, so it is worth wondering why it is. This whole book that you are holding in your hands is predicated on the conjunction of life and literature; reaching middle age, writers start to reflect on middle age and to make it the basis for the continuing evolution of their art. Even allowing for this concatenation of perspectives, however, what fiction (or drama or poetry) can offer that personal recollection cannot is access to alternative epistemologies: we can write our way into another way of seeing the world. That we can also read our way into alternative perspectives is, of course, the premise of the present book. But it is contingent on the original impetus of the imagination.

In the case of *The Mandarins*, this impetus is divided into two competing voices, since the novel alternates between chapters narrated from the points of view of Henri and of Anne. If this suggests a split consciousness, a constant oscillation between male and female perspectives – between what one might call, in Jungian terms, the *anima* and the *animus* of middle age – it is one that is weighted towards Beauvoir's own, female experience, since it is only Anne who is allowed to narrate in the first person. Henri, for his part, remains locked in the classical *style indirect libre* of nineteenth-century realism. In narrative terms, it is as though Beauvoir were privileging the recuperation of feminine authority, reserving for herself – or, at least, for her female avatar – the scrupulous subjectivity of the writer. All perspectives on middle age are equal, but some are more equal than others.

This relativity theory of experience emerges, in fact, as the underlying concern of the novel. At the end, Anne implicitly concedes that we cannot escape our own consciousness – 'For twenty years, I believed we were living together; but no, each of us is alone, imprisoned in his body' – and in terms that make the attainment of middle age (via, once again, the regulation twenty years of maturity) the prerequisite for this realization.[27] What Beauvoir's double-narrative perspective makes possible is the exploration of just how gendered this middle age necessarily is. If the narration is contrapuntal, contrasting male objectivity with female subjectivity, then so is the understanding of midlife maturity that emerges.

Competing statements from Chapters Two and Three exemplify the differences. Writing from her first-person perspective, Anne experiences the arrival of middle age with sudden urgency:

All at once I understood why my past sometimes seemed to me to be someone else's. Because now I am someone else [*une autre*], a woman of thirty-nine, a woman who's aware of her age!

'Thirty-nine years!' I said aloud. Before the war I was too young for the years to have weighed upon me. And then for five years, I forgot myself completely. And now I've found myself again, only to learn that I'm condemned. Old age is awaiting me; there's no escaping it. Even now I see the beginnings in the depths of the mirror . . . 'It's even too late for regrets. There's nothing left to do but to keep going [*il n'y a qu'à continuer*].'[28]

Anne's epiphany, perhaps unsurprisingly, closely echoes Beauvoir's own recollections, right down to the regulation reduction of all anxiety to the magic number, 39. It is emphatically not a merely physiological experience linked to the menopause – indeed, it pre-dates the menopause – but rather a psychological experience linked to changing perception of time. The caesura of the war divides her life neatly – perhaps too neatly – into periods of youth and maturity; if the war functioned as a temporal black hole, foreclosing any question of narcissistic anxiety, in the post-war period there is now nothing to stop Anne from seeing her ageing self ahead of her. In strikingly Beckettian terms, all she can do is keep going: *il n'y a qu'à continuer*.

Notice, however, what happens when we compare this with Henri's evocation of the same subject:

But now, he had to admit to himself that he was a mature man [*un homme fait*]: young people treated him as an elder, adults as one of them, and some even treated him with respect. Mature, bounded, finite, himself and no one else [*pas un autre*], nothing but himself. But who was he?[29]

From the Prime of Life to Old Age

The difference jumps out immediately: where Anne is now 'an other', Henri is emphatically *not* an other. Where Anne has become someone else, Henri has become himself, 'nothing but himself'. Anne's view of middle age is presented from the inside out, defined by her own vision of herself, whereas Henri's is presented from the outside in, defined by how others see him. The female and male perspectives on middle age are thus, in effect, mirror images of each other; in both cases, its arrival is experienced as restrictive, but for diametrically opposed reasons.

It is hard, to be sure, to disentangle the comment from the claim. Does Beauvoir think middle-aged men and women see themselves in this way, or rather that men and women see each other in this way? She is not Tiresias, so she cannot ultimately know, in any subjective sense, how men experience middle age. What she can know, however, is how (male) society views our differences in status as we age: men become more experienced, while women become less alluring. As they grow older, that is to say, men become more themselves, while women become less so. The lessness, *pace* Beckett, is all on the distaff side.

Beauvoir and Beckett may be unlikely bedfellows – especially given the latter's attested animosity towards the former, following her decision to edit his work without consulting him – but Anne can at times be startlingly reminiscent of the Irishman in her views on ageing:[30]

> I hasten to tell myself, 'I'm finished, I'm old.' In that way, I cancel out those thirty or forty years when I will live, old and finished, grieving over a lost past; I'll be deprived of nothing since I've already renounced everything... By rejecting the compromises of old age, I deny its very existence.[31]

If Anne's position here echoes Beckett's evocation, in the letter to Duthuit of August 1948, of his desire to reach old age earlier, 'while there are still refusals we can make', in doing so it collapses the differences between the sexes, producing an ungendered, 'third sex' response to being in the middle of life's way. To view middle age as proleptic old age is to attempt to forestall it, to take the wind from its sagging sails. Both sexes can, and demonstrably do, engage in such tactics, but the difference lies in Anne's sense of holding her position *as* a tactic: 'Under my wilting skin, I affirm the survival of a young woman with her demands still intact, a rebel against all concessions, and disdainful of those sad forty-year-old hags.' Beauvoir is astute enough, then, to see that maturity is only skin-deep.[32]

Beauvoir's and Beckett's shared attempt to renounce middle age in favour of old age suggests the common cause between the genders when faced with the exigencies of time. We may be different, but we are all getting older: such might be the message of *The Mandarins*. The beauty of Beauvoir's double perspective is that it allows us to experience midlife from the point of view of both genders. The virtual-reality machine of fiction enables us, for the duration of the novel, to become a middle-aged Tiresias. We do not need to be male to identify with Henri's shifting sense of how adults now treat him as an equal, or the young as an elder; we do not need to be female to identify with Anne's sense of becoming another person. We have all had, or will have had, such unsettling experiences.

How do we come to terms with them? For Beauvoir, Sartre and all the other existentialists, a happy midlife is a *committed* midlife, committed to major external causes such as art and politics. To live in this selfless, disinterested manner – in the manner, in short, of a 'mandarin' – is to relegate one's own sense of ageing to the most minor of personal concerns. Progressive politics, innovative aesthetics: for left-wing intellectuals, these are the things that make life worth living. What *The Mandarins* also shows, however, is that our relationship to them changes as we grow older. When they start learning about the gulags in the

Soviet Union, for instance, the younger Henri wants to speak out – although he hesitates, something he feels he would never have done at twenty – while the older Robert decides against it on the grounds that it would damage the left-wing cause. 'In effect, we had to decide what can and what should be the role of an intellectual today,' he concludes.[33] Is it to document things or to change them?

Our answer to this question surely evolves as we age. The old adage that we are progressive and 'emotional' when young and regressive and 'rational' when old tells only half the story; it is perfectly possible to invert the evolution, such that youthful conservatism becomes ageing radicalism. The point is rather that maturity imposes, indeed arguably *implies*, the acknowledgement that one's own position can only ever be partial. To reach middle age is to step back from oneself – as both Anne and Henri do, as Beauvoir demonstrably does – and see that one's passions and prejudices are merely part of a broader continuum. Literature, with its numerous narrative perspectives and complex consciousness, with its access to voices both male and female, young and old, has always known this. That is why it can help us not only to attain maturity, but to understand what maturity is in the first place. Art and ageing offer different routes, in short, to the same realization: that no one has a monopoly on wisdom.

Beauvoir not only writes *about* the middle of life's way, then; she writes her way *through* it. By coming at middle age from several perspectives – personal (*Force of Circumstance*), biological (*The Second Sex*), political and philosophical (*The Mandarins*) – she seeks meaning in its various imperatives. Chief among those is the drive to be happy. The happiness of middle age is an under-discussed subject, no doubt since it smacks of smugness and complacency. Are we simply 'settling'? How do we know when enough is enough? The secret, perhaps, is to keep wanting more from life as we grow older, but from a position of satisfaction, rather than dissatisfaction, with what we already have. Becoming and being, we learn as we age, need not necessarily be opposites.

The existentialism that emerged out of the war clarified this notion of *becoming* what one *is*, principally owing to its sense of responsibility towards its historical position, which is to say to the privilege of survival. Pronounced in the French manner *survivre*, to sur-vive is to 'live beyond' – beyond the war, of course, but also beyond youth. For how do we survive ourselves? By the time we reach middle age, we are refugees from our earlier existence, endlessly reiterating the same appetites and urges. 'To survive is, after all, perpetually to begin to live again.'[34] *The Mandarins* culminates with Anne pondering, in true existentialist fashion, whether she should simply kill herself; if she decides against it in the end, it is because she is 'condemned to death; but also condemned to live'.[35] In such equivocal existentialism lies a lesson for us all. Between her *Prime of Life* and her *Old Age*, between her feminism and her activism, Simone de Beauvoir teaches us that to understand middle age is to understand how to survive ourselves.

11
Streams of Consciousness
Middle Age in a New Millennium

I

On 29 July 1966 *Time* magazine announced that it had uncovered 'a conspiracy of silence'. This conspiracy, it contended, controls every aspect of our lives, from our tastes and our politics to our health and careers. The ultimate monopoly, it 'dares not, or prefers not, speak its name'; with unimaginable power and influence, it insinuates itself into our very thoughts. Utterly at its mercy, we can achieve almost nothing without its approval. The name of this conspiracy? Middle age.[1]

For all the general view of the 1960s as a time of youthful excess, for all the twentieth century's shift towards an obsession with staying 'young', the *Time* cover story put its finger on an inconvenient truth of modernity. The 'Command Generation', then as now, continues to command. And it continues, of course, to be gendered: men are judged on their skill, women on their looks. The emblematic figure of the 'pleasures and perils of middle age' in the 1960s may have been JFK, but the story was nonetheless announced by an arresting cover image of Lauren Bacall, a grey-but-glamorous vision of maturity as 'authentic as well as beguilingly lovely'. Audiences, we are told, did not think of Bacall 'as a woman of 41' – as though that would be an insult – owing to her 'poise, inner amusement, and enriched femininity'. In the era of the midlife crisis (codified by Elliott Jaques just a year earlier, in 1965), middle age had never looked so good.

Does it still look good? In an age in which the command generation has so singularly failed, in an era in which middle-aged privilege has so strikingly abrogated not just its political but its planetary responsibilities, it is becoming ever harder to make the argument. Immaturity is the new maturity; the only way to save the world, as teenagers such as Greta Thunberg have shown us, is to do things differently. More of the same – of the same middle-class, middle-aged, middle-of-the-road consensus of the last fifty years – simply will not cut it. For things to stay the same, they will have to change.

Perhaps, though, this might also be true of middle age itself. What if it were reconceived not as a synonym of crisis and complacency, but in the manner of the writers discussed in this book as a spur to new forms of creativity? What if it were reclaimed not as a time of loss and decline, but as a period of rediscovered zeal? We have explored the past of middle age, outlining some of the ways in which it has been imagined over the centuries; but what of its present and its future? Seven centuries after Dante, we should now consider what it means to be in the middle of life's way in a new millennium.

In one sense, of course, the future of middle age is simply old age. But it is a future that will be determined, paradoxically, by those who are young today – which means that, when viewed from another perspective, the future of middle age is the present of youth. The question, as it has always been, is how much today's youth will have changed by the time it becomes tomorrow's middle age. The midlife mind is not the teenage mind; so much the better, no doubt. But there are losses as well as gains in the transition from adolescence to maturity. Chief among these, one might assume, is energy.

That this is not actually the case is one of the many counter-intuitive discoveries of recent research. We live in a golden era of neuroscience, allowing us to study what happens to the brain when it is submitted to any number of more or less plausible

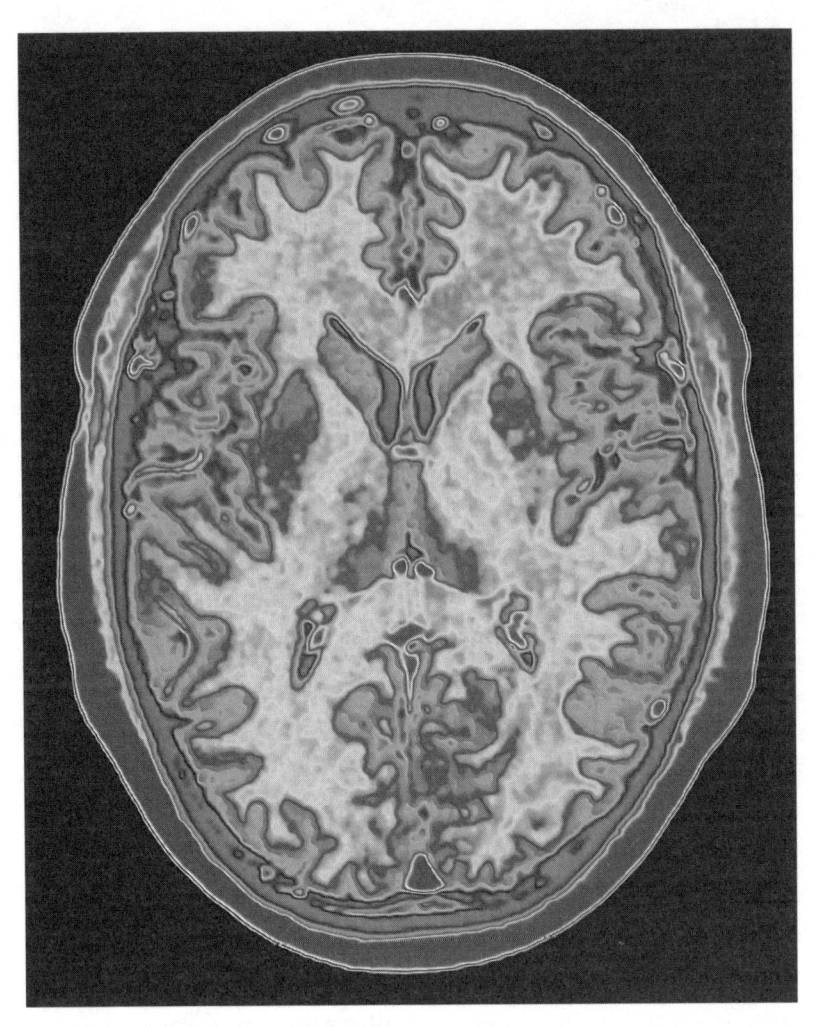

MRI scan showing the midlife brain.

stimuli. Understandably, the focus of this new science in its early days tended to be on what happened to the brain when it was either developing (in early life) or decaying (in late life), since change generally tells us more than stasis. Yet what has since become clear is that this change also occurs in *mid*life. Research conducted at the Harvard Medical School has shown that the brain undergoes a second growth spurt in middle age – the first, of course, having come during adolescence.[2] While the brain overall begins to shrink after the age of forty – by about 2 per cent every decade – certain parts of it can start performing better, especially those areas linked to judgement and control. 'Neuroplasticity', the idea that the brain continues to change and develop depending on its exposure to external stimuli, has become the new watchword – but, of course, it is a plasticity that cuts both ways. The prefrontal cortex, for instance, exemplifies the paradox: it reaches full maturity only in a person's thirties, but it is also – for this reason? – particularly vulnerable to middle-aged decay.[3] The neurology thus supports the mythology; the mistake of the *Time* cover image was to stop at Bacall's shiny surface, rather than burrowing into her ageing brain. Maturity is *not* only skin-deep.

The midlife mind is no longer a mere metaphor, then; it is a perceived reality.[4] But of what? Neuroscience, to be sure, can tell us what happens to our brains as we age; and this, in turn, may alter our self-image, producing a cognitive feedback loop through which we become what we perceive ourselves to be. What it cannot do, however, is tell us how it *feels* to be inside the brain. For that, we are still reliant on the traditional methods of description and diagnosis, of emotions and images. We are still reliant, in short, on words.

The brain scan may function as a subjective correlative (to adapt T. S. Eliot's terms), showing us inside our subjectivity from the outside, but it cannot capture the emotions as they are felt. Consciousness, to put it another way, is one thing; stream of consciousness, quite another. Observe what happens when we lay alongside the brain scan a passage chosen, almost at random, from perhaps the most representative of all 'stream-of-consciousness' writers, Virginia Woolf. Here is a paragraph taken from Bernard's peroration at the end of *The Waves* (1931):

> Nevertheless, life is pleasant, life is tolerable. Tuesday follows Monday; then comes Wednesday. The mind grows rings; the identity becomes robust; pain is absorbed in growth. Opening

and shutting, shutting and opening, with increasing hum and sturdiness, the haste and fever of youth are drawn into service until the whole being seems to expand in and out like the mainspring of a clock.[5]

The syntax here is almost sentient, so closely does it track the thought processes of middle age. It begins with the tone of faint praise so characteristic of midlife monotony; in another great midlife text of this time, Hesse will write in *Steppenwolf* (1927) of 'the moderately pleasant, the wholly bearable and tolerable, lukewarm days of a discontented middle-aged man'.[6] Life is 'pleasant', certainly, but the seductive odour of everything it is not – ecstatic, inventive, *new* – lurks at its barely suppressed edges. The seemingly never-ending cycle of the days and weeks announces itself not only in Woolf's present participles, 'opening and shutting' incessantly, but in the punctuation, and in particular in the recurring use of the semicolon. The semicolon is Woolf's secret weapon, her 'trademark';[7] cleaving phrases in both senses of that ambivalent verb, it serves both to separate and to combine, to pause and to progress. As such, it functions as the very motor of her stream of consciousness, enacting the hesitant but unrelenting rhythm of her mature thought. What the semicolon helps to render – and what Woolf's syntax captures more generally, as the 'haste and fever of youth' become part of the 'whole being' – is the interior monologue of midlife.

If the syntax is suggestive, so are the similes. Three comparisons are introduced, either explicitly or implicitly: the mind 'grows rings' like a tree, 'opening and shutting' like a camera as it 'expand[s] in and out' like a clock. By conflating organic and inorganic imagery, the terms Woolf chose literalize the metaphor of a 'body clock', functioning as something like a cognitive MRI scan of the midlife brain. Its age (those arboreal 'rings') is built into its 'identity', and the whole passage not only describes, but enacts the waves announced in the title. The 'brainwaves' perceived from the outside by the scan are now conceived from the inside of the skull. We use the term colloquially to indicate a great new idea understood as a state of exception, but Woolf helps us to see that it is more properly applied to the great grey mass of repetitive, everyday thoughts, the brainwaves of banality. What she helps us to understand, in short, is the monotonous sublime of middle age.

We could read this passage, then – and there are many others like it – as a commentary on the midlife brain scan shown here. But actually it is much closer to a *phenomenology* of the midlife mind, showing us how it feels from the inside out rather than how it looks from the outside in. Woolf gives us a – broadly positive – description of maturity, in which dither and drift, process and pain are all absorbed into a robust, sturdy identity. Importantly, this identity is – or at least, it *seems* – endlessly repeatable, like a well-oiled machine, pistons pumping in and out as the days and weeks pass by. While the passage thus symbolizes time, it also softens it, smoothing out mortality into mundanity. Literature can function, as we have known at least since Aristotle, as a shock absorber.

Accepting repetition and integrating it into the fabric of our lives in this manner is arguably one of the key components of a successful middle age. Life may not be a dress rehearsal, but we do spend much of our time rehearsing the same arguments and emotions, the same riddles and relationships. The stream of consciousness is circular, not linear; it is only in middle age, as the curve of our lives flattens out into a plateau, that this becomes irrefutably clear. Woolf's writing forces this realization upon us; the titular image of the waves suggests the rhythm of repetition, 'the little fierce beat – tick-tack, tick-tack – of the pulse of one's mind'.[8] But it also suggests the extent to which we abrogate agency – or perhaps one should say, the *impression* of agency – as we age. 'How fast the stream flows from January to December!' continues the passage cited above. 'We are swept on by the torrent of things grown so familiar that they cast no shadow. We float, we float.'[9]

Woolf's somewhat mixed metaphor – time is like water on to which light is projected – betrays the unease beneath the surface of her stream of consciousness. 'Life is pleasant; life is good,' Bernard keeps asserting, not entirely convincingly. Overfamiliar things may cast no shadow, but mortality certainly does: 'I now made the contribution of maturity to childhood's intuitions – satiety and doom; the sense of what is inescapable in our lot; the knowledge of limitations; how life is more obdurate than one had thought it.'[10] Beyond the fairly standard intimations of maturity reminiscent of so many we have encountered over the course of this book, it is the malleability of the mind, its infinite adjustability as it ages, that strikes a genuinely new note here. For Woolf does not just explore the midlife mind; she also explores the *delusions* of the midlife mind, depicting how we trick ourselves into thinking that now, finally, we see the true nature of things. Bernard tells himself at one point that 'I was like one admitted behind the scenes: like one shown how the effects are produced,' as though he were suddenly divested of all illusion.[11] But then he concedes that this, too, is an illusion:

> Time has given the arrangement another shake. Out we creep from the arch of the currant leaves, out into a wider world. The true order of things – this is our perpetual illusion – is now apparent. Thus in a moment, in a drawing room, our life adjusts itself to the majestic march of day across the sky.[12]

The passage reads almost as a commentary on some of the more dramatic midlife epiphanies documented in this book. Beckett's moment in his mother's bedroom, for instance: was this the true fallacy? Was he merely kidding himself when he felt he had suddenly grasped the true order of his writing? Is maturity, in short, an optical illusion?

The only way to rebut this reproach is to acknowledge that we are not, ourselves, the final arbiters of our own maturity. The mind may grow rings, but identity is precisely *not* robust; it is forever contingent on the changing perspective it inhabits. Such, ultimately, is Woolf's epistemology, spread across the six characters of *The Waves*. 'It is not one life that I look back upon,' concludes Bernard. 'I am not one person, I am many people.'[13] That Woolf links this profusion of perspectives to her advancing age suggests the extent to which the midlife mind should not be understood as singular, but as multiple: 'I'm getting old myself – I shall be fifty next year,' she told one correspondent shortly after publication of the novel, 'and I come to feel more and more how difficult it is to collect oneself into one Virginia.'[14] At the age of 49, at the very peak of her Aristotelian *akmē*, Woolf comes to the realization that middle age is not so much a stream as *streams* of consciousness.

We can thus learn as much about the midlife mind, if not more, by considering it from the inside out as we can by examining it from the outside in. Such might be the lesson of literature. But Woolf's competing perspectives – the six narrative voices of *The Waves* – also suggest something more, namely the necessary multiplicity of maturity. Not only must we all feel our own way through midlife, but we must feel *more than one* way through midlife: this, in essence, is the true marker of middle age. Getting older is not an exam question. None of us has the answers to ageing. There is no single path through the middle of life's way; the best we can do is triangulate a range of coordinates and try to navigate accordingly. The epiphany, if there is one, is an antiepiphany: that there is – that there can be – no triumphant midlife moment in which we finally feel *aha*, we have it all figured out. In *Middlemarch* Casaubon, we must remember, fails; there is no key to all middle ages. Literature, understood as a way of making sense of time, is ultimately predicated on its *in*ability to make sense of time: 'life is not susceptible ... to the treatment we give it when we try to tell it.'[15] Maturity begins the moment we accept this.

II

What happens when we do accept it? The ultimate incommensurability of life and literature – one is linear, the other circular – is the reason why art even exists; mortality, in this sense, is what makes us. But it is also, of course, what makes us middle-aged, the very concept of which is predicated on our growing sense of an ending. We use literature, as the critic Frank Kermode famously showed, as a way of taming time, of breaking it down into finite, end-stopped narratives.[16] The tick of a beginning anticipates the tock of an ending, and this our brains can cope with. Much harder for us to process, however, is the sense of a middle, defined as it is by barely perceptible movement. How do we hear the moment *between* the tick and the tock?

Maturity, if it is about anything, is about listening to this silence. The melodrama of youth has abated; the pathos of old age is still distant. To all intents and purposes, we are installed in a perpetual present, a seemingly endless succession of days and weeks. Middle age, in this regard, has a curious relationship to time: on the one hand, it is defined as the period in which mortality really hits us; on the other, it is the period in which time seems to stand still. 'If by eternity is understood not endless temporal duration but timelessness,' notes Wittgenstein in his *Tractatus*, 'then he lives eternally who lives in the present.'[17] Adapting his subsequent sentence just slightly, we could say that our midlife has no end in the way in which our visual field has no limits; equidistant between birth and death, we are as timeless as we will ever be.

The lesson here, then, is that to be mature – to be middle-aged in the best sense of the term – is to pursue existential self-sufficiency. Eternal midlife belongs to those who live in the

Shades of grey: Susan Sontag in the 1980s.

present; dwelling nostalgically in the past, or indeed anticipating proleptically the future, makes the middle a mere shadow-beginning or shadow-end, rather than a fully realized period on its own terms. The cumulative model of existence built into the human brain – that we are the sum total of all our experiences and memories – distracts us from the fact that we can also choose to live as conscious animals, constantly in the middle of our lives. Not for nothing is this the advice of so many religions and philosophies: live in the present tense.

To live in this manner in an incessant stream of consciousness is, of course, untenable on an everyday basis, but it can provide an aspirational model for the midlife mind. Rather than viewing writing as accumulative, we might view it as a way of getting *rid* of thoughts and ideas; rather than counting up our achievements, we might cultivate a zero degree of creativity, looking to expunge our ageing selves rather than to exhibit them. Talking at the age of 45, Susan Sontag – the very emblem of midlife *Geist* in the 1970s and '80s, with her iconic skunk streak of grey offset by her enduringly glamorous image – expresses precisely this desire: 'I write partly in order to change myself so that once I write about something I don't have to think about it anymore. And when I write, it actually *is* to get rid of those ideas.'[18] The ancient Aristotelian idea of catharsis thus receives a new twist: it is now the author, and not the spectator, who expunges her emotions. Middle age becomes a perpetual purgation.

Purge, purgation, purgatory: we have been here before, with Dante. What his example – and that of all those writers who follow in his wake – ultimately illustrates is that the discourse of middle age creates its own pressures. As we reach what we think of as middle age – for which turning forty is as good a symbolic threshold as any – we become conscious not just that we have (at least notionally) reached the middle of life, but that we are now 'middle-aged'. Centuries of culturally conditioned clichés come crashing down on us, and all of a sudden we find ourselves in a dark forest of 'crises' and 'conversions'. How we respond depends on our own preferences and disposition – not everyone, mercifully, feels the need to write a book about it – but there is no doubt that the idiom of midlife predetermines the experience. 'Middle age' produces, and thus polices, the metaphors we age by.

The role of writers, of course, is to resist such tired metaphors, or at least to revivify them. But there is a limit to how many different images we can find for ageing, since there is a limit to how many different ways we can conceptualize time. The sun sits in judgement, having no alternative, on the nothing new; as I watch it rise and set over my house, as I watch the seasons come and go in my garden, I am doing what humans have always done, ascribing meaning to indifference, setting my body clock to nature. But I am also, more pointedly, setting it to culture, to all the ways in which artists and writers – Shakespeare's sun imagery, T. S. Eliot's rose garden – have struggled with time. For the set of images that recur as metaphors for middle age is in fact surprisingly small; even in the twenty-first century – perhaps *especially* in the twenty-first century – we seem to turn, time and again, to predetermined models of maturity. Zadie Smith, writing in 2016, provides an interesting case in point:

> My novels were once sunnier places and now the clouds have rolled in. Part of this I chalk up simply to the experience of middle age: I wrote *White Teeth* as a child, and have grown up alongside it. The art of midlife is surely always cloudier than the art of youth, as life itself gets cloudier. But it would be disingenuous to pretend it is only that. I am a citizen as well as an individual soul and one of the things citizenship teaches us, over the long stretch, is that there is no perfectibility in human affairs. This fact, still obscure to the twenty-one-year-old, is a little clearer to the woman of forty-one.[19]

Having established herself so spectacularly in her early twenties with the publication of *White Teeth* (2000), Smith was forced to do much of her growing up in public (as she almost, but tactfully not quite, says). Nearly twenty years later, she now looks back on her youth as a time of untroubled sunshine, in contrast to the cloud control of her middle years. If the metaphor itself is somewhat cloudy (does 'cloudier' mean darker, or murkier, or more variegated?), it tells us much about the manner in which we conceptualize middle age – or indeed romanticize youth – through recourse to a predetermined set of images, without fully enquiring what we mean by these images. Beyond this, what is particularly striking is the way that Smith goes on to juxtapose her own perspective on ageing with that of her species in general, conflating the micro-history of human time with the macro-history of historical time. What maturity has taught her – and by extension what it might teach us all – is to step back from her own point of view and see the *longue durée*.

Smith's observations implicitly reinforce the incommensurability of life and literature. 'Citizen' and 'the individual soul' may sound like a millennial remake of Eliot's 'tradition' and 'the individual talent', but they represent the two poles of public and private experience. Middle age, we notice, has subtly different effects on them: where it *obscures* insight for the latter, it *clarifies* it for the former; where midlife becomes 'cloudier' for the individual soul, it becomes 'clearer' for the citizen. Our aesthetic imagination, so the implication goes, develops in ever more mysterious ways as we age, whereas our political understanding evolves towards a greater appreciation of why definitive, clear-cut solutions are ultimately impossible. 'Imperfectibility' – its acknowledgement, its integration – becomes a synonym for maturity.

Such an acknowledgement is, of course, easier read than done. To accept the grindingly slow, one-step-forwards-two-steps-back nature of what Smith terms 'incremental progress' is to accept that our youthful dreams of changing the world will, almost certainly, never become reality.[20] The incremental inch is all we have. Writers who reflect on the power of the imagination can help us to see this, since our experience of middle age is itself largely a function of the imagination. The secret to a successful midlife is to embrace the increments, to relish, rather than to resent, the many minor steps that define us. Examining our consciousness, and the ways that literature streams it, is one way of hearing the silence between the tick and the tock.

III

If neuroscience provides perhaps the boldest new model of the midlife mind, then, it is one that requires supplementing by descriptive commentary. But what of the midlife *body*? Neurology still implies psychology; but it also, quite obviously, implies biology. Any appeal to science as a way of conceptualizing middle age must triangulate information from these three fields. It must also, however, insist on the extent to which our *understanding* of science is predetermined by the culture we inhabit. For such, we have seen, is the logic of the discourse: middle age is a biological fact; 'middle age' is a cultural construct. The midlife mind may be *under* the microscope, but it is also the thing looking *through* the microscope, with all its assorted prejudices. We should not kid ourselves that just because we can now look into the mind, we can also step out of it. We remain, as before, 'middle-aged', clinging to our quotation marks.

The single most important aspect of these quotation marks to have been reassessed in recent decades is surely their gendered nature. The post-war emergence of feminism as a serious cultural force had the effect of re-orientating our understanding of ageing as a specifically gendered phenomenon – not just in the sense that the two sexes experience it differently, but (and perhaps above all) in the sense that society constructs it differently. Readers will have noticed that this book has become increasingly female as it has progressed: George Eliot, Beauvoir, Bacall, Woolf, Sontag and Smith provide a salutary – and historically speaking, long overdue – corrective to centuries of male middle age. I have tried to avoid fetishizing them as 'women writers' – we do not, after all, speak of 'men writers' – but there is no doubt that they, and others like them, have given a very different inflection to the idea of ageing (even male writers in the twenty-first century now emerge against the backdrop of the supposed 'feminization' of masculinity, with autobiographical authors such as Karl Ove Knausgård railing bitterly against their feeling of midlife emasculation). What these and other female writers have done is effectively to restore the cliché 'life begins at forty' to its original context – that 'the best part of a *woman's* life begins at forty'.

The transition from claim to cliché tells its own story about the historical hegemony of male middle age. What it also shows us, however, is the extent to which the female perspective on midlife is baked into the concept, albeit in subterranean ways. The claim that life begins at forty, popularized by Walter Pitkin in 1932, was originally made by a certain 'Mrs Theodore Parsons' in an interview with the *Pittsburgh Press* in April 1917:

> The average woman does not know how to breathe, sit, stand or walk. Now I want women to train for the special duties which may devolve upon them in war time. Death begins at thirty, that is, deterioration of the muscle cells sets in. Attention to diet and exercise would enable men and women to live a great deal longer than they do today. The best part of a woman's life begins at forty.[21]

The author of *Brain Culture through Scientific Body Building* (1912), a Nietzschean encomium to the power of the will, Parsons wanted to persuade women to prolong and enhance their quality of life through physical education. What is also apparent, however, is that she wanted to turn them into men, or at least into what society of the time saw as the next best thing to men – with their 'special duties which may devolve upon them in war time' – while the real thing was away fighting. The idea that life begins at forty may have emerged as a specifically female cliché, then, but it had a very male sense of maturity as its default setting.

Has this changed a hundred years later? The successive waves of feminism that washed over the course of the twentieth century certainly challenged the assumption that only men are allowed to get older. Beauvoir's pioneering work of the 1940s was followed by the 'second-wave' feminists of the 1960s, and the introduction of the contraceptive pill at the start of that decade marked an obvious turning point in women's relationship to their own bodies. By the end of the decade, Germaine Greer had diagnosed Western woman as *The Female Eunuch*, infantilized and oppressed; two years later, in 1972, Sontag published an essay decrying 'The Double Standard of Ageing'. It is worth reflecting on what this essay tells us not just about the obvious differences in the ways the two sexes are said to get older, but about how we understand middle age more generally.

The first striking fact is biographical. Born in 1933, Sontag was precisely 39 at the time of writing the essay. Yet again, then, it would seem that George Miller Beard was right: 39 is the magic number. But Sontag saw a psychological reason beyond the maths: if forty represents the symbolic threshold, it is the *anticipation* of this threshold that occasions the real torture, offering as it does 'a whole year in which to meditate in glum astonishment that one stands on the threshold of middle age'. Such borders are obviously arbitrary, but no less powerful for it: 'although a woman on her fortieth birthday is hardly different from what she was when she was still thirty-nine, the day seems like a turning point. But long before actually becoming a woman of forty, she has been steeling herself against the depression she will feel.'[22] As far as ageing is concerned, then, it is worse to travel than to arrive.

Sontag's analysis of the double standard of ageing was predicated on understanding it as 'an ordeal of the imagination – a moral disease, a social pathology'. Viewing ageing as culturally constructed in this manner allowed her, like Beauvoir before her, to identify the ways in which this disease afflicts women much more than men. We are all 'haunted by numbers' (at least in a Western society in which we carefully mark each birthday), but the ghost of getting older is particularly frightening for women, since unlike men they are supposed 'to maintain an ideal, static appearance, against the progress of age'. This ideal, of course, is that of youth, more specifically that of late adolescence and early adulthood, deemed by society – which is to say, by men – to be the sexually desirable norm. Women are thus encouraged to be 'moral idiots', more concerned with their appearance than with their intelligence. Female ageing, in short, is 'more a social judgement than a biological eventuality'.

Sontag does allow for differences in time and place, although these amount to little more than cultural clichés and national stereotypes; turning forty is easier for a French woman, she argues, since 'her role is to initiate an inexperienced or timid young man.' The Marschallin in Richard Strauss's opera *Der Rosenkavalier* (1911), similarly, suddenly sees that her youth is over at the age of 34, an idea that we would now, Sontag feels, find 'merely neurotic, or even ridiculous'. What such examples help her to emphasize, in any case, is that ageing is a crisis of the imagination rather than of the body – and that, as such, 'it has the habit of repeating itself again and again.' Thirty becomes forty becomes fifty; just as we are coming to terms with one landmark, the next one arrives. The female version of this anxiety, however, exhibits a curious tension, or at least it did in the 1970s. On the one hand, women are subject to immense pressure to 'stay' – that is, to look – young, which means that they remain 'girls as long as possible, who then age humiliatingly into middle-aged women'; on the other hand, women are thereby 'exempted from the dreary panic of middle-aged men whose "achievements" seem paltry', since they are not supposed to be ambitious in the first place. If male middle age is measured by 'achievements', female middle age is assessed by appearances.

Such, at least, was the view from the 1970s. It is a sign of the success of feminism that fifty years later women can now experience their own 'dreary panic' at the thought that they have achieved too little. Middle age has been normalized, and women, too, can now feel like professional failures. No one in the twenty-first century bats an eyelid at the idea of mid-career women experiencing disappointment or frustration; it is the inevitable corollary of equality and emancipation. It is a strange cause for celebration, no doubt, but a sure sign of progress nonetheless.

That is not to say, of course, that women now experience middle age in the same way as men do, nor indeed that we talk about their experience of it in the same way. For one thing, we still focus to a remarkable extent on appearance. The public images of Beauvoir and Bacall, or of Sontag and Smith, are significantly defined by their looks, in a way unimaginable for comparable male figures. For all the advances in understanding the female midlife mind, the middle-aged woman remains demonstrably defined by her body. Male reason, here as elsewhere, is still placed in opposition to female passion.

Beyond neuroscience, beyond social science, perhaps the biggest single development in the discussion of middle age in recent years has been the breaking of the taboo around the menopause. Sontag, interestingly, mentions it only once in her essay of nearly 10,000 words on the gendered nature of ageing, alluding *en passant* to the 'sense of loss suffered during menopause (which, with increased longevity, tends to arrive later and later)'.[23] For all the air of emancipation surrounding the 1960s – and for all the work of pioneers such as Marie Stopes, who had argued in her best-selling *Change of Life in Men and Women* (1936) that the discourse concerning the menopause created the very crisis it purported to diagnose – it would seem that the 1970s were not ready to acknowledge the biology of female ageing. The menopause was not yet mentionable.

All this changed with the publication, in the early 1990s, of two best-selling books: Greer's *The Change: Women, Ageing, and Menopause* (1991) and Gail Sheehy's *The Silent Passage* (1992). The titles spoke for themselves, putting what Greer called the 'climacteric' centre stage in debates about female middle age. Determined to wrest control from the pharmaceutical and advertising companies – with their obvious interest in keeping women anxiously receptive to palliatives and placebos of one sort or another – the two writers sought to reclaim the menopause from the 'menopause industry', asserting individual acceptance of ageing over the social imperative of agelessness. That their books found such a broad echo tells its own story.

Greer identified a number of earlier texts that discussed the menopause either implicitly or explicitly, such as Iris Murdoch's *Bruno's Dream* (1969) and Doris Lessing's novel *The Summer Before the Dark* (1973). It is only really since her study, however, that the menopause has become widely discussed, to the point where it has now become a commonplace of newspaper columns and agony aunts. Perhaps the most incisive recent work on the topic is Marina Benjamin's *The Middlepause* (2016), which is incisive in the truest sense of the adjective; pitched somewhere between memoir and *memento mori*, it traces the author's response to having her uterus excised at the age of 48. With brutal simplicity, the hysterectomy sliced her life in two. Despite her avowedly cavalier attitude towards the operation, she came out, unsurprisingly, a changed woman.

Benjamin's book offers a moving meditation on the impact of the hysterectomy on her mental landscape. Drawing on literature and psychology, social science and neuroscience, she presents an eyewitness account of how it feels to undergo the menopause, and in such an uncompromising manner. Rather than rehearsing her story, however, I want to reflect by way of conclusion on the way in which her memoir exemplifies the changing metaphors of middle age. Our vocabulary determines our world view, and the limits of our language, to adapt Wittgenstein's famous phrase, are the limits of our oldness. For Benjamin, for understandable reasons, the idiom of ageing is one of incision: she is 'mesmerised by [her] puncture wounds', by the 'reddish slash that looks like a half-cocked smile' across her stomach.[24] Her experience of middle age, by extension, is that of a caesura, defined by the *Oxford English Dictionary* as 'a pause near the middle of a line' and deriving from the Latin verb *caedere*, meaning to cut. As she notes wryly, you cannot argue with scars.

Benjamin's descriptive language conveys the strong sense, then, that her experience of the menopause was punctual, not gradual. Intellectually speaking, the event itself is both vividly present and curiously absent. Unlike most people's experience of middle age, the 'middlepause' for her is – at least initially – almost exclusively physiological rather than psychological: 'There was no real menopausal process, only a Before and After.'[25] Middle age, in this model, becomes a decisive, incisive, *excisive* experience of metamorphosis: one morning she awakes from an uneasy operation to find herself transformed into a monstrous middle-aged woman. 'The change' has occurred.

Such an idiom of incision represents the counterpart to the metaphor – whether Heraclitean or Woolfian – of life as a 'stream'. The knife of middle age cuts into the life of the body; there is a before and after, but no 'during'. But what is midlife if not the very essence of enduring? Alongside the model of middle age as change, then, there is also the model of continuity, whereby we gradually get used to ageing as we gradually get older. Do the two models divide along gender lines? Is it as simple as saying that women *change* where men *continue*? There is biological truth to this, perhaps, but the real distinction is surely between those of either sex who – through character or sheer force of circumstance – experience midlife as transformative, and those who experience it as more, or less, of the same. Middle age may be a metamorphosis, but it is also, undoubtedly, a metaphor. It is up to us, in the end, how we perceive it.

Epilogue
The End of the Middle

I wandered beneath the sun-dappled shade from the tree, surrounded by the warm fragrances of the forest, thinking that I was in the middle of my life. Not life as an age, not halfway along life's path, but *in the middle of my existence*.

My heart trembled.

KARL OVE KNAUSGÅRD[1]

A friend once told me a magnificent joke. Walking along the street together one blustery day, he suddenly started bending over, hunching his back into a caricature of a wizened old man. When I asked him what he was doing, he replied with a single word: 'practising'.

Can we practise middle age? In one sense, it is impossible to disassociate the practice of middle age from the performance. We get older whether we rehearse or not: *on joue perdant*. We may, however, at least hope to get better at it as time passes, if only through our increasing awareness and acceptance of the inevitability of ageing. Through studying the examples of others, through reflecting on our own trajectories, we can learn to assert some degree of agency over the stories we tell ourselves. Sparked by self-knowledge, fuelled by fatalism, with a bit of luck we might just drive off happily into our anecdotage.

Yet there is also the more sombre sense, the more minor key, of *merely* practising. What if our attempt to come to terms with midlife, to attain mastery of maturity, is simply so much

Epilogue

shadow boxing, empty sparring in a softly lit mirror? What if the practice is simply a pose? Jean-Paul Sartre famously theorized the notion of 'bad faith', taking as his example a Paris waiter who self-consciously plays at being a waiter, dressing and holding himself as though he were playing a part, rather than simply getting on with the job of taking people drinks and being rude to them.[2] What if I am similarly indulging in the *mauvaise foi* of middle age?

Early middle age, it seems to me, is particularly susceptible to this charge. As we feel ourselves starting to get older, as we move away from the plateau of established adulthood, we start casting around for new models of maturity. In our forties and fifties, the person we want to be – the person we *can* be – is not the same as in our twenties or thirties, if only because we are no longer 'becoming' but now *are*. 'This awareness', writes Gombrowicz in his early fifties, 'that I have already become myself. I already am. Witold Gombrowicz, these two words, which I carried on myself, are now accomplished. I am. I am too much ... I am made, finished, delineated.'[3] We could all substitute our own names for those two words, since we all suffer, sooner or later, from the sensation of having become who we are. If it takes a while to accept this shift of tense from future to present, to get used to the new selves that succeed each other, it is because we are always a few years younger in our minds than in our bodies, as though we were still catching up with the latest time zone in which we find ourselves landing. For that very reason, though, the life of the mind can offer us orientation, mapping out the changing coordinates as we fly through time. In the middle of life's way, literature offers the example of others, like Gombrowicz, who have been there before us.

What literature can also teach us, more fundamentally, is to stop practising middle age and to start living it. From Dante onwards, midlife is often configured as a crisis – but more common for most of us is surely the problem of *stasis*. Ennui and repetition are the real enemies of adulthood, not the occasional moment of reckoning that is, by definition, exceptional. Most of the time we are too busy *being* middle-aged – commuting to work, planning our next holiday, wondering when our children will be able to outrun us – that we omit to reflect on what it actually means. Precisely here is where literature has so much to offer: not as a self-help manual of crisis management telling us how to lead our lives differently, but as a means of enriching the life we are leading anyway. With a bit of effort, the midlife mind can start to lead the midlife *of* the mind.

Why, after all, do we read? Why do we write? In Dr Johnson's famous words, the end of literature is to enable readers 'better to enjoy life or better to endure it'.[4] We engage with literature, that is to say, in order to become smarter, nobler, *better* people; we engage with literature in order to evolve. The implicit promise of the creative life is that we can continue developing; the implicit premise of the creative *mid*life is that we can continue changing. If the nightmare of middle age is to fossilize into brittle versions of our younger selves, the dream of middle age is surely to take on new selves. That this takes practice is merely another reason for reading on.

As we reach midlife, then, what we might usefully learn is to practise middle age in the sense in which a doctor practises medicine; skilled, experienced and self-confident, we should look to maximize, rather than minimize, our maturity. We like to think of the ageing process as an irregular verb – I am still young, you are getting older, he/she/it is over the hill – but closer inquiry into the various ways in which it has been constructed can help us, paradoxically, to reconstruct it for ourselves. Through due reflection, we can hope to overcome the midlife crisis by embracing the midlife stasis – if by stasis we mean the calm self-assurance of being in the *akmē* of existence. To practise middle age in this sense is to analyse it, absorb it and apply it; like medicine, it is best learned by looking over the shoulders of more experienced practitioners. Literature, in this regard, is the perfect tutor, since it offers a record of midlife history from the inside out, a phenomenology of ageing. Its lessons can be surprising; even the numbers are not always where we might expect them – the biblical 35, the 'beginning' of 40 – but lie rather in the subtler psychology of the authorial 39 or the Aristotelian 49. Middle age is not a round number; the meaning of life, as Douglas Adams famously joked in *The Hitchhiker's Guide to the Galaxy*, is 42.

The models of middle age explored in this book are nothing if not multiple, since none of us has a monopoly on maturity. 'Crisis' (and its more metaphysically loaded counterpart, 'grief') is the most obvious mode of response to midlife, but it is for that reason perhaps the least interesting. Middle age is more than mere crisis management; it is also the sense that we can begin again (with Dante), that we can achieve a newfound humility (with Montaigne) or that we can reach a renewed awareness of the tragicomedy of existence (with Shakespeare). It is the realization that we can take a year off (like Goethe), that we can attain a more Realistic view of ageing (like the Victorians) or that we can convert to a whole new set of beliefs (like T. S. Eliot). And it is the sense that less may in fact be more (in the manner of Samuel Beckett), that the menopause may in fact be liberating (in the manner of Simone de Beauvoir) and that middle age may in fact need to reinvent itself for the new millennium (in the manner of its long-overdue feminization). What writing this book has taught me, in short, is that middle age is what we make of it.

What *I* have made of it, I now realize, is something different from what I had anticipated. I thought I was writing about middle age, but I have also been writing about maturity. I thought I was undertaking an intellectual enquiry into aesthetics, but I have also been pursuing a moral enquiry into ethics. I have surprised myself – and I hope you, too – into rediscovering the midlife mind as the mature mind, as an Archimedean point from

Jean Marais, *Le passe-muraille* (The Passer through Walls), 1999, street sculpture in Montmartre, Paris.

which both youth and old age may be dispassionately surveyed. Kant famously claimed that enlightenment is the 'emergence out of self-incurred immaturity' – but is it possible to emerge out of self-incurred *maturity*?[5] What if this were the harder task?

This book has tried to show that FOMO (fear of missing out) need not necessarily mutate into FOMA (fear of middle age), since such fear is predicated on defining midlife as a period of loss. In so many ways, however, it is a period of gain: of children, of creativity, of confidence. To ask what it means to be middle-aged is to ask, in the final analysis, what it means to be a man or a woman, since the middle is the period of life that defines us as adults. From Aristotle to Adams, the meaning of life has long been located in our forties, since this is the time when we can hope to attain the clearest perspective on what does and does not matter, on how we should or should not want to spend such time as is granted us. The meaning of *mid*life, by extension, is to acquire this perspective, the better to look both to the future and to the past. If middle age remains such an elusive concept, it is because it both confirms and confounds our understanding of time more generally. As the full extent of our finitude dawns on us, as we start to realize that our future is not unlimited, we take refuge in the infinity of the present, relegating mortality to the margins by positioning ourselves in the centre of life's parabola. As John Calvin puts it: 'the world is sloped on either side, therefore place yourself in the middle.'[6]

The final lesson of the midlife mind, then, is that it is only as wise as we make it. Beyond all the clichés of crisis, beyond all the dreams of renewal, we must make our own meaning out of ageing. It is up to us to place ourselves in the middle. What this means will vary from person to person and from gender to gender, but for all of us its realization is predicated on its conceptualization. To be fully in the middle, we need to know what it *means* to be fully in the middle – which means learning to see ourselves from the outside. This, of course, is where literature can help, by offering us models for our changing sense of time. Like the 43-year-old hero of Marcel Aymé's short story 'Le Passe-muraille' (1941), immortalized by Jean Marais' sculpture in Montmartre, we are caught in the very thick of things, struggling to pierce through the wall of our midlife minds. Art, in all its ambivalence, can help us to see this wall.

But it can also help us to see that the wall is of our own making. We can only break through it once we have understood that middle age is a metaphor; we can only come to terms with midlife once we have understood that what we mean by 'middle age' changes with the centuries and cultures. After this, the onus is on us to reconstruct our own, composite sense of what it means to get older. For me at least, this sense amounts to the realization that emotion is as valid as reason – that affect, as we age, trumps intellect. The midlife mind teaches us, ultimately, that there is more to midlife than the mind – that middle age, in the end, is an emotional as well as an intellectual category. We must imagine the middle-aged, in short, as Camus tells us that we must imagine Sisyphus: as happy. 'The way we are living, timorous or bold, will have been our life' – but it will also have been our midlife.[7] For the end of middle age is not old age; it is the acceptance, both liberating and terrifying, of the fact that we must now take responsibility for who we are, in all our ambivalent maturity. The secret of midlife, like the secret of the good life, is to accept ourselves.

References

Prologue: The Incremental Inch

1. See Angela Monaghan, 'Deputy Bank Governor Apologises for "Menopausal Economy" Comment', www.theguardian.com, 16 May 2018.
2. Susan Sontag, *The Complete Rolling Stone Interview*, ed. Jonathan Cott (New Haven, CT, 2013), p. 4. The interview took place in 1978; I have adapted the personal pronouns.
3. See Joseph Conrad, *The Shadow-Line*, ed. Jeremy Hawthorn (Oxford, 2003).
4. Sontag, *The Complete Rolling Stone Interview*, p. 130.
5. Jean Starobinski, *La Parole est moitié à celui qui parle: Entretiens avec Gérard Macé* (Paris, 2009), p. 37: 'Or quels sont les objets qui appellent notre pesée? C'est la vie que nous sentons en nous, qui s'affirme, et qui en même temps s'écoule.'

1 Crisis and Grief: The Invention of Midlife

1. For this and all subsequent references, see Elliott Jaques, 'Death and the Midlife Crisis', *International Journal of Psychoanalysis*, XLVI (January 1965), pp. 502–14.
2. George Miller Beard, *American Nervousness* (New York, 1881), pp. 228–9.
3. See Walter Pitkin, *Life Begins at Forty* (New York, 1932).
4. G. Stanley Hall, *Senescence: The Last Half of Life* (New York, 1922), p. 12.
5. Ibid., pp. 29–30.
6. Carl Jung, *Modern Man in Search of a Soul*, trans. C. F. Baynes with W. S. Dell (London, 1933), p. 125.
7. Ibid., pp. 66–7.
8. Cesare Pavese, *This Business of Living: Diaries 1935–50*, trans. John Taylor (New Brunswick, NJ, 2009), p. 265. Diary entry of 22 November 1945.
9. Cited (slightly simplified) from J. P. Griffin, 'Changing Life Expectancy Throughout History', *Journal of the Royal Society of Medicine*, CI/12 (1 December 2008), p. 577.
10. See Judith Rowbotham and Paul Clayton, 'An Unsuitable and Degraded Diet? Part Three: Victorian Consumption Patterns and

Their Health Benefits', *Journal of the Royal Society of Medicine*, CI/9 (1 September 2008), pp. 454–62.
11 See www.japanesewithanime.com/2018/04/ossan-meaning.html, accessed 7 November 2019. Susan Scutti and Yoko Wakatsuki, 'The Real Reason People Rent Middle-aged Men in Japan', CNN Health, 3 August 2018.
12 Griffin, 'Changing Life Expectancy'.
13 See Patricia Cohen, *In Our Prime: The Fascinating History and Promising Future of Middle Age* (New York, 2012).
14 Yehuda Halevi, 'When a Lone Silver Hair Appeared on My Head', trans. Peter Cole, in *The Dream of the Poem: Hebrew Poetry from Muslim and Christian Spain, 950–1492* (Princeton, NJ, 2007), p. 149.
15 See Elisabeth Kübler-Ross, *On Death and Dying* (New York, 1969).
16 Mary Shelley, *The Last Man* (Oxford, 1994), p. 240.
17 Ibn Khaldūn, *The Muqaddimah*, trans. Franz Rosenthal (Princeton, NJ, 2015), p. 285.
18 See Roland Barthes, 'Chateaubriand: Life of Rancé', in *New Critical Essays*, trans. Richard Howard (Evanston, IL, 2009), pp. 41–54.
19 The graph here is taken from Cari Romm, 'Where Age Equals Happiness', *The Atlantic*, 6 November 2014. As this article shows, the data varies considerably from continent to continent.
20 Roland Barthes, 'Longtemps, je me suis couché de bonne heure', in *Roland Barthes: The Rustle of Language*, trans. Richard Howard (Berkeley, CA, 1989), pp. 277–90, here p. 284.
21 See Jean Améry, *Über das Altern: Revolte und Resignation* (Stuttgart, 1968).
22 William Shakespeare, *As You Like It*, Act II, scene 7.

2 The Piggy in the Middle: The Philosophy of Midlife

1 See, for instance, Lynne Segal, *Out of Time: The Pleasures and the Perils of Ageing* (London, 2013).
2 Aristotle, *Ethics*, trans. J.A.K. Thomson (London, 1976), p. 100.
3 Aristotle, *Eudemian Ethics*, trans. Anthony Kenny (Oxford, 2011), II.5, p. 21.
4 Aristotle, *Rhetoric*, trans. Richard Claverhouse Jebb (Cambridge, 1909), II:xiv, p. 102. All citations in this paragraph are taken from this page.
5 Aristotle, *Physics*, trans. Robin Waterfield (Oxford, 1996), IV/11, p. 106.
6 See, for instance, his famous definition of the 'practical imperative': 'Act that you use humanity, in your own person as well as in the person of any other, always at the same time as an end, never merely as a means.' Immanuel Kant, *Groundwork of the Metaphysics of Morals*, trans. Mary Gregor, ed. Jens Timmermann (Cambridge, 2012), p. 41.
7 See René Descartes, *Meditations on First Philosophy*, trans. John Cottingham (Cambridge, 1996), esp. the second meditation.
8 John Locke, *An Essay Concerning Human Understanding*, ed. Kenneth P. Winkler (Indianapolis, IN, 1996), p. 142.
9 See Derek Parfit, *Reasons and Persons* (Oxford, 1984), esp. Chapter Ten: 'What we believe ourselves to be'.

10 Henri Bergson, *An Introduction to Metaphysics*, trans. T. E. Hulme (New York, 1912), pp. 44–5.
11 Hans Jonas, *The Phenomenon of Life: Toward a Philosophical Biology* (New York, 1966), p. 22.
12 For up-to-date information on the activities and experiments of the Institute on Aging, see www.aging.wisc.edu.
13 This paragraph draws on the summary presented in Chapter Nine of Patricia Cohen, *In Our Prime: The Fascinating History and Promising Future of Middle Age* (New York, 2012), pp. 140–59.
14 Ludwig Wittgenstein, *Philosophical Investigations*, trans. G.E.M. Anscombe (Oxford, 2001), 109, p. 40e.
15 Cited from Lawrence Shainberg, 'Exorcizing Beckett', *Paris Review*, 104 (1987), p. 106.
16 Witold Gombrowicz, *Diary*, trans. Lillian Vallee (New Haven, CT, 2012), p. 47.

3 Halfway Up the Hill: How to Begin in the Middle

1 Dante Alighieri, *Le Opere di Dante Alighieri*, ed. E. Moore and P. Toynbee (Oxford, 1924), p. 1. All subsequent citations in Italian are from this edition.
2 Dante Alighieri, *The Divine Comedy*, trans. Allen Mandelbaum (New York, 1995). All translations are taken from this edition.
3 Dante, *Il Convivio (The Banquet)*, trans. Richard H. Lansing (New York and London, 1990), IV/24, pp. 218–19. The four stages of life, as Dante sees them, are *adolescenza, gioventute, senettute* and *senio*. For each of these stages he draws on a different classical writer, respectively Statius, Virgil, Ovid and Lucan.
4 For discussion of Aeneas and maturity, see Dante, *Il Convivio*, IV/26, pp. 225–8.
5 Joseph Conrad, *The Shadow-Line*, ed. Jeremy Hawthorn (Oxford, 2003), p. 45.
6 Giacomo Leopardi, *Zibaldone*, ed. Michael Caesar and Franco D'Intino (New York, 2015), 30 November 1828, pp. 1991–2.
7 Charles Baudelaire, *Oeuvres*, ed. Claude Pichois (Paris, 1975), p. 134. My translation.
8 Chateaubriand, *Mémoires d'outre-tombe* (Paris, 1998), IV, p. 224.
9 Friedrich Schlegel, *Lectures on the History of Literature Ancient and Modern* (New York, 1841), p. 160. More generally – and for the paragraphs that follow – for Schlegel on the Middle Ages, see Lecture Seven.
10 René Descartes, *Discourse on Method and Related Writings*, trans. Desmond M. Clarke (London, 1999), p. 20.
11 Friedrich Hölderlin, *Selected Poems and Fragments*, trans. Michael Hamburger (London, 1998), p. 171.
12 Henry Wadsworth Longfellow, *Poems and Other Writings* (New York, 2000), p. 671.
13 Henry Wadsworth Longfellow, *Dante's Inferno* (New York, 2003), p. 3.

14 See Hölderlin, 'Bread and Wine', in *Selected Poems and Fragments*, p. 157. Hamburger translates the famous phrase 'Wozu Dichter in dürftiger Zeit?' as 'Who wants poets at all in lean years?'

4 A Room at the Back of the Shop: Midlife Modesty

1 Quoted in Philippe Desan, *Montaigne: A Life*, trans. Steven Rendall and Lisa Neal (Princeton, NJ, 2017), p. 197.
2 Michel de Montaigne, 'On Solitude', in *The Complete Essays*, ed. and trans. M. A. Screech (London, 1991), pp. 266–78. All subsequent references to the Essays are taken from this edition and cited by book and number.
3 Seneca, *Epistles 1–65*, trans. Richard M. Gummere (Cambridge, MA, 1917), p. 325.
4 Samuel Beckett, *Murphy* (London, 1973), p. 36.
5 Stefan Zweig, *Montaigne*, trans. Will Stone (London, 2015), p. 38.
6 See George Orwell, *Collected Essays, Journalism and Letters*, vol. IV: *1945–1950* (London, 1971), p. 515.
7 Seneca, *Epistles*, p. 237.
8 See Aristotle, *Poetics*, trans. Anthony Kenny (Oxford, 2013), pp. 29–30.

5 Getting On: The Tragicomedy of Middle Age

1 See William Empson, *Seven Types of Ambiguity* (London, 1995).
2 William Shakespeare, *The Oxford Shakespeare: The Complete Works*, ed. Stanley Wells and Gary Taylor (Oxford, 1988), p. 751. All subsequent references are to this edition.
3 Many other writers have of course followed Shakespeare in taking the sun as a metaphor for middle age, and not only male ones. See, for instance, Emily Dickinson's brief poem of almost unbearable pathos: 'Consulting summer's clock, / But half the hours remain. / I ascertain it with a shock – / I shall not look again. // The second half of joy / Is shorter than the first. / The truth I do not dare to know / I muffle with a jest.' Emily Dickinson, *The Poems of Emily Dickinson* (Cambridge, MA, 1999), p. 625.
4 See Aristotle, *Poetics*, trans. Anthony Kenny (Oxford, 2013), p. 23; and Martha Nussbaum, *Love's Knowledge: Essays on Philosophy and Literature* (Oxford, 1990).
5 See Friedrich Nietzsche, 'On the Uses and Disadvantages of History for Life' (1874), in *Untimely Meditations*, trans. R. J. Hollingdale (Cambridge, 1997), pp. 57–124.
6 Plato, *Phaedo*, trans. David Gallop (Oxford, 1993), p. 89c.

6 Perpetual Incipience: The Midlife Gap Year

1 Johann Wolfgang von Goethe, *Italienische Reise*, in *Werke* XI, ed. Erich Trunz [Hamburger Ausgabe] (Munich, 1998), p. 64. All subsequent references to Goethe in German are to this edition. Unless otherwise specified, the translation is my own.

2 Ibid., p. 126.
3 Ibid., p. 146.
4 J. W. Goethe, *Italian Journey*, trans. W. H. Auden and Elizabeth Mayer (London, 1970), p. 151.
5 For this translation, see Rüdiger Safranski, *Goethe: Life as a Work of Art*, trans. David Dollenmayer (New York, 2017).
6 Goethe, *Italienische Reise*, p. 446.
7 Ibid., p. 125.
8 Ibid., p. 154.
9 Ibid., p. 456.
10 Ibid., p. 135.
11 Ibid., p. 353.
12 Ibid., p. 366.
13 Ibid., p. 373.
14 Cited, in Dollenmayer's translation, from Safranski, *Goethe: Life as a Work of Art*, p. 290.
15 Goethe, *Italienische Reise*, p. 399.
16 Ibid., p. 430.
17 See ibid., p. 133.
18 Ibid., p. 242.
19 J. W. von Goethe, *The Poems of Goethe*, trans. Edgar Alfred Bowring (London, 1874), pp. 181–2.
20 J. W. von Goethe, *Select Minor Poems: Translated from the German of Goethe and Schiller*, trans. John S. Dwight (Boston, MA, 1839), pp. 111–12.
21 See Arthur Lovejoy, *The Great Chain of Being* (Cambridge, MA, 1936).
22 See J. W. von Goethe, *Elective Affinities*, trans. Victoria C. Woodhull (Boston, MA, 1872), p. 1.
23 See Edward Said, *Out of Place* (New York, 2000), p. 8.
24 See Safranski, *Goethe*, Chapter 26.
25 See ibid., Chapter 29.
26 Johann Peter Eckermann, *Conversations with Goethe*, trans. John Oxenford (London, 1930), pp. 165–6.

7 Realism and Reality: The 'Middle Years'

1 Stefan Zweig, *The World of Yesterday: Memories of a European*, trans. Benjamin W. Huebsch and Helmut Ripperger (London, 1943), p. 37.
2 Ibid.
3 See Patricia Cohen, *In Our Prime: The Fascinating History and Promising Future of Middle Age* (New York, 2012), pp. 33–4.
4 Mary Shelley, *The Journals of Mary Shelley, 1814–1844*, ed. Paula R. Feldman and Diana Scott-Kilvert (Oxford, 1987), vol. II, p. 478.
5 George Eliot, *Middlemarch*, ed. Rosemary Ashton (London, 1994), p. 144.
6 Ibid., pp. 40, 29.
7 Ibid., p. 64.
8 Ibid., p. 278.
9 Ibid., p. 279.

10 Ibid., p. 278.
11 Ibid., p. 94.
12 George Eliot, *Daniel Deronda*, ed. Barbara Hardy (London, 1967), p. 491.
13 Thomas Hardy, 'Middle-age Enthusiasms', in *Wessex Poems* (London, 1912), p. 80.
14 Henry James, 'The Middle Years', in *Tales of Henry James*, ed. Christof Wegelin and Henry B. Wonham (New York, 2003), pp. 211–28, here p. 211.
15 Ibid., p. 214.
16 See Rainer Maria Rilke, *The Book of Hours*, trans. Susan Ranson (Rochester, NY, 2008), p. 163.
17 James, 'The Middle Years', p. 216.
18 Ibid., p. 221.
19 Ibid., p. 226.
20 Eliot, *Middlemarch*, p. 138.
21 See Franz Kafka, 'Before the Law', in *A Hunger Artist and Other Stories*, trans. Joyce Crick (Oxford, 2012), pp. 20–22.
22 James, 'The Middle Years', p. 227.
23 Joseph Conrad, *The Shadow-Line*, ed. Jeremy Hawthorn (Oxford, 2003), p. 23.
24 Stefan Collini, *The Nostalgic Imagination: History in English Criticism* (Oxford, 2019), p. 4.
25 Henry James, 'The Diary of a Man of Fifty', in *Complete Stories*, vol. II: *1874–1884* (New York, 1999), pp. 453–84, here p. 454.
26 Virginia Woolf, *The Waves*, ed. Kate Flint (London, 1992), p. 123.
27 See Hayden White, *Metahistory: The Historical Imagination in Nineteenth-century Europe* (Baltimore, MD, 1973).

8 'The Years that Walk Between': Midlife Conversion

1 *Werke* III, ed. Erich Trunz [Hamburger Ausgabe] (Munich, 1998), p. 24.
2 See St Augustine, *Confessions*, VIII:12 (London, 1961), p. 177.
3 Ezra Pound to Harriet Monroe, 30 September 1915, in *The Selected Letters of Ezra Pound: 1907–41*, ed. D. D. Paige (New York, 1971), p. 40.
4 T. S. Eliot to Ezra Pound, 15 November 1922, in *The Letters of T. S. Eliot*, ed. Valerie Eliot (London, 1988), p. 597. T. S. Eliot to John Quinn, 12 March 1923, in *The Letters of T. S. Eliot*, vol. II: *1923–1925*, ed. Valerie Eliot and Hugh Haughton (London, 2011). Cited hereafter as *Letters*, vol. II.
5 T. S. Eliot, *For Lancelot Andrewes: Essays on Style and Order* (London, 1929), p. vii.
6 T. S. Eliot, *The Poems of T. S. Eliot*, ed. Christopher Ricks and Jim McCue (London, 2015), pp. 265–6, 270–71.
7 See Edward Helmore, 'T. S. Eliot's Hidden Love Letters Reveal Intense, Heartbreaking Affair', *The Guardian*, 2 January 2020, www.theguardian.com.

8 *The Poems of T. S. Eliot*, p. 179.
9 Virginia Woolf to Vanessa Bell, 18 May 1923, quoted by Lyndall Gordon, *T. S. Eliot: An Imperfect Life* (London, 1998), p. 208.
10 T. S. Eliot to Alfred Kreymborg, 6 February 1923. See *The Poems of T. S. Eliot*, p. 712.
11 T. S. Eliot to Henry Eliot, 1 January 1936. See *The Poems of T. S. Eliot*, p. 714.
12 *The Poems of T. S. Eliot*, p. 81.
13 T. S. Eliot to John Middleton Murry, April 1925, in *Letters*, vol. II, p. 627.
14 *The Poems of T. S. Eliot*, p. 191.
15 See the essays 'Hamlet and His Problems' and 'Tradition and the Individual Talent', in T. S. Eliot, *The Sacred Wood: Essays on Poetry and Criticism* (London, 1920).
16 *The Poems of T. S. Eliot*, p. 87.
17 T. S. Eliot to Henry Eliot, 19 October 1929. See *The Poems of T. S. Eliot*, p. 735.
18 T. S. Eliot to Laurence Binyon, 16 May 1930; T. S. Eliot to Paul Elmer More, 2 June 1930. See *The Poems of T. S. Eliot*, p. 730.
19 T. S. Eliot, 'Dante' (1929), in *Selected Essays, 1917–32* (New York, 1932), pp. 199–240, here p. 235.
20 T. S. Eliot to William Force Stead, 7 January 1927. See *The Poems of T. S. Eliot*, p. 1221.
21 T. S. Eliot to Marquis W. Childs, 8 August 1930, in *The Letters of T. S. Eliot*, vol. V: *1930–31* (London, 2014), p. 382.
22 T. S. Eliot, 'Yeats', *Selected Prose*, ed. Frank Kermode (New York, 1975), pp. 248–57, here p. 249.
22 Ibid., p. 251.
23 Ibid., pp. 252–3.
24 See *The Poems of T. S. Eliot*, p. 1222.
25 T. S. Eliot to John Hayward, 25 November 1940. See *The Poems of T. S. Eliot*, p. 1225.
26 *The Poems of T. S. Eliot*, p. 191.
27 T. S. Eliot to Pamela Murray, 4 February 1938. See *The Poems of T. S. Eliot*, p. 951.
28 See *The Poems of T. S. Eliot*, p. 952.
29 Ibid., pp. 187–8.
30 T. S. Eliot, 'John Bramhall', in *Selected Essays* (London, 1932), p. 316. Quoted by Gordon, *T. S. Eliot*, p. 229.
31 T. S. Eliot, 'Commentary', in *Criterion* (March 1928). See *The Poems of T. S. Eliot*, p. 950.
32 Sir Arthur Conan Doyle, *The Hound of the Baskervilles* (New York, 2008), p. 68.

9 Lessons in Lessness: Midlife Minimalism

1 James Knowlson, *Damned to Fame: The Life of Samuel Beckett* (London, 1997), p. 352.
2 Samuel Beckett, *Krapp's Last Tape*, in *Collected Shorter Plays* (London, 1984), p. 60.

3 Knowlson, *Damned to Fame*, p. 353. Originally cited from an interview with Israel Shenker, *New York Times*, 5 May 1956.
4 Samuel Beckett, 'Three Dialogues: Samuel Beckett and Georges Duthuit', in *Proust and Three Dialogues with Georges Duthuit* (London, 1965), p. 125. First published in *Transition*, v (1949).
5 Samuel Beckett to Georges Duthuit, 2 August 1948, trans. George Craig. Cited from *The Letters of Samuel Beckett, 1941–1956*, ed. George Craig, Martha Dow Fehsenfeld, Dan Gunn and Lois More Overbeck (Cambridge, 2011), p. 92.
6 For further discussion of this language – both in Beckett and in other modernists – see Shane Weller, *Language and Negativity in European Modernism* (Cambridge, 2019).
7 Samuel Beckett to Georges Duthuit, 9 March 1949, in *Letters, 1941–1956*, p. 140.
8 Beckett, 'Three Dialogues', p. 125.
9 Samuel Beckett to Georges Duthuit, 2 March 1949, in *Letters, 1941–1956*, p. 133.
10 Beckett, 'Three Dialogues', p. 103.
11 Samuel Beckett to Axel Kaun, 7 July 1937, in *Letters, 1929–1940*, p. 518 in English, pp. 513–14 in German.
12 Cited by Theodor W. Adorno, 'Notes on Kafka', in *Prisms*, trans. Samuel and Shierry Weber (Cambridge, MA, 1983), pp. 243–71, here p. 271.
13 Samuel Beckett, *Trilogy: Molloy, Malone Dies, The Unnamable* (London, 1973), p. 176.
14 Beckett, *Trilogy*, p. 418.
15 Ibid., p. 36.
16 Ibid., p. 302.
17 See Lucretius, *On the Nature of Things*, trans. Martin Ferguson Smith (Indianapolis, IN, and Cambridge, 2001), p. 29.
18 Samuel Beckett, *How It Is* (London, 2009), p. 112.
19 Ibid., p. 115.
20 Ibid., p. 112.
21 Charles Baudelaire, 'L'héautontimorouménos', in *Les Fleurs du mal* (Paris, 1857), pp. 123–4.
22 Beckett, *Trilogy*, p. 149.
23 Ibid., p. 125.
24 Samuel Beckett to Georges Duthuit, 11 August 1948, in *Letters, 1941–1956*, p. 98.
25 Samuel Beckett to Georges Duthuit, 6 April 1950, in *Letters, 1941–1956*, p. 195.
26 T. S. Eliot, *Murder in the Cathedral* (New York, 1935), p. 44.

10 From the Prime of Life to Old Age: How to Survive the Menopause

1 See Virginia Woolf, *A Room of One's Own* (London, 1929).
2 Simone de Beauvoir, *Force of Circumstance*, trans. Richard Howard (London, 1965), p. 19.
3 Ibid., pp. 177, 291.

4 Ibid., p. 669.
5 Ibid., pp. 5, 17.
6 Ibid., p. 137.
7 Simone de Beauvoir, *The Second Sex*, trans. H. M. Parshley (London, 1993), p. lix.
8 Ibid., p. 35.
9 Beauvoir, *Force of Circumstance*, p. 266.
10 Ibid., p. 297.
11 Ibid.
12 Ibid., p. 480.
13 Beauvoir, *The Second Sex*, p. 32.
14 Ibid., p. 605.
15 Ibid., p. 610.
16 Simone de Beauvoir, *The Woman Destroyed*, trans. Patrick O'Brian (New York, 1969), p. 241.
17 Michel Leiris, *Manhood*, trans. Richard Howard (Chicago, IL, 1984), p. 3.
18 Beauvoir, *The Second Sex*, p. 739.
19 Beauvoir, *Force of Circumstance*, p. 661.
20 Ibid., p. 671.
21 Ibid., p. 671.
22 Ibid., p. 195.
23 Ibid., p. 448.
24 Ibid., pp. 601–2.
25 Ibid., p. 384.
26 Beauvoir, *The Second Sex*, p. 760.
27 Simone de Beauvoir, *The Mandarins*, trans. Leonard M. Friedman (London, 1957), p. 700.
28 Ibid., p. 93.
29 Ibid., p. 169.
30 See Samuel Beckett to Simone de Beauvoir, 25 September 1946, in *The Letters of Samuel Beckett, 1941–1956*, ed. George Craig, Martha Dow Fehsenfeld, Dan Gunn and Lois More Overbeck (Cambridge, 2011), pp. 40–42.
31 Beauvoir, *The Mandarins*, p. 618.
32 Skin (and its rejuvenation) is accordingly one of Beauvoir's favourite images for the passing of time. See, for instance, her description of Anne's relationship with the American author Lewis Brogan (the double for Nelson Algren): 'Avec ma vie déjà usée, avec ma peau plus toute neuve, je fabriquais du bonheur pour l'homme que j'aimais: quel bonheur! . . . Moi aussi j'exultais. Quel dépaysement! Quand les étoiles fixes se mettent à valser dans le ciel, et que la terre fait peau neuve, c'est presque comme si on changeait de peau soi-même.' 'With my lived-in life, with my skin that was no longer the youngest, I was creating happiness for the man that I loved: what joy! . . . I, too, was delighted. What a change of scene! When the fixed stars start dancing in the sky, when the earth sheds its skin, it's almost as though one changes one's own skin.' *Les Mandarins*, pp. 423–4.
33 Ibid., p. 498.

34 Ibid., p. 266.
35 Ibid., p. 703.

11 Streams of Consciousness: Middle Age in a New Millennium

1 For this and subsequent references, see 'The Pleasures and Perils of Middle Age', *Time*, 29 July 1966, www.time.com/3105861 (accessed 1 May 2019). Inspired by Patricia Cohen, *In Our Prime: The Fascinating History and Promising Future of Middle Age* (New York, 2012), p. 109.
2 See F. Benes, M. Turtle, Y. Khan and P. Farol, 'Myelination of a Key Relay Zone in the Hippocampal Formation Occurs in the Human Brain During Childhood, Adolescence and Adulthood', *Archives of General Psychiatry*, LI/6 (June 1994), pp. 477–84. Quoted in Marina Benjamin, *The Middlepause: On Life after Youth* (London, 2016), pp. 114–15.
3 See Cohen, *In Our Prime*, pp. 140–59, esp. pp. 142 and 149. For further discussion of the midlife brain, see Barbara Strauch, *The Secret Life of the Grown-up Brain: Discover the Surprising Talents of the Middle-aged Mind* (London, 2011).
4 See 'Health Matters: Midlife Approaches to Reduce Dementia Risk', National Institute for Health Research, https://news.joindementiaresearch.nihr.ac.uk, accessed 29 January 2020.
5 Virginia Woolf, *The Waves*, ed. Kate Flint (London, 1992), p. 198.
6 Hermann Hesse, *Steppenwolf*, trans. Basil Creighton (New York, 2002), p. 26.
7 See Jane Goldman, '1925, London, New York, Paris: Metropolitan Modernisms – Parallax and Palimpsest', in *The Edinburgh Companion to Twentieth-century Literature in English*, ed. Brian McHale and Randall Stevenson (Edinburgh, 2006), p. 71.
8 Woolf, *The Waves*, p. 199.
9 Ibid., p. 198.
10 Ibid., p. 206.
11 Ibid., p. 204.
12 Ibid., p. 209.
13 Ibid., p. 212.
14 Virginia Woolf to G. L. Dickinson, 27 October 1931, in *The Letters of Virginia Woolf*, ed. Nigel Nicolson and Joanne Trautmann (London, 1975–80), IV, p. 397.
15 Woolf, *The Waves*, p. 205.
16 See Frank Kermode, *The Sense of an Ending* (Oxford, 1967).
17 Ludwig Wittgenstein, *Tractatus Logico-Philosophicus* 6.4311, trans. C. K. Ogden (New York, 1999), p. 106.
18 Susan Sontag, *The Complete Rolling Stone Interview*, ed. Jonathan Cott (New Haven, CT, 2013), p. 123.
19 Zadie Smith, 'On Optimism and Despair', in *Feel Free* (London, 2018), pp. 35–41, here pp. 37–8.
20 Ibid.
21 I am grateful to Mark Jackson for bringing this passage to my attention.
22 Susan Sontag, 'The Double Standard of Ageing', *Saturday Review*, 23 September 1972, p. 33. All subsequent citations are taken from here.

23 Ibid., p. 32.
24 Marina Benjamin, *The Middlepause: On Life after Youth* (London, 2016), p. 9.
25 Ibid.

Epilogue: The End of the Middle

1 Karl Ove Knausgård, *A Man in Love* (*My Struggle*, II), trans. Don Bartlett (London, 2013), p. 221.
2 See Jean-Paul Sartre, *Being and Nothingness*, trans. Hazel E. Barnes (New York, 1956), pp. 101–3.
3 Witold Gombrowicz, *Diary*, trans. Lillian Vallee (New Haven, CT, 2012), p. 211.
4 Samuel Johnson, review of Soame Jenyns's *A Free Enquiry into the Nature and Origin of Evil*, in *Miscellaneous and Fugitive Pieces* (London, 1774), p. 23.
5 See Immanuel Kant, *An Answer to the Question: What Is Enlightenment* (1784), trans. H. B. Nisbet (London, 2009).
6 Quoted in Susan Sontag, *The Complete Rolling Stone Interview*, ed. Jonathan Cott (New Haven, CT, 2013), p. 126.
7 Seamus Heaney, 'Elegy', in *Field Work* (London, 1979), p. 31.

Further Reading

General books on middle age

Améry, Jean, *Über das Altern: Revolte und Resignation* (Stuttgart, 1968)
Benjamin, Marina, *The Middlepause: On Life after Youth* (London, 2016)
Cohen, Patricia, *In Our Prime: The Fascinating History and Promising Future of Middle Age* (New York, 2012)
Greer, Germaine, *The Change: Women, Ageing, and Menopause* (New York, 1991)
Jaques, Elliott, 'Death and the Midlife Crisis', *International Journal of Psychoanalysis*, XLVI (January 1965), pp. 502–14
Jung, Carl, *Modern Man in Search of a Soul*, trans. C. F. Baynes with W. S. Dell (London, 1933)
Pitkin, Walter, *Life Begins at Forty* (New York, 1932)
Segal, Lynne, *Out of Time: The Pleasures and the Perils of Ageing* (London, 2013)
Setiya, Kieran, *Midlife: A Philosophical Guide* (Princeton, NJ, 2018)
Sontag, Susan, 'The Double Standard of Ageing', *Saturday Review*, 23 September 1972, pp. 29–38
Strauch, Barbara, *The Secret Life of the Grown-up Brain: Discover the Surprising Talents of the Middle-aged Mind* (London, 2011)

Selected works of literature related to middle age

Aymé, Marcel, *Le passe-muraille* (Paris, 1941)
de Beauvoir, Simone, *The Mandarins*, trans. Leonard M. Friedman (London, 1957)
—, *Force of Circumstance*, trans. Richard Howard (London, 1965)
—, *The Woman Destroyed*, trans. Patrick O'Brian (New York, 1969)
—, *The Second Sex*, trans. H. M. Parshley (London, 1993)
Beckett, Samuel, *Trilogy: Molloy, Malone Dies, The Unnamable* (London, 1973)
Colette, *Break of Day*, trans. Enid McLeod (New York, 2002)
Conrad, Joseph, *The Shadow-Line*, ed. Jeremy Hawthorn (Oxford, 2003)
Dante Alighieri, *The Divine Comedy*, trans. Allen Mandelbaum (New York, 1995)

Eliot, George, *Middlemarch*, ed. Rosemary Ashton (London, 1994)
Eliot, T. S., *The Poems of T. S. Eliot*, ed. Christopher Ricks and Jim McCue (London, 2015), esp. 'Ash Wednesday' and 'Four Quartets'
Goethe, *Elective Affinities*, trans. Victoria C. Woodhull (Boston, MA, 1872)
—, *Italian Journey*, trans. W. H. Auden and Elizabeth Mayer (London, 1970)
Gombrowicz, Witold, *Diary*, trans. Lillian Vallee (New Haven, CT, 2012)
Hesse, Hermann, *Steppenwolf*, trans. Basil Creighton (New York, 2002)
Hölderlin, Friedrich, 'Half of Life', in *Selected Poems and Fragments*, trans. Michael Hamburger (London, 1998), p. 171
James, Henry, 'The Middle Years', in *Tales of Henry James*, ed. Christof Wegelin and Henry B. Wonham (New York, 2003), pp. 211–28
Kafka, Franz, *The Metamorphosis*, trans. Susan Bernofsky (New York, 2015)
Knausgård, Karl Ove, *A Man in Love* (*My Struggle*, II), trans. Don Bartlett (London, 2013)
Leiris, Michel, *L'âge d'homme* (Paris, 1939); published in English as *Manhood*, trans. Richard Howard (Chicago, IL, 1984)
Longfellow, Henry Wadsworth, 'Mezzo Cammin', in *Poems and Other Writings* (New York, 2000), p. 671
Mann, Thomas, *Death in Venice*, trans. David Luke (London, 1998)
Montaigne, Michel de, *The Complete Essays*, ed. and trans. M. A. Screech (London, 1991)
Pavese, Cesare, *This Business of Living: Diaries 1935–50*, trans. John Taylor (New Brunswick, NJ, 2009)
Shakespeare, William, *The Oxford Shakespeare: The Complete Works*, ed. Stanley Wells and Gary Taylor (Oxford, 1988), esp. Sonnets I–XVII
Woolf, Virginia, *The Waves*, ed. Kate Flint (London, 1992)

Acknowledgements

This book was conceived in Canterbury, continued in Saint-Jean-de-Luz and concluded in Paris. It was completed during the Great Confinement of 2020, a *crise de la quarantaine* if ever there were one. The enforced solitude made me realize just how grateful I am to friends and family in all three places for supporting me, and for tolerating my curious obsession with time. Books are products not just of those who write them, but also of those who live with them, and this is especially true as we reach middle age. Marie, Max and Hugo have helped me realize this.

I am particularly grateful to the book's first readers, Shane Weller and Mathilde Régent, as well as to Anna Katharina Schaffner, who read drafts of early chapters. From different points on the shadow-line they were kind enough to show an interest in someone else's midlife mind. Such neuroses as remain, needless to say, are all my own.

Mads Rosendahl Thomsen, in Aarhus, indulged my middle ageing with genial hospitality; Michael Leaman, in London, with gentle humour. Zinovy Zinik pointed me to Hazlitt, at the beginning of the book's gestation; William Marx reminded me of Bergson, at its end. Edward Kanterian was kind enough to effect a necessary introduction, and to follow the book's gestation from afar. To all the other friends and colleagues whom I have bored with the topic: many apologies.

One of the defining moments of middle age is the realization that, like it or not, you are now the adult in the room. In this regard, my greatest debt is a long-distance one – to the adults who came before me. With all its imperfections, this book is dedicated to Claire and Alwin Hutchinson, for helping me reach maturity.

Photo Acknowledgements

The author and publishers wish to express their thanks to the below sources of illustrative material and/or permission to reproduce it. Some locations of artworks are also given below, in the interest of brevity:

From George M. Beard, *American Nervousness: Its Causes and Consequences* (New York, 1881): p. 19; CSU Archives/Everett Collection/Alamy Stock Photo: p. 216; Gallerie dell'Accademia, Venice: p. 13; INTERFOTO/Alamy Stock Photo: p. 238; from Arthur Thomas Malkin, *The Gallery of Portraits: With Memoirs*, vol. V (London, 1835): p. 96; Musée du Louvre, Paris: p. 58; Museo del Prado, Madrid: p. 215; Odescalchi Balbi Collection, Rome: p. 170; from [Conrad Reitter], *Mortilogus F. Conradi Reitterii Nordlingensis Prioris monasterii Caesariensis: Epigrammata ad eruditissimos uaticolas* . . . (Augsburg, 1508): p. 46; photo Sipa/Shutterstock: p. 88; Städel Museum, Frankfurt: p. 121; after Arthur A. Stone, Joseph E. Schwartz, Joan E. Broderick and Angus Deaton, 'A Snapshot of the Age Distribution of Psychological Well-being in the United States', in *Proceedings of the National Academy of Sciences*, VCVII/22 (June 2010): p. 31; from George Newnes, ed., *The Strand Magazine: An Illustrated Monthly*, vol. XXII (London, 1901): p. 186; TCD/Prod.DB/Alamy Stock Photo: p. 108; photo Guilhem Vellut/CC BY 2.0 [https://flic.kr/p/SgfWeZ]: p. 254; photo Roger Viollet/Lipnitzki via Getty Images: p. 190.

Index

Page numbers in *italics* indicate illustrations

19th century *see under* realism and models of middle age
age 39 significance 17, 19, 51, 84, 172, 192, 209, 224, 244, 253
ageing
　anxiety 103–4, 105–6, 110, 152–7
　brain changes 47–8, 230–32, 231, 233–4
　process 38–9, 47–50, 241–2, 244–9
The Ages of Woman and Death (Baldung) 213–16, *215*
akmē 42, 236, 252
Aristotle 41–2, 57, 92–3, 135, 239
Aymé, Marcel, *Le passe-muraille* (Marais) 254, 256

Bacall, Lauren 229
Baldung, Hans, *The Ages of Woman and Death* 213–16, *215*
Barthes, Roland 29–30, 32, 95
Baudelaire, Charles 64–5, 193–4, 200
Beard, George Miller 18–19, *19*, 84, 172, 192, 209, 244
Beauvoir, Simone de 208–28, *216*
　existentialist ethics 210–11, 214, 219–21, 226–7, 228
　The Mandarins 222–7, 228
　Sartre relationship 208, 209, 211, 217, 222

The Second Sex 209, 210, 211, 216, 227
　see also menopause
Beckett, Samuel 50–51, 85–6, 99, 183, 189–205
　Krapp's Last Tape 191, 220
　language change to French 195–6, 199, 209
　Molloy trilogy 196–7, 198, 200, 201–3
　present tense, use of 197–8, 199
　'Three Dialogues with Georges Duthuit' 192–4
　Waiting for Godot 189, *190*, 196
　see also minimalism
Benjamin, Marina, *The Middlepause* 247–8
Bergson, Henri 46
brain changes 47–8, 230–34, *231*

Cohen, Patricia, *In Our Prime* 24, 147
Colette 218
Conrad, Joseph, *The Shadow-Line* 13, 62, 159
creativity interest 18, 31, 32–3, 35–7, 217–18

Dante 52–9, 65–70, 193, 207–8
　The Banquet 57–9, 92–3, 183
　Divine Comedy 52–7, 64, 65–6, 68–70, 152
　Divine Comedy, Inferno 53, 74, 78, 194

274

Index

Divine Comedy, Purgatory 53, 54, 56, 65–6, 74, 79, 239
terza rima (third rhyme) 54–6
Vita Nuova 119, 177–8, 185
see also experiencing middle of life
On Death and Dying (Kübler-Ross) 25–6, 35
'Death and the Midlife Crisis' (Jaques) 16, 17–18, 21–2, 36, 74, 153, 188
Descartes, René 69–70
and mind-body dualism 43–6, 47, 197, 212
Divine Comedy (Dante) see under Dante

Eliot, George, *Middlemarch* 149–51, 156, 236
Eliot, T. S. 170–87, *174*, 203
Ash Wednesday 177–8
Four Quartets 61–2, 174, 178, 182, 183, 185
Four Quartets, 'East Coker' 182, 183, *186*, 187
The Hollow Men 175–7
'Prufrock' 171, 172
religious conversion 171–80, 184, 185–7
The Waste Land 168, 171, 172–3
see also midlife conversion
escaping oneself 117–42
and biological clock 118–19
literature evolution and rebirth 133–5, 141–2
maturity and temperament development 127–30, 138–9
middle age as accumulated experiences 140–41
mortality, acceptance of 130–33
new life 117–28, 136–8, 141–2, 253
time, passage of 123–36
see also Goethe
existentialist ethics 210–11, 214, 219–21, 226–7, 228
experience acquisition 49–51, 89, 92–8, 140–41, 158–9
experiencing middle of life 52–75
adolescence connection 62–5

literature and changing perception of Great Books 63–5
maturity as conscious idea 59–62, 63–4, 152
maturity, qualities defining 57–9, 92–3, 183
'middle' as starting point 55–6, 59, 65–6, 68–70, 78, 184, 197, 253
midlife angst 73–5
perception of life 71–3
see also Dante

Faust (Goethe) 65, 134–7, *136*, 138, 168
free indirect discourse 150, 161
Freud, Sigmund 18, 30, 48, 85, 86, 93

gendering of middle age 27–8, 90, 147, 223–6
19th century see under realism and models of middle age
and feminism 242–6
see also menopause
'getting on' metaphor 99, 100–101, 104
Goethe, Johann Wolfgang von 82, 117–42, *121*
Elective Affinities 133, 134, 138
escape to Italy 117–24, 125–6, 127–8, 253
Faust 65, 134–7, *136*, 138, 168
'The Limits of Man' 130–32
'Prometheus' 128–30, 132
pseudonym 117–18
Roman Elegies 121–2, 134
The Sorrows of Young Werther 125–6, 127
world literature advocate 138–40
see also escaping oneself
Gombrowicz, Witold 51, 251
Greer, Germaine 244, 247

Halevi, Yehuda 25, 28
'Half of Life' (Hölderlin) 71–3, 74
Hall, G. Stanley, *Senescence* 19–20
happiness measurement 221–3, 226–8

275

Hardy, Thomas, 'Middle-age
  Enthusiasms' 152
Hazlitt, William, *Liber Amoris* 148
Hegel, Georg 40, 43
Hölderlin, Friedrich 75
  'Half of Life' 71–3, 74

Ibn Khaldūn, *Muqaddimah* 29
identity *see* self-image

James, Henry, 'The Middle Years'
  152–6, 158, 161–2
Japan, *ossan* 23
Jaques, Elliott, 'Death and the
  Midlife Crisis' 16, 17–18, 21–2,
  36, 74, 153, 188
Jonas, Hans 47
Joyce, James 63, 65, 181, 189, 191
Jung, Carl 20–21, 179, 223

Kafka, Franz 156, 196
  Metamorphosis 9, 59
Kant, Immanuel 43, 90, 255
Knausgård, Karl Ove 243, 250
Kübler-Ross, Elisabeth, *On Death
  and Dying* 25–37

Leiris, Michael 217
Leonardo da Vinci, *Vitruvian Man*
  11–12, *13*, 77
'life begins at forty' 19, 243–4, 245
life expectancy 17–19, 22–4, 22–4,
  105–6
  see also mortality
lifestyle changes 171–80, 184, 185–7
literature
  and changing perception of
    Great Books 63–5
  evolution and rebirth 133–5,
    141–2
  happiness measurement 221–3,
    226–8
  and midlife conversion 168–9,
    170–71, 183, 185
  reading habits as we age 87–91
  realism and mid-19th century
    novels 149–52, 161–4, 208
  shaping maturity and morals
    99–100, 112–15

Locke, John 44–5
Longfellow, Henry, 'Mezzo
  Cammin' 73–5
male dominance 149–52, 207, 208,
  209, 211, 214, 216
male focus, midlife crisis 17–23
male menopause 17
  see also menopause
The Mandarins (Beauvoir) 222–7,
  228
maturity 253–5
  acceptance of 83–4, 85–9, 152
  as conscious idea 59–62, 63–4,
    152
  and living in the present 237–9
  qualities defining 57–9, 92–3, 183
  and temperament development
    127–30, 138–9
  triggers 167–71
menopause 11, 206–28, 253
  control, sense of losing 219–21
  creativity interest 217–18
  and depersonalization 216–17,
    218–19
  happiness measurement and
    literature 221–3, 226–8
  and invisibility 48
  male dominance, continuing
    207, 208, 209, 211, 214, 216
  male menopause 17
  'new' experiences, seeking
    212–14
  and New Millennium 246–8
  and sexual relationships 211–14
  society's view of women 216–17
  and third sex 214–16, 218–19, 221,
    226
  see also Beauvoir, Simone de;
    gendering of middle age
'Mezzo Cammin' (Longfellow) 73–5
Middle Ages 52, 57, 66–70, 207–8
'middle' as starting point 55–6, 59,
  65–6, 68–70, 78, 184, 197, 253
'middle style' development and
  sense of failure 182–5
'The Middle Years' (James) 152–6,
  158, 161–2
'Middle-age Enthusiasms' (Hardy)
  152

Middlemarch (Eliot) 149–51, 156, 236
middleness philosophy 39–42, 43
The Middlepause (Benjamin) 247–8
midlife conversion 165–87
   'change' and 'repudiation', distinction between 179–81
   emptiness of middle age 175–6
   lifestyle changes 171–80, 184, 185–7
   literature, learning from 168–9, 170–71, 183, 185
   maturity triggers 167–71
   middle age as rite of passage 169–70
   'middle style' development and sense of failure 182–5
   sense of self 166–7, 169, 180, 181
   see also Eliot, T. S.
midlife crisis 11, 16–37
   acceptance stage 35–7
   anger stage 28–31
   creativity post-crisis 18, 31, 32–3, 35–7
   denial stage 26–8
   depression stage 33–5
   as invention 16–17, 24–5
   life expectancy 17–19, 22–4, 22–4
   male focus 17–23
   and mortality 18, 20, 21–2, 25, 28, 31
   as self-realization period 20–21, 26, 31–3, 36
   well-being ladder (U-shaped) 30, *31*, 33, 36, 154–5, 221
'Midlife in the United States' research 47–8
mind-body dualism 43–6, 47, 197, 212
minimalism (starting again) 188–205
   accumulation of knowledge, recognizing 192–3
   defence against, and responsibility to others 204–5
   and fidelity to failure 192–3, 194–5, 235

   inverted pride danger 203–4
   less is more 191–2, 202–3, 204
   perpetual present/purgatory 193–4, 196–200, 202
   refusal response to challenge of middle age 194–5, 202–5, 225–6
   see also Beckett, Samuel
models of middle age *see* realism and models of middle age
modesty and asking what we want 76–98
   ageing, indignity of 93
   experience and judgement 89, 92–8
   literature, and reading habits as we age 87–91
   maturity, acceptance of 83–4, 85–9, 152
   mortality acceptance 78–9, 83–4, 183
   psychoanalysis 85–6, 92
   self-knowledge quest 81–2, 89, 90–91, 95
   solitude and renouncing ambition 80
   and Stoicism 81–3, 93, 97
   see also Montaigne, Michel de
Molloy trilogy (Beckett) 196–7, 198, 200, 201–3
Montaigne, Michel de, *Essais* 76–98, *89*, 96–7
   mathematical metaphors 94–5
   'On Books' 89–91
   'On Experience' 89, 92–8
   Seneca's *Moral Epistles*, influence of 81–2, 89, 90, 95
   see also modesty and asking what we want
moral purpose, Victorian 145–7
mortality
   acceptance 78–9, 83–4, 110, 130–33, 183, 237
   and midlife crisis 18, 20, 21–2, 25, 28, 31
   see also life expectancy

'new' experiences, seeking, and menopause 212–14

277

new life, and escaping oneself 117–28, 136–8, 141–2, 253
New Millennium 229–49
  ageing, incremental nature 241–2, 244–9
  anticipation of middle age 244–6
  brain changes 47–8, 230–34, *231*
  citizenship and individuality comparison 240, 241–2
  delusions of the midlife mind 235–7
  gendered nature of middle age and feminism 242–6
  'life begins at forty' 243–4, 245
  maturity and living in the present 237–9
  and menopause 246–8
  middle age as purgatory 239–40
  mortality, acceptance of 237
  repetition and banality, acceptance of 234–5
  stream of consciousness 232–6, 239
  time, making sense of 236–9, 240
Nietzsche, Friedrich 25, 38, 114, 159, 161

Paul, St 169–70, *170*, 172
Le passe-muraille (Aymé, Marais) *254*, 256
philosophy of midlife 38–51
  ageing process 38–9, 47–50
  identity and narcissism 44–5
  known unknowns 49–51
  menopause and invisibility 48
  and middleness 39–42, 43
  mind-body dualism 43–6, 47, 197, 212
  self-consciousness 42–5, 49–51
Pitkin, Walter, *Life Begins at Forty* 19, 243–4
Pound, Ezra 171
power acquisition in middle age 100–105
practising middle age 250–53
  midlife stasis, embracing 252–3

Proust, Marcel, *In Search of Lost Time* 65, 87
purgatory, middle age as 193–4, 196–200, 202, 224, 239–40
Purgatory (Dante) 53, 54, 56, 65–6, 74, 79

Radiohead 165–8, 181
  'Paranoid Android' 167–8
realism and models of middle age 143–64
  anxiety of ageing 152–7
  experience acquisition and imposter syndrome 158–9
  feminization of middle age 147
  gender roles, 19th century 147–53
  identity changes 144–5, 161–4
  incremental nature of ageing 151, 157
  literature, mid-19th century 149–52, 161–4, 208
  male middle age and power, 19th century 149–52
  moral purpose, Victorian 145–7
  'new woman' 147
  regrets, dealing with 155–7
  self-confidence and sense of certainty, Victorian 159–61, 253
  self-image re-adjustment 154–5, 157–9, 161–3
  sexual and class imbalance, 19th century 148–51
  youth, romantic delusions of 157–8
refusal response to challenge of middle age 194–5, 202–5, 225–6
regrets, dealing with 155–7
Reitter, Conrad, *Mortilogus* 46

Sartre, Jean-Paul 251
  and Simone de Beauvoir 208, 209, 211, 217, 222
Schlegel, Friedrich 67–8
The Second Sex (Beauvoir) 209, 210, 211, 216, 227
self-awareness 12–14, 110–12, 114–15, 166–7, 169, 180, 181, 253–6

Index

self-confidence, Victorian 159–61, 253
self-consciousness 42–5, 49–51, 204
self-image 44–5, 144–5, 154–5, 157–9, 161–3, 161–4
self-knowledge quest 81–2, 89, 90–91, 95
self-realization, midlife crisis as 20–21, 26, 31–3, 36
self-renewal, and escape 136–8, 141–2
Seneca, *Moral Epistles* 81–2, 89, 90, 95
The Shadow-Line (Conrad) 13, 62, 159
Shakespeare, William 36, 63, 100–115, 253
  ambivalence in writing 100–102
  Hamlet 101, 106, 107
  Macbeth 100, 109
  'procreation sonnets' 102–4, 150
  sun metaphor 104–5
  virtue of moderation in characters 114–15
  The Winter's Tale 104–5, 106
  see also tragicomedy of middle age
Sheehy, Gail, *The Silent Passage* 247
Shelley, Mary, *The Last Man* 28
Smith, Zadie, *White Teeth* 240–42
Sontag, Susan 12, *238*, 239
  'The Double Standard of Ageing' 244–5, 246
starting again *see* minimalism
Stoicism 81–3, 93, 97
stream of consciousness 232–6, 239

third sex, and menopause 214–16, 218–19, 221, 226
time
  body clock 27–8, 118–19
  making sense of 236–9, 240
  passage of 108–9, 123–36, 180
Time magazine 229, 232
tragicomedy of middle age 99–116, 253
  ageing process 103–4, 105–6, 110
  comedy and tragedy, distinction between 107
  'getting on' metaphor 99, 100–101, 104
  literature shaping maturity and morals 99–100, 112–15
  mortality 105–6, 110
  passage of time 108–9, 180
  power acquisition 100–105
  self-perception 110–12, 114–15
  see also Shakespeare, William

U-shaped well-being ladder 30, *31*, 33, 36, 154–5, 221

Vitruvian Man (Leonardo) 11–12, *13*, 77

Waiting for Godot (Beckett) 189, *190*, 196
Wittgenstein, Ludwig 50, 237, 248
women *see* gendering of middle age
Woolf, Virginia 149, 162, 175, 207
  The Waves 232–5, 236

Yeats, W. B. 180–81, 182–3, 183–4